Agronomy in Brief

For JRF, SRF, NET, ARS and other competitive exams

Agronomy in Brief

For JRF, SRF, NET, ARS and other competitive exams

Compiled & Edited by

B. Raghavendra Goud
Scientist (Agronomy), ICAR

Y. Ashoka Reddy
Ph.D Scholar, Agronomy,
TNAU, Coimbatore.

G. Prabhakara Reddy
Professor, Agronomy,
S.V. Agricultural College, Tirupati, AP.

M. Srinivasa Reddy
Assistant Professor, Agronomy,
Agricultural College, Mahanandi, AP.

G. Krishna Reddy
Principal Scientist, Agronomy,
RARS, Tirupati, AP.

S. Satish
Ph.D Scholar, Soil Science,
S.V. Agricultural College, Tirupati, AP.

BSP BS Publications
A unit of **BSP Books Pvt. Ltd.**
4-4-309/316, Giriraj Lane,
Sultan Bazar, Hyderabad - 500 095.

Agronomy in Brief ***For JRF, SRF, NET, ARS and other competitive exams by*** **B. Raghavendra Goud, Y. Ashoka Reddy, G. Prabhakara Reddy, M. Srinivasa Reddy, G. Krishna Reddy and S. Satish**

First Reprint 2022

Published by:

BSP BS Publications
A unit of **BSP Books Pvt., Ltd.**
4-4-309/316, Giriraj Lane, Sultan Bazar,
Hyderabad - 500 095
Phone: 040 - 23445688
e-mail: info@bspbooks.net
Website: www.bspbooks.net

Printed at

Aditya Offset Process (I) Pvt. Ltd.
Hyderabad.

Price: Rs. 450.00
ISBN: 978-93-8681-948-2 (Paperback)

Preface

There are few books in Agronomy which satisfies the requirements of students particularly preparing for competitive examinations. This book is designed to satisfy their need and is presented in a systematic manner to understand every fundamental aspect related to agronomy. This book covers all the basic concepts of agronomy viz., tillage, sowing, soil fertility and nutrient management, water management, weed management, dryland agriculture and sustainable agriculture. Some of the new topics like climate change, herbicide resistance and herbicide tolerant crops were also included. Current statistics related to agriculture is also provided for the benefit of the students. This book will be very much useful for those students preparing for NET, ARS, JRF, SRF and PG and Ph.D entrance examinations. The authors acknowledge their indebtedness to the authors of various books, bulletins, monographs and periodicals from which most of the material have been drawn.

Tirupati,
Andhra Pradesh.

Authors

CONTENTS

1	*Introduction to Agronomy*	1-5
2	*Agricultural Research Institutes*	6-16
3	*Botanical Names of Crops*	17-21
4	*Text Books and their Authors*	22-23
5	*Journals and their Publishers*	24-27
6	*Agricultural Meteorology*	28-53
7	*Soil Environment and its Modification*	54-79
8	*Problematic soils and Management*	80-83
9	*Tillage*	84-89
10	*Seeds and Sowing*	90-97
11	*Plant Population*	98-102
12	*Soil Fertility and Nutrient Management*	103-155
13	*Growth and Development of Crops*	156-167
14	*Dryland Agriculture*	168-181
15	*Soil Conservation*	182-190
16	*Water Management*	191-215
17	*Weed Management*	216-259
18	*Cropping and farming Systems*	260-268
19	*Maturity and Harvesting*	269-278
20	*Quality of Agricultural Produce*	279-281
21	*Sustainable Agriculture*	282-286
22	*Agroforestry*	287-291
23	*Climate Change*	292-296
24	*Other Important Concepts*	297-337
25	*Agricultural Statistics*	338-344
26	*Recent Stastistics and General Agriculture*	345-368
	Selected References	369-369

About the Editors

Mr. B. Raghavendra Goud is working as Scientist in ICAR. He completed his graduation in 2010 from Agricultural College, Mahanandi of Acharya N.G.Ranga Agricultural University, Andhra Pradesh. He secured 28th rank in ICAR-JRF examination and completed his M.Sc.(Agronomy) in 2012 from UAS, GKVK, Bangalore. He worked as Agriculture Extension Officer in AP State Department of Agriculture for a period of two and half years and then joined Ph.D at S.V.Agricultural College, Tirupati. He secured All India 1st rank in Agriculture Research Service – 2015 examination conducted by ASRB of ICAR and currently undergoing training as scientist in NAARM, Hyderabad

Mr. Y. Ashoka Reddy is a Ph.D Scholar in the department of Agronomy at TNAU, Coimbatore. He obtained his B.Sc.(Ag.) degree in 2009 from Agricultural College, Mahanandi, ANGRAU, A.P. and M.Sc.(Agronomy) in 2011 from S.V. Agricultural College, Tirupati, ANGRAU, A.P. He has published 3 books, 11 research papers in different reputed national journals and 5 research papers in international journals.

Dr. G. Prabhakara Reddy is presently working as Professor, Department of Agronomy, S.V. Agricultural College, Tirupati Campus of ANGR Agricultural University (AP). He completed B.Sc.(Ag.) and M.Sc.(Ag.) from ANGR Agricultural University during the years 1998 and 1990 respectively and obtained his Ph.D from IARI, New Delhi during the year 1996. He was awarded Chinese Govt. Post Doctoral fellowship under the ministry of HRD, Govt. of India, during the year, 1997. He has more than 20 years of teaching experience in different courses of Agronomy more specifically dryland agriculture. He has guided 15 M.Sc.(Ag.) and 5 Ph.D Students. He published more than 40 research papers in national and international journals. He prepared study manual on Dryland Farming and Watershed Management for under graduate students of ANGR Agricultural University.

Dr. G. Krishna Reddy, Ph.D. (Agronomy) is working as Professor of Agronomy, Acharya NG Ranga Agricultural University, Andhra Pradesh, having nearly two decades of teaching and research experience along with potential extension practice and served various research centres of university. He contributed nearly 20 scientific research articles to national and international peer reviewed journals besides about 100 popular articles in various mmagazines. A couple of post graduates and doctoral students have been enriched under his able guidance. He received a couple of gold medals for his academic excellence and honored with several awards, appreciations for his commendable achievements in allied areas of Agronomy. Dr. GK Reddy is a popular agronomist with the farmers of Andhra Pradesh.

Dr. Mallu Srinivasa Reddy has a vast experience in teaching, research and extension. Having completed his Ph.D. in Agronomy during the year 2002 at S.V. Agricultural College, Tirupati, ANGRAU has worked for 4 years in the department of Agriculture, Government of A.P. as Mandal Agricultural officer (2002-2006). He is working as Assistant Professor at Agricultural College, Mahanandi since 2006 till today. Presently he is Associate Professor and Head (FAC) of Agronomy at the same college. He has guided 8 students as chairman and 7 students as member of the Advisory committee for M.Sc(Ag.).

Mr. S. Satish has obtained his B.Sc.(Ag.) in 2008 from Agricultural College, Mahanandi of Acharya N.G.Ranga Agricultural University, Hyderabad, A.P. and M.Sc.(Ag.) in the discipline of Soil Science and Agricultural Chemistry in 2011 from S.V. Agricultural College, Tirupati, Acharya N.G.Ranga Agricultural University, AP. He worked as a Research Associate for a period of four years and has published many articles in national and international journals. At present he is pursuing Ph.D(Ag.) in the discipline of Soil Science and Agricultural Chemistry at S.V. Agricultural College, Tirupati of Acharya N.G.Ranga Agricultural University, AP.

Chapter 1

Introduction to Agronomy

- The term **agriculture** is derived from the **Latin** words **'ager'** or **'agri'** meaning **'soil'** and **'cultura'** meaning **cultivation**.
- **Agriculture** is a very broad term encompassing all aspects of crop production, livestock farming, fisheries, forestry *etc.*
- **Agronomy** is a branch of agricultural science which deals with principles and practices of soil, water and crop management.
- **Agronomy** can also be defined as a branch of agricultural science that deals with methods which provide favourable environment to the crop for higher productivity.
- **Agronomy** is derived from **Greek** words **agros** meaning **'field'** and **nomos** meaning **'to manage'**.
- **Norman** (1980) has defined **agronomy** as the science of manipulating the crop environment complex with dual aim of improving agricultural productivity and gaining a degree of understanding of the process involved.
- **Agronomy** deals with different management practices like tillage, seeds and sowing, nutrient management, water management, weed management, harvesting, storage and marketing.
- **Agronomy** is a synthesis of several disciplines like soil science, agricultural chemistry, crop physiology, plant ecology, entomology and plant pathology.
- **Agronomy** is an **art, science** and a **business.**
- As an **art**, **agronomy** refers to the knowledge of the way to perform the operations of the farm in a skillful manner but do not necessarily include an understanding of the principles underlying farm practices.
- Both **physical** and **mental skills** are essential for successful crop production.
- **Agronomy** is a **science**, because scientific principles are freely used for production of quality crops.

- **Agronomy** is a **business**, because small and marginal farmers take crop production on subsistence levels but progressive and large farmers consider it to maximize production as well as profit.
- **Pietro 'De' Crescenzi** is regarded as **father of Agronomy.**
- **Agrostology** is a branch of science which deals with the study of grasses, their classification, management and utilization.
- **Environment** is defined as the aggregate of all the external conditions and influences affecting the life and development of an organism.
- **Crop production** is basically conversion of environmental inputs like solar energy, carbon dioxide, water and soil nutrients into economic products in the form of human or animal food or industrial raw materials.
- Season for raising each crop has to be selected to attain highest productivity from available climatic resources.
- The earliest man, ***Homo erectus*** emerged around **one and half million years** ago and by about a million years ago he spread throughout world tropics and later to temperate zones.
- ***Homo sapiens***, the direct ancestor of modern man lived **250 thousand years** ago.
- ***Homo sapiens sapiens***, the modern man, appeared in Africa about **35 thousand years** ago.
- **India's** most important contribution to world agriculture is **rice**, the staple food crop of most of south, south-east and east-Asia.
- **Sugarcane**, **number of legumes** and tropical fruit like **mango** are natives of India.
- **Indian agriculture** is predominantly of **subsistence type**.
- Several crops like potato, sweet potato, tomato, chillies, groundnut, cashewnut, tobacco, American cotton, arrow root, cassava, pumpkin, papaya, pineapple, guava, custard apple and rubber were introduced into India by **Portuguese** during **16th century A.D**.
- In pre-scientific agriculture, six persons could produce enough food for themselves and for four others. In years of bad harvest, they could produce only enough for themselves.
- With the development of agricultural science and application of advanced technology, five persons are able to produce enough food for 95 others.

- Scientific agriculture began in India when sugarcane, cotton and tobacco were grown for export purposes.

Important events in history of agriculture

8700 B.C. – Domestication of sheep
7700 B.C. – Domestication of goat
7500 B.C. – Cultivation of crops (wheat and barley)
6000 B.C. – Domestication of cattle and pigs
4400 B.C. – Cultivation of maize
3500 B.C. – Cultivation of potato
3400 B.C. – Wheel was invented
2900 B.C. – Plough was invented
2200 B.C. – Cultivation of rice
1800 B.C. - Cultivation of fingermillet
1725 B.C. – Cultivation of sorghum
1500 B.C. – Cultivation of sugarcane. Irrigation from wells.
1400 B.C. – Use of iron
15 Century A.D. – Cultivation of sweet orange, sour orange, wild brinjal, pomegranate
16 Century A.D. – Introduction of crops into India by Portuguese.

- Experiments pertaining to plant nutrition in a systematic way were initiated by **Van Helmont** (1577-1644 A.D.).
- **Van Helmont** claimed that plants require only water to grow and concluded that the main principle of vegetation is water.
- **Francis Bacon** stated that **water** was the **principal nourishment for plants**.
- **Glauber** claimed that plants needed only **saltpeter (potassium nitrate)** to grow.
- **Jethro Tull** suggested that plant roots directly absorb soil particles.
- **Jethro Tull** conducted experiments on cultural practices, developed **seed drill** and **horse drawn cultivator**.
- **Jethro Tull** published a book '**Horse Hoeing Husbandry**'.
- **Woodward** stated that terrestrial matter or earth rather than water was the principle of vegetation.

- **Thaer** regarded soil humus as the source of **carbon** for plants.
- **Theory of humus** formulated in the year **1809**.
- **Boussingault** first stated that plants derive carbon from air.
- **Liebig** is regarded as the **founder of modern agricultural chemistry** and enunciator of the **Law of minimum (1843).**
- **Arthur Young** (1741-1820 A.D.) conducted **pot culture experiments** to increase the yield of crops by applying several materials like poultry dung, nitre, gun powder *etc.*
- **Arthur young** published his work in 46 volumes as **'Annals of Agriculture'**.
- In 1837, **Lawes** began to experiment on the effect of manures on crops.
- In 1842, **Lawes** patented a process of treating phosphate rock to produce superphosphate and thus initiated the synthetic fertilizer industry.
- World's **oldest permanent field experiments** located at **Rothamsted, UK.**
- Establishment of long-term field experiments at Rothamsted (UK) in **1834** by **Lawes and Gilbert.**
- Long-term fixed plot 'manurial' experiments were started at **Kanpur** in UP, **Pusa** in Bihar, **Coimbatore** in Tamil Nadu, **Padegaon** in Maharashtra, **Shanjahanpur** in UP.
- **Oldest manurial trials** established in India in **Kanpur**, UP.
- All manurial trials except Coimbatore had been demolished. Long-term manurial experiment at **Coimbatore** is **still continuing.**
- **YL Nene (Virologist)** first discovered field-scale **zinc deficiency** in India at **Pantnagar.**
- **Bray** developed nutrient mobility concept in soils.
- **Hellriegel and Wilfarth** discovered that legumes can fix atmospheric N with the help of bacteria.
- **Beijerinck** isolated the bacteria responsible for N fixation in symbiosis with legumes.
- ***Bacillus radicicola*** was the **earlier name** of **rhizobium.**
- **Beijerinck** isolated ***Rhizobium***, ***Azotobacter*** and ***Azospirillum.***
- **Gregor Johann Mendel** discovered **laws of heredity** in 1866.

- In 1876, **Charles Darwin** published the results of experiments on **cross and self-fertilization** in plants.
- **Robert Ransome** patented a **cast iron share** in 1785.
- **DDT** was first synthesized in 1874 by **Dr. Paul Muller**.
- **Wholer** first synthesized urea in **1928.**
- In **1870**, a **joint department of agriculture, revenue and commerce** was established in India.
- In **1905**, **Imperial Agricultural Research Institute** was started at **Pusa, Bihar**.
- In **1912**, **Sugarcane Breeding Institute** was established in **Coimbatore** as a branch of Imperial Agricultural Research Institute.
- Several agricultural colleges and agricultural research stations were started in **1929**.
- After the **earthquake of 1936**, **Imperial Agricultural Research Institute** was **shifted** from Pusa to Delhi.
- **Agricultural Universities** were started in India from **1964** onwards in different states.

ROLE OF AGRONOMIST

- **Agronomist** aims at obtaining **maximum production** at **minimum cost**.
- **Agronomist** is concerned with production of food and fibre to meet the needs of the growing population.
- **Agronomist** is a key person working with knowledge of all agricultural disciplines and **coordinator** of different subject matter specialists.

Chapter 2

Agricultural Research Institutes

INTERNATIONAL INSTITUTES

AVRDC Asian Vegetable Research and Development Centre, Taiwan

CGIAR Consultative Group of International Agricultural Research, Washington, USA

CIAT International Centre for Tropical Agriculture, Columbia, South America

CIMMYT International Centre for the Improvement of Maize and Wheat, Mexico

CIP International Potato Centre, Peru, South America

FAO Food and Agricultural Organization of the United Nations, Rome, Italy

IBPGR International Board for Plant Genetic Resources, Rome, Italy

IBRD International Bank for Reconstruction and Development (The World Bank), Washington DC, USA

IBSNAT International Benchmark Soils Network for Agrotechnology Transfer, Hawaii, USA

ICARDA International Centre for Agricultural Research in the Dry Areas, Aleppo, Syria

ICBA International Centre for Biosaline Agriculture, Dubai, UAE

ICRAF International Centre for Research in Agroforestry, Nairobi, Kenya

ICRISAT International Crops Research Institute for the Semi-Arid Tropics, Patancheru, Andhra Pradesh, India

IDRC International Development Research Centre, Ottawa, Canada

IFDC International Fertilizer Development Centre, Alabama, USA

IFPRI International Food Policy Research Institute, Washington DC, USA

IITA International Institute of Tropical Agriculture, Ibadan, Nigeria

ILRI International Livestock Research Institute, Nairobi, Kenya

IRRI International Rice Research Institute, Manila, Philippines

ISNAR International Service for National Agricultural Research, The Hague, Netherlands

ISRIC International Soils Reference and Information Centre, Netherlands

ISSS International Society of Soil Science, Rome

IWMI International Water Management Institute, Digama, Sri Lanka

LRDC Land Resources Development Centre, UK

TPRI Tropical Pesticides Research Institute, Arusha, Tanzania

WAC World Agroforestry Centre (ICRAF), Nairobi, Kenya

WARDA West Africa Rice Development Association, Monrovia, Liberia

WMO World Meteorological Organization, Geneva

NATIONAL INSTITUTES

BARC Bhabha Atomic Research Centre, Trombay, Mumbai, Maharashtra

CARI Central Agroforestry Research Institute, Jhansi, Uttar Pradesh

CARI Central Avian Research Institute, Izatnagar, Uttar Pradesh

CAZRI Central Arid Zone Research Institute, Jodhpur, Rajasthan

CCRI Central Citrus Research Institute, Nagpur, Maharashtra

CFTRI Central Food Technological Research Institute, Mysore, Karnataka

CIAE Central Institute of Agricultural Engineering, Bhopal, Madhya Pradesh

CIAH Central Institute of Arid Horticulture, Bikaner, Rajasthan

CIARI Central Island Agricultural Research Institute, Port Blair, Andaman and Nicobar Islands

CIBA Central Institute of Brackish water Aquaculture, Chennai, Tamil Nadu

CICR Central Institute for Cotton Research, Nagpur, Maharashtra

CIFA Central Institute of Freshwater Aquaculture, Bhubaneswar, Odisha

CIFRI Central Inland Fisheries Research Institute, Barrack pore, West Bengal

CIFT Central Institute of Fisheries Technology, Willingdon Island, Cochin, Kerala

CIMAP Central Institute of Medicinal and Aromatic Plants, Lucknow, Uttar Pradesh

CIPHET Central Institute of Post-harvest Engineering and Technology, Ludhiana, Punjab

CIRB Central Institute for Research on Buffaloes, Hisar, Haryana

CIRC Central Institute for Research on Cattle, Meerut, Uttar Pradesh

CIRCOT Central Institute for Research on Cotton Technology, Matunga, Mumbai, Maharashtra

CIRG Central Institute for Research on Goats, Makhdoom, Farah, Uttar Pradesh

CISTH Central Institute of Sub-Tropical Horticulture, Lucknow, Uttar Pradesh

CITH Central Institute of Temperate Horticulture, Srinagar, Jammu & Kashmir

CIWA Central Institute for Women in Agriculture, Bhubaneswar, Odisha.

CMFRI Central Marine Fisheries Research Institute, Cochin, Kerala

CPCRI Central Plantation Crops Research Institute, Kasargod, Kerala

CPPTI Central Plant Protection Training Institute, Hyderabad, Telangana

CPRI Central Potato Research Institute, Shimla, Himachal Pradesh

CRIDA Central Research Institute for Dryland Agriculture, Hyderabad, Telangana

CRIJAF Central Research Institute for Jute and Allied Fibres, Barrack pore, West Bengal

CSIR Council of Scientific and Industrial Research, New Delhi

CSSRI Central Soil Salinity Research Institute, Karnal, Haryana

CSWCRTI Central Soil and Water Conservation Research and Training Institute, Dehradun, Uttarakhand

CSWRI Central Sheep and Wool Research Institute, Avikanagar, Rajasthan

CTCRI Central Tuber Crops Research Institute, Thiruvananthapuram, Kerala

CTRI Central Tobacco Research Institute, Rajahmundry, Andhra Pradesh

CTRL Cotton Technological Research Laboratory, Matunga, Mumbai, Maharashtra

DARE Department of Agricultural Research and Education, New Delhi

FRI Forest Research Institute, Dehradun, Uttarakhand

IASRI Indian Agricultural Statistics Research Institute, New Delhi

ICAR Indian Council of Agricultural Research, New Delhi

ICAR-RCER ICAR Research Complex for Eastern Region, Patna, Bihar

ICAR-RCNEHR ICAR Research complex for NEH region, Umiam, Meghalaya

IGFRI Indian Grassland and Fodder Research Institute, Jhansi, UP

IIAB Indian Institute of Agricultural Biotechnology, Ranchi, Jharkhand

IIFSR Indian Institute of Farming Systems Research, Modipuram, UP

IIHR Indian Institute of Horticultural Research, Bangalore, Karnataka

IIMR Indian Institute of Maize Research, Ludhiana, Punjab.

IIMR Indian Institute of Millets Research, Hyderabad, Telangana

IINRG Indian Institute of Natural Resins and Gums, Ranchi, Jharkhand

IIOPR Indian Institute of Oil Palm Research, Pedavegi, West Godavari, Andhra Pradesh

IIOR Indian Institute of Oilseeds Research, Hyderabad, Telangana

IIPR Indian Institute of Pulses Research, Kanpur, Uttar Pradesh

IIRR Indian Institute of Rice Research, Hyderabad, Telangana

IIRS Indian Institute of Remote Sensing, Dehradun, Uttarakhand

IISR Indian Institute of Seed Research, Mau, Uttar Pradesh

IISR Indian Institute of Spices Research, Calicut, Kerala

IISR Indian Institute of Sugarcane Research, Lucknow, Uttar Pradesh

IISS Indian Institute of Soil Science, Bhopal, Madhya Pradesh

IISWC Indian Institute of Soil and Water Conservation, Dehradun, Uttarakhand

IIVR Indian Institute of Vegetable Research, Varanasi, Uttar Pradesh

IIWBR Indian Institute of Wheat and Barley Research, Karnal, Haryana

IIWM Indian Institute of Water Management, Bhubaneswar, Odisha

ISI Indian Statistical Institute, Kolkata, West Bengal

MANAGE National Institute of Agricultural Extension Management, Hyderabad, Telangana

NAARM National Academy of Agricultural Research Management, Hyderabad, Telangana

NBRI National Botanical Research Institute, Lucknow, Uttar Pradesh

NCOF National Centre of Organic Farming, Ghaziabad, Uttar Pradesh

NIAG National Institute of Animal Genetics, Karnal, Haryana

NIANP National Institute of Animal Nutrition & Physiology, Adugodi, Bengaluru, Karnataka

NIASM National Institute of Abiotic Stress Management, Malegaon, Baramati, Pune, Maharashtra

NIBSM National Institute of Biotic Stress Management, Baronda, Raipur, Chhattisgarh

NIHSAD National Institute of High Security Animal Diseases, Bhopal, MP

NIRJAFT National Institute for Research on Jute Allied Fibres Technology, Kolkata, West Bengal

NIVEDI National Institute of Veterinary Epidemiology and Disease Informatics, Hebbal, Bengaluru, Karnataka

NOFRI National Organic Farming Research Institute, Gangtok, Sikkim

NRRI National Rice Research Institute, Cuttack, Odisha

NRSC National Remote Sensing Centre, Balanagar, Hyderabad, Telangana

NSI National Sugar Institute, Kanpur, Uttar Pradesh

PRII Potash Research Institute of India, Gurgaon, Haryana

SBI Sugarcane Breeding Institute, Coimbatore, Tamil Nadu

VPKAS Vivekananda Parvatiya Krishi Anusandhan Shala, Almora, Uttarakhand

DEEMED UNIVERSITIES – 4

IARI Indian Agricultural Research Institute, New Delhi

NDRI National Dairy Research Institute, Karnal, Haryana

IVRI Indian Veterinary Research Institute, Izatnagar, Uttar Pradesh

CIFE Central Institute on Fisheries Education, Mumbai, Maharshtra

DIRECTORATES/PROJECT DIRECTORATES

Directorate of Groundnut Research, Junagadh, Gujarat

Directorate of Cashew Research, Puttur, Dakshina Kannada Dist, Karnataka

Directorate of Coldwater Fisheries Research, Bhimtal, Uttarakhand

Directorate of Floricultural Research, Pune, Maharashtra

Directorate of Knowledge Management in Agriculture, Pusa, New Delhi

Directorate of Medicinal & Aromatic Plants Research, Anand, Gujarat

Directorate of Mushroom Research – Solan, Himachal Pradesh

Directorate of Onion and Garlic Research, Pune, Maharashtra

Directorate of Poultry Research, Rajendranagar, Hyderabad, Telangana

Directorate of Rapeseed & Mustard Research, Bharatpur, Rajasthan

Directorate of Soybean Research, Indore, Madhya Pradesh

Directorate of Weed Science Research, Jabalpur, Madhya Pradesh

Directorate of Wheat Research, Karnal, Haryana

Project Directorate on Foot and Mouth Disease, Mukteswar, Kumaon, Uttarakhand

NATIONAL BUREAUS

NBAGR National Bureau of Animal Genetic Resources, Karnal, Haryana

NBAIR National Bureau of Agricultural Insect Resources, Hebbal, Bengaluru, Karnataka

NBAIMO National Bureau of Agriculturally Important Micro-Organisms, Mau Nath Bhanjan, Uttar Pradesh

NBFGR National Bureau of Fish Genetic Resources, Lucknow, Uttar Pradesh

NBPGR National Bureau of Plant Genetic Resources, New Delhi

NBSS & LUP National Bureau of Soil Survey and Land-Use Planning, Nagpur, Maharashtra

NATIONAL RESEARCH CENTRES

National Centre for Integrated Pest Management, Pusa, New Delhi

National Research centre for Agricultural Economics & Policy Research, Pusa, New Delhi

National Research Centre for Banana, Tiruchirapalli, Tamil Nadu

National Research Centre for Camel, Bikaner, Rajasthan

National Research Centre for Equines, Hisar, Haryana

National Research Centre for Grapes, Pune, Maharashtra

National Research Centre for Litchi, Muzaffarpur, Bihar

National Research Centre for Mithun, Jharnapani, Medziphema, Nagaland

National Research Centre for Orchids, Pakyong, Gangtok, Sikkim

National Research Centre for Pig, Guwahati, Assam

National Research Centre for Pomegranate, Sholapur, Maharashtra

National Research Centre for Seed Spices, Ajmer, Rajasthan

National Research Centre for Yak, Dirang, West Kameng Dist. Arunachal Pradesh

National Research Centre on Integrated Farming (ICAR-NRCIF), Motihari, Bihar

National Research Centre on Meat, Hyderabad, Telangana

National Research Centre on Plant Biotechnology, Pusa, New Delhi

AICRP's - All India Co-ordinated Research Project

- All India Co-ordinated Research Project on Agricultural Meteorology, Santoshnagar, Hyderabad, Telangana
- All India Co-ordinated Research Project on Agro-forestry, Jhansi, UP
- All India Co-ordinated Research Project on Application of Plastics in Agriculture, Ludhiana, Punjab
- All India Co-ordinated Research Project on Arid Fruits, Bikaner, Rajasthan
- All India Co-ordinated Research Project on Arid Legumes, Jodhpur, Rajasthan
- All India Co-ordinated Research Project on Cashew, Puttur, Karnataka
- All India Co-ordinated Research Project on Cattle Research, Meerut, UP
- All India Co-ordinated Research Project on Chickpea, Kanpur, UP
- All India Co-ordinated Research Project on Cotton, Coimbatore, Tamil Nadu
- All India Co-ordinated Research Project on Dryland Agriculture, Hyderabad, Telangana
- All India Co-ordinated Research Project on Farm Implements and Machinery, Bhopal, Madhya Pradesh

- All India Co-ordinated Research Project on Floriculture, IARI, New Delhi
- All India Co-ordinated Research Project on Foot and Mouth Disease, Mukteshwar, UP
- All India Co-ordinated Research Project on Forage Crops, Jhansi, UP
- All India Co-ordinated Research Project on Goat Improvement, Mathura, Uttar Pradesh
- All India Co-ordinated Research Project on Ground Water Utilisation, Bhubaneswar, Odisha
- All India Co-ordinated Research Project on Groundnut, Junagadh, Gujarat
- All India Co-ordinated Research Project on Home Science, Pusa, New Delhi
- All India Co-ordinated Research Project on Honeybees, Hisar, Haryana
- All India Co-ordinated Research Project on Integrated Farming System Research, Modipuram, Uttar Pradesh
- All India Co-ordinated Research Project on IPM and Biocontrol, Bengaluru, Karnataka
- All India Co-ordinated Research Project on Linseed, Kanpur, UP
- All India Co-ordinated Research Project on Long-term Fertilizer Experiments, Bhopal, MP
- All India Co-ordinated Research Project on Maize, New Delhi
- All India Co-ordinated Research Project on Medicinal and Aromatic Plants including Betelvine, Bengaluru, Karnataka
- All India Co-ordinated Research Project on Micronutrients and Secondary Nutrients and Pollutant Elements, Bhopal, MP
- All India Co-ordinated Research Project on Mullarp, Kanpur, UP
- All India Co-ordinated Research Project on Mushrooms, Solan, Himachal Pradesh
- All India Co-ordinated Research Project on Nematodes, IARI, New Delhi
- All India Co-ordinated Research Project on NSP (Crops), Mau, Uttar Pradesh
- All India Co-ordinated Research Project on Palms, Kasargod, Kerala

- All India Co-ordinated Research Project on Pearl millet, Jodhpur, Rajasthan
- All India Co-ordinated Research Project on Pigeonpea, IIPR, Kanpur, UP
- All India Co-ordinated Research Project on Pigs, Izatnagar, UP
- All India Co-ordinated Research Project on Potato, Shimla, Himachal Pradesh
- All India Co-ordinated Research Project on Poultry, Hyderabad, Telangana
- All India Co-ordinated Research Project on Rapeseed and Mustard, Bharatpur, Rajasthan
- All India Co-ordinated Research Project on Rice, Hyderabad, Telangana
- All India Co-ordinated Research Project on Sesame and Niger, Jabalpur, MP
- All India Co-ordinated Research Project on Small Millets, GKVK, Bangalore, Karnataka
- All India Co-ordinated Research Project on Soil Test and Crop Response, Bhopal, MP
- All India Co-ordinated Research Project on Sorghum, Rajendranagar, Hyderabad, Telangana
- All India Co-ordinated Research Project on Soybean, Indore, MP
- All India Co-ordinated Research Project on Spices, Calicut, Kerala
- All India Co-ordinated Research Project on Sugarcane, Lucknow, UP
- All India Co-ordinated Research Project on Sunflower, Safflower, Castor, Hyderabad, Telangana
- All India Co-ordinated Research Project on Tropical Fruits, IIHR, Bangalore, Karnataka
- All India Co-ordinated Research Project on Tuber Crops, Thiruvananthapuram, Kerala
- All India Co-ordinated Research Project on Use of Salt-affected Soils and Saline Water, Karnal, Haryana
- All India Co-ordinated Research Project on Vegetable and NSP, Varanasi, Uttar Pradesh

- All India Co-ordinated Research Project on Water Management Research, Bhubaneswar, Odisha
- All India Co-ordinated Research Project on Weed Science, Jabalpur, MP
- All India Co-ordinated Research Project on Wheat and Barley, Karnal, Haryana

NETWORK PROJECTS

- All India Network Project on Jute and Allied Fibres, Barrack pore, West Bengal
- All India Network Project on Pesticides Residues, New Delhi
- All India Network Project on Rodent Control, Jodhpur, Rajasthan
- All India Network Project on Tobacco, Rajahmundry, Andhra Pradesh
- All India Network Project on Under utilised Crops, New Delhi
- Network on Agricultural Acarology, Bangalore, Karnataka
- Network on Economic Ornithology, Hyderabad, Telangana
- Network Programme on Sheep Improvement, Avikanagar, Rajasthan
- Network Project on Animal Genetic Resources, Karnal, Haryana
- Network Project on Bio-fertilizers, Bhopal, Madhya Pradesh
- Network Project on Buffaloes Improvement, Hisar, Haryana
- Network Project on Harvest and Post Harvest and Value Addition to Natural Resins & Gums, Ranchi
- Network Project on Improvement of Onion and Garlic, Pune, Maharashtra
- Network Project on R&D Support for Process upgradation of Indigenous Milk Products for Industrial Application, Karnal, Haryana

Chapter 3

Botanical Names of Crops

English/Hindi Name	Botanical Name	Family
CEREAL CROPS		
Rice (Found in Asia, America and Europe)	*Oryza sativa*	Poaceae (Gramineae)
Rice (Found in West Africa)	*Oryza glaberrima*	Poaceae (Gramineae)
Common bread wheat/ Mexican dwarf wheat	*Triticum aestivum*	Poaceae (Gramineae)
Macaroni/durum wheat	*Triticum durum*	Poaceae (Gramineae)
Indian dwarf wheat	*Triticum sphaerococcum*	Poaceae (Gramineae)
Emmer wheat	*Triticum dicoccum*	Poaceae (Gramineae)
Einkorn wheat	*Triticum monococcum*	Poaceae (Gramineae)
Maize	*Zea mays*	Poaceae (Gramineae)
Sorghum	*Sorghum bicolor*	Poaceae (Gramineae)
Barley	*Hordeum vulgare*	Poaceae (Gramineae)
Oat	*Avena sativa*	Poaceae (Gramineae)
Triticale	*Tritico secale*	Poaceae (Gramineae)
Rye	*Secale cereale*	Poaceae (Gramineae)
MILLETS		
Pearl millet	*Pennisetum glaucum*	Poaceae (Gramineae)
Finger millet/Ragi	*Eleusine coracana*	Poaceae (Gramineae)
Foxtail millet (Italian millet)	*Setaria italica*	Poaceae (Gramineae)
Kodo millet	*Paspalum scrobiculatum*	Poaceae (Gramineae)
Little millet/ kutki	*Panicum sumatrense*	Poaceae (Gramineae)
Proso millet/cheena	*Panicum miliaceum*	Poaceae (Gramineae)
Barnyard millet/Sawan	*Echinocloa frumentacea*	Poaceae (Gramineae)

PULSE CROPS		
Chickpea	*Cicer arietinum*	Fabaceae (Leguminosae)
Pigeon pea (Red gram)	*Cajanus cajan*	Fabaceae (Leguminosae)
Lentil	*Lens culinaris*	Fabaceae (Leguminosae)
Green gram (Moong)	*Vigna radiata*	Fabaceae (Leguminosae)
Black gram (Urd)	*Vigna mungo*	Fabaceae (Leguminosae)
Cowpea	*Vigna unguiculata*	Fabaceae (Leguminosae)
Field pea	*Pisum sativum var. arvense*	Fabaceae (Leguminosae)
Garden pea	*Pisum sativum var. hortense*	Fabaceae (Leguminosae)
Cluster bean/Guar	*Cyamopsis tetragonoloba*	Fabaceae (Leguminosae)
Common/Kidney/French bean	*Phaseolus vulgaris*	Fabaceae (Leguminosae)
Lathyrus (Grass pea)	*Lathyrus sativus*	Fabaceae (Leguminosae)
Moth bean	*Vigna acontifolia*	Fabaceae (Leguminosae)
Rice bean	*Vigna umbellata*	Fabaceae (Leguminosae)
Horse gram	*Macrotyloma uniflorum*	Fabaceae (Leguminosae)
Lablab bean	*Lablab purpureus*	Fabaceae (Leguminosae)
OILSEED CROPS		
Rapeseed and mustard	*Brassica* sp.	Brassicaceae (Cruciferae)
Mustard		
Indian mustard/Leaf mustard/ Brown mustard	*Brassica juncea*	Brassicaceae (Cruciferae)
Black mustard/true mustard/banarasi rai	*Brassica nigra*	Brassicaceae (Cruciferae)
Ethiopian mustard/African mustard	*Brassica carinata*	Brassicaceae (Cruciferae)
Rapeseed		
Yellow sarson	*B. rapa ssp. oleifera var. yellow sarson*	Brassicaceae (Cruciferae)
Brown sarson	*B. rapa ssp. oleifera var. brown sarson*	Brassicaceae (Cruciferae)
Indian rape/Toria	*B. rapa ssp. oleifera var. toria*	Brassicaceae (Cruciferae)
Summer rape/Winter rape/Swede rape/Gobhi sarson	*B. napus ssp. oleifera*	Brassicaceae (Cruciferae)

Rocket salad/Tarmira	*Eruca sativa*	Brassicaceae (Cruciferae)
Sesame	*Sesamum indicum*	Pedaliaceae
Sunflower	*Helianthus annuus*	Asteraceae (Compositae)
Ground nut	*Arachis hypogaea*	Fabaceae (Leguminosae)
Linseed	*Linum usitatissimum*	Linaceae
Safflower	*Carthamus tinctorius*	Asteraceae (Compositae)
Niger	*Guizotia abyssinica*	Asteraceae (Compositae)
Soybean	*Glycine max*	Fabaceae (Leguminosae)
Castor	*Ricinus communis*	Euphorbiaceae
FIBRE CROPS		
White Jute	*Corchorus capsularis*	Tiliaceae
Tossa Jute	*Corchorus olitorius*	Tiliaceae
Upland/American Cotton	*Gossypium hirsutum*	Malvaceae
Desi Cotton	*Gossypium arboreum*	Malvaceae
Asiatic cotton	*Gossypium herbaceum*	Malvaceae
Sea Island or Egyptian Cotton	*Gossypium barbadense*	Malvaceae
Mesta	*Hibiscus sabdariffa*	Malvaceae
Sunnhemp	*Crotalaria juncea*	Fabaceae (Leguminosae)
Kenaf	*Hibiscus cannabinus*	Malvaceae
White Ramie	*Boehmeria nivea*	Urticaceae
Green Ramie	*Boehmeria utilis*	Urticaceae
Sisal	*Agave sisalina*	Agavaceae
Urena (Congo jute)	*Urena lobata*	Tiliaceae
SUGAR AND STARCH CROPS		
Sugarcane (Noble cane)	*Saccharum officinarum*	Poaceae (Gramineae)
Sugarcane (North Indian cane)	*Saccharum barberi*	Poaceae (Gramineae)
Sugarcane (Chinese cane)	*Saccharum sinensis*	Poaceae (Gramineae)
Sugarcane (Edible cane)	*Saccharum edule*	Poaceae (Gramineae)
Sugarbeet	*Beta Vulgaris*	Chenopodiaceae
Potato	*Solanum tuberosum*	Solanaceae
Buck wheat	*Fagopyrum esculentum*	Polygonaceae
Cassava (Tapioca)	*Manihot esculenta*	Euphorbiaceae
NARCOTIC CROPS		
Tobacco	*Nicotiana tabacum/rustica*	Solanaceae
Canabis	*Cannabis sativa*	Cannabaceae

BEVERAGE CROPS		
Tea	*Camellia sinensis*	Theaceae
Coffee	*Coffea arabica*	Rubiaceae
Cocoa	*Theobroma cacao*	Sterculiaceae
Chicory	*Chicorium intybus*	Asteraceae (Compositae)
FORAGE AND GRASSES		
Egyptian Clover / Berseem	*Trifolium alexandrium*	Fabaceae (Leguminosae)
Alfalfa/Lucerne	*Medicago sativa*	Fabaceae (Leguminosae)
Cowpea/Lobia	*Vigna unguiculata*	Fabaceae (Leguminosae)
Cluster bean/Guar	*Cyamopsis tetragonoloba*	Fabaceae (Leguminosae)
Sweet clover/Senji	*Melilotus alba*	Fabaceae (Leguminosae)
Para grass/Buffalo grass	*Brachiaria mutica*	Poaceae (Gramineae)
Napier grass	*Pennisetum purpureum*	Poaceae (Gramineae)
Oats	*Avena sativa*	Poaceae (Gramineae)
Red Clover	*Trifolium pratense*	Fabaceae (Leguminosae)
Sericea	*Lespedeza cuneata*	Fabaceae (Leguminosae)
Velvet bean	*Mucna pruriens*	Fabaceae (Leguminosae)
Common Vetch	*Vicia sativa*	Fabaceae (Leguminosae)
Kudzu	*Pueraria thumb ergiana*	Fabaceae (Leguminosae)
Indigo (Hairy)	*Indigofera hirsuta*	Fabaceae (Leguminosae)
Rhodes grass	*Chloris gayana*	Poaceae (Gramineae)
Rye	*Secale cereale*	Poaceae (Gramineae)
Italian Ryegrass	*Lolium multiflorum*	Poaceae (Gramineae)
Sudan grass	*Sorghum sudanense*	Poaceae (Gramineae)
Torpedo grass	*Panicum repens*	Poaceae (Gramineae)
Triticale	*Tritico secale*	Poaceae (Gramineae)
Love grass/weeping grass	*Eragrostis curvula*	Poaceae (Gramineae)
Johnson grass	*Sorghum halepense*	Poaceae (Gramineae)
Guinea grass	*Panicum maximum*	Poaceae (Gramineae)
Bermuda grass	*Cynodon dactylon*	Poaceae (Gramineae)
Bahia grass	*Paspalum notatum*	Poaceae (Gramineae)
Lemon grass	*Cymbopogon citratus*	Poaceae (Gramineae)
Asparagus	*Asparagus officinalis*	Poaceae (Gramineae)
Marvel grass	*Dicanthium annulatum*	Poaceae (Gramineae)
Teosinte	*Zea mexicana*	Poaceae (Gramineae)
Buffel grass/ Anjan grass	*Cenchrus ciliaris*	Poaceae (Gramineae)

GREEN MANURE CROPS		
Cluster bean/Guar	*Cyamopsis tetragonoloba*	Fabaceae (Leguminosae)
Sesbania	*Sesbania speciosa*	Fabaceae (Leguminosae)
Dhaincha (Root nodulating species)	*Sesbania aculeata*	Fabaceae (Leguminosae)
Dhaincha (Stem + root nodulating species)	*Sesbania rostrata*	Fabaceae (Leguminosae)
Pillipesara	*Phaseolus trilobus*	Fabaceae (Leguminosae)
Sunnhemp	*Crotalaria juncea*	Fabaceae (Leguminosae)
VEGETABLES		
Cabbage	*Brassica oleracea var. capitata*	Brassicaceae (Cruciferae)
Cauliflower	*Brassica oleracea var. botrytis*	Brassicaceae (Cruciferae)
Broccoli	*Brassica oleracea var. italica*	Brassicaceae (Cruciferae)
Turnip	*Brassica rapa*	Brassicaceae (Cruciferae)
Radish	*Raphanus sativus*	Brassicaceae (Cruciferae)
Chilli	*Capsicum spp.*	Solanaceae
Eggplant	*Solanum melongena*	Solanaceae
Tomato	*Solanum lycopersicum*	Solanaceae
Carrot	*Daucus carota*	Apiaceae (Umbelliferae)
Fennel	*Foeniculum vulgare*	Apiaceae (Umbelliferae)
Fenugreek	*Trigonella foenumgraecum*	Fabaceae (Legimonasae)
Drumstick tree	*Moringa oleifera*	Moringaceae
Onion	*Allium cepa*	Amaryllidaceae
Garlic	*Allium sativum*	Amaryllidaceae
Okra	*Abelmoschus esculentus*	Malvaceae
Spinach	*Spinacia oleracea*	Amaranthaceae
Bitter gourd	*Momordica charantia*	Cucurbitaceae
Cucumber	*Cucumis sativus*	Cucurbitaceae

Chapter 4

Text Books and their Authors

Text Book	Author
Advances in Pulse Production Technology Commercial Crops, Volume I and II	L.M. Jeswani and B. Baldev D. Lenka
Dryland Farming – Perspectives and Prospects	B.L. Sharma
Dryland Agriculture	S.R. Reddy and G. Prabhakara Reddy
Ecology and Environment	P.D. Sharma
Organic Agriculture	J.C. Tarafdar, K.P.Tripathi and Mahesh Kumar
New Vistas of Organic Farming	Mukund Joshi
Principles & Practices of Agronomy	S.S. Singh
Principles of Agronomy	S.R. Reddy
Principles of Agronomy	T. Yellamanda Reddy and G.H. Sankara Reddi
Principles of Crop Production	S.R.Reddy and G.K.Reddy
Principles of Field Crop Production	J.E. Pratley
Efficient Use of Irrigation Water	T. Yellamanda Reddy and G.H. Sankara Reddi
Research Techniques in Agronomy	D.K. Shelke
Agrometeorology	S.R. Reddy and D.S. Reddy
Climate, Weather and Crops	D. Lenka
Introduction to Agrometeorology	H.S. Mavi
Fundamentals of Soil Science	Indian Society of Soil Science, New Delhi
The Nature and Properties of Soils	Nyle C. Brady and Ray R. Weil
Tillage and Crop Production	N.R. Das
Tillage Systems in the Tropics	Rattan Lal
A Text Book of Rice Agronomy	Rajendra Prasad
Cropping and Farming Systems	S.C. Panda
Cropping System Research	R.S. Dixit
Cropping System, Theory and Practice	B.N. Chatterjee, S. Maiti and B.K. Mandal
Modern Techniques of Raising Field Crops	Chhidda Singh, Prem Singh and Rajbir Singh

Text Book	Author
Resource Conserving Techniques in Crop Production	A.R. Sharma and U.K. Behera
Resource Conservation Technology in Pulses	P.K. Ghosh
Textbook of Field Crops Production – Food Grain Crops Volume I	Rajendra Prasad
Textbook of Field Crops Production – Commercial Crops Volume II	Rajendra Prasad
Crop Nutrition – Principles & Practices	Rajendra Prasad
Salt Affected Soils Reclamation and Management	S.K. Gupta and I.C. Gupta
Soil Fertility and Fertilizers	Samuel L. Tisdale, Werner L. Nelson, James D. Beaton and John L. Havlin
Soil Fertility and its Management for Sustainable Agriculture	Rajendra Prasad and James F. Power
Soil Fertility and Nutrient Management	S.S. Singh
Irrigation – Theory and Practice	A.M. Michael
Irrigation Agronomy	S.R. Reddy and G.K. Reddy
Irrigation of Field Crops	S.S. Prihar and B.S. Sandhu
Irrigation – Principles and Practices	Vaughn E. Hansen, Orson W. Israelson and Glen E. Stringham
Physiological Aspects of Dryland Farming	U.S. Gupta
Rainfed Agriculture in India	J. Venkateswarlu
Modern Weed Management	O.P. Gupta
Manures and Fertilizers	K.S. Yawalkar, J.P. Agarwal and S. Bodke
Principles of Weed Science	V.S.Rao
Scientific Weed Management in the Tropics and Sub-Tropics	O.P. Gupta
Weed Management	U.S. Walia
Weed Science – Basics and Aplications	T.K. Das
Weed Science Principles	R. Jayakumar and R. Jagannathan
Vermiculture and Organic Farming	T.V. Sathe
A Text Book of Agricultural Statistics	R. Rangaswamy
Statistical Procedures for Agricultural Research	K.A. Gomez and A.A. Gomez
Hand Book of Agriculture	ICAR

Chapter 5

Journals and their Publishers

Journal	Publisher	Periodicity
Agricultural Science Digest	Agricultural Research Communication Centre, Karnal, India	Quarterly
Annals of Agricultural Research	Indian Society of Agricultural Sciences, IARI, New Delhi	Quarterly
Asian Agri-History	Asian Agri-History Foundation, Udaipur, Rajasthan	Quarterly
Annals of Arid Zone	Arid Zone Research Association of India, CAZRI, Jodhpur	Quarterly
Annals of Agricultural Research	The Indian Society of Agricultural Science, IARI, New Delhi	Quarterly
Allelopathy Journal	International Allelopathy Foundation, Haryana, India	Bi-monthly
Cotton Research Journal	Indian Society for Cotton Improvement	Half -yearly
Current Science	Current Science Association, Indian Academy of Sciences, Bangalore	Half -yearly
Current Advances in Agricultural Sciences	The Society of Agricultural Professionals, Chandra Sekhar Azad University of Agriculture & Technology, Kanpur	Half-yearly
Forage Research	Indian Society of Forage Research, CCSHAU, Hisar	Quarterly
ICAR News	ICAR	Quarterly
ICAR Reporter	ICAR	Quarterly
Kheti	ICAR	-
Phal Phool	ICAR	-
Krishi Chayanika	ICAR	-
Indian Agriculturist	Agricultural Society of India	Quarterly

Indian Farming	ICAR	Monthly
Indian Horticulture	ICAR	Quarterly
Indian Farmers Digest	G.B.Pant University of Agriculture & Technology	Monthly
Indian Coconut Journal	Coconut Development Board, Kochi, India	Monthly
Indian Journal of Agricultural Sciences	DIPA, ICAR, Krishi Anusandhan Bhawan, New Delhi	Monthly
Indian Journal of Agricultural Research	Agricultural Research Communication Centre, Karnal, India	Bi-monthly
Indian Journal of Agroforestry	Indian Society of Agroforestry, NRCAF, Jhansi	Half -yearly
Indian Journal of Agronomy	Indian Society of Agronomy, IARI, New Delhi	Quarterly
Indian Journal of Dryland Agricultural Research & Development	CRIDA, Hyderabad	Half-yearly
Indian Journal of Fertilizers (Formerly Fertilizer News)	Fertilizer Association of India, Delhi	Monthly
Indian Journal of Hill Farming	Indian Society of Hill Farming, Shillong	Half-yearly
Indian Journal of Soil Conservation	Indian Association of Soil & Water Conservationists, CSWCRTI, Dehradun	Tri-annual
Journal of Rice Research	Society for Advancement of Rice Research	Half-yearly
Journal of Root Crops	Indian Society for Root crops Publication	Half-yearly
Journal of Soil and Crops	Association of Soils and Crops Research Scientists, Nagpur, India	Half-yearly
Indian Journal of Weed Science	Indian Society of Weed Science, NRCWS, Jabalpur	Quarterly
Indian Journal of Soil Conservation	Indian Association of Soil & Water Conservationists, Dehradun, Uttarakhand	Triannually

Journal of Agrometeorology	Association of Agrometeorologists, AAU, Anand	Half-yearly
Journal of Farming Systems Research and Development	Farming Systems Research and Development Association, Modipuram, Meerut	Half-yearly
Journal of Indian Society of Soil Science	Indian Society of Soil Science, IARI, New Delhi	Quarterly
Journal of Cotton Research and Development	Cotton Research and Development Association, Hisar, Haryana	Half-yearly
Journal of Oilseeds Research	Indian Society of Oilseed research, DOR, Hyderabad	Half-yearly
Journal of Plantation Crops	Indian Society of Plantation Crops, CPCRI, Kasargod	Triannually
Journal of Potassium Research	Potash Research Institute of India, Gurgaon	Quarterly
Journal of Root Crops	Indian Society for Root Crops, CTCRI, Thiruvananthapuram	Half-yearly
Journal of Soil and Water Conservation, India	Soil Conservation Society of India, NASC Complex, New Delhi	Quarterly
Journal of Spices and Aromatic Crops	Indian Society for Spices, NRCS, Calicut	Half-yearly
Journal of Tropical Agriculture	Kerala Agricultural University, Thrissur	Half-yearly
Madras Agricultural Journal	Madras Agricultural Students Union, TNAU, Coimbatore	Quarterly
Mausam (Formerly Indian Journal of Meteorology, Hydrology and Geophysics)	Indian Meteorological Department, New Delhi	Quarterly
Oryza	Association of Rice Research Workers, CRRI, Cuttack	Quarterly
Pesticide Research Journal	Society of Pesticide Science, India, New Delhi	Half - yearly
Pestology	Pesticide Association of India, New Delhi	Monthly

Advances in Water Resources	Elsevier	Monthly
Agricultural and Forest Meteorology	Elsevier	Monthly
Agricultural Water Management	Elsevier	Monthly
Agriculture, Ecosystem and Environment	Elsevier, The Netherlands	Monthly
Agroforestry Systems	Springer, The Netherlands	Bi-monthly
Agronomy for Sustainable Development	EDP Sciences	Quarterly
Agronomy Journal	American Society of Agronomy & High Wire Press	Bi-monthly
Allelopathy Journal	International Allelopathy Association	Bi-monthly
American Journal of Alternative Agriculture	Henry Wallace Institute for Alternative Agriculture	Quarterly
Legume Research	Agricultural Research Communication Centre, Karnal, Haryana	Quarterly
Nature	Nature Publishing Group	Half-yearly

Chapter 6

Agricultural Meteorology

- Modification of **weather**, except to a limited extent, is difficult and uneconomical.
- We can get higher crop yields by adjusting cropping patterns and by following suitable agronomic practices to mitigate the adverse effects of weather.
- **Weather** is a state or condition of atmosphere at a given place and at a given time.
- **Weather** is daily variations or conditions of lower layers of atmosphere.
- **Weather** pertains to smaller area like village, city, or even a district and **smaller duration** of time *i.e.,* part of a day or complete day.
- **Weather** is expressed by **numerical values** of meteorological parameters.
- Examples of weather are hot day, rainy day, cloudy weather, dry weather etc.
- **Climate** is generalized weather or summation of weather conditions over a given region during a comparatively **longer period**.
- **Climate** is weather conditions related to larger areas like zone, state, country, part of continent or whole of continent, longer duration of time like month, season or year.
- Climate is expressed by **normals** and **averages** *e.g.*, cold season, tropical climate etc.
- **Meteorology** is the science that deals with laws and principles as they apply to atmospheric phenomenon.
- **Meteorology** is the science of atmosphere and its attendant activities.
- **Meteorology** also defined as a branch of physics that deals with physical process in the atmosphere that produce weather.

- **Agricultural meteorology** is a branch of applied meteorology which deals with response of crops to the physical environment.
- **Agriculture meteorology** is the study of physical process of the atmosphere that produces weather in relation to agricultural production, and also deals with agroclimatology, instrumentation and weather forecasting.
- **Climatology** is the science dealing with the factors which determine and control distribution of climate over the earth's surface.
- **Agroclimatology** deals with relationship of climatic regimes and agricultural production. It also includes instrumentation and weather forecasting.
- **Atmosphere** extends up to a height of about **1600 km**.
- **99 per cent** of total atmospheric mass is within **40 km** from the surface of earth.
- Volume of **Nitrogen** in atmosphere is **78%.**
- Weight of **Nitrogen** in atmosphere is **75.5%.**
- Volume of **Oxygen** in atmosphere is **21%.**
- Weight of **Oxygen** in atmosphere is **23.1%.**
- Volume of **Argon** in atmosphere is **0.93%.**
- Weight of **Argon** in atmosphere is **1.28%.**
- Volume of **Carbon dioxide** in atmosphere is **0.03%.**
- Weight of **Carbon dioxide** in atmosphere is **0.045%**.
- Volume of **water vapour** in lower layer of atmosphere is **0 to 4%**.
- Based on vertical temperature differences **atmosphere** is divided into **4 layers** *i.e.,* troposphere, stratosphere, mesosphere and thermosphere.
- **Troposphere** is the **lower layer** of atmosphere.
- Troposphere extends up to a height of **8 to 18km** from earth surface depending on latitude.
- Troposphere is **thicker at equator** than poles.
- Troposphere contains **85%** of **atmospheric mass**.
- **Weather phenomenon** like clouds, fog, dew, mist, rain etc. **occur in troposphere**.
- Temperature **decreases** with **increase in altitude** of **troposphere**.

- Temperature at the boundary of troposphere is **-60°C**.
- **Tropopause** is a thin layer between troposphere and stratosphere.
- **Temperature** does **not vary** with height in **tropopause**.
- Stratosphere layer lies above tropopause.
- Stratosphere lies **beyond 8 to 18 km** extending **up to 50km** depending on latitude.
- **Stratosphere** is dustless, cloudless and warmest layer.
- **Temperature increases** with height in **stratosphere**.
- **Stratosphere** contains **15%** of atmospheric mass.
- **Stratosphere** has low density of gases.
- Mass of air up to 40 km is more than **99%** of total atmospheric mass.
- **Stratosphere** absorbs **ultra violet radiation** of the sun.
- Stratosphere air does not move above, because air at higher altitude is **warmer** than air below.
- **Stratopause** separates stratosphere and mesosphere.
- **Mesosphere** is the layer that lies above stratosphere.
- In **mesosphere temperature decreases** with increase in altitude up to 80km.
- **Mesopause** separates mesosphere from thermosphere.
- **Thermosphere** is the **outer layer** of atmosphere.
- **Temperature increases** with altitude in **thermosphere**.
- **Ionosphere** is the **lower layer of thermosphere** through which **long distance radio communication** is possible.

WEATHER PARAMETERS

- **Solar constant** is defined as the energy falling in **one minute** on a surface area of **one square centimeter** at the **outer boundary of atmosphere** held **normal to the sunlight** at the **mean distance of the earth from the sun**.
- Value of solar constant is **1.94 cal /cm^2/min**.
- **Direct solar radiation** is the radiation received directly from sun by a surface normal to the incident radiation.

- **Diffused radiation** or **sky radiation** is the radiation scattered by suspended particles in the atmosphere.
- Quantity of diffused radiation depends on **latitude**, **season** and **cloudiness**.
- In **high latitudes diffused radiation** is **important source of solar radiation** and forms substantial part of solar radiation during **winter months**.
- **Cloudiness** increases ratio of diffused to direct radiation.
- **Before sunrise and after sunset** all the solar radiation received is **diffused or sky radiation**.
- In plant canopies **diffused** radiation penetrates **effectively** than direct radiation.
- **Diffused radiation** contains **65% photosynthetically active radiation (PAR)**.
- **Direct radiation** contains **42% photosynthetically active radiation (PAR)**.
- **Global radiation** is the **total** of **direct** and **diffused solar radiation** received on a horizontal surface from the sun directly and from the sky as scattered radiation.
- **Albedo** or **reflected solar radiation** is the solar radiation that is reflected **without** any **change in its quality**.
- **Clouds** are effective reflectors of solar radiation.
- **Snow** is a very effective reflector, particularly **when** it is **fresh**.
- **Water surfaces** and **sea** are **poor reflectors.**
- **Rocks, sand, soil** and **vegetation** reflect from **10 to 30 per cent** of the incident solar radiation.
- **Reflected solar radiation** is important in **remote sensing**.
- **Terrestrial radiation** is the thermal radiation **emitted by the earth**.
- **Earth absorbs** solar **radiation** in **short waves** and **emits** back in the form of **long waves**.
- **Terrestrial radiation** heats the atmosphere.
- **Net radiation** is the radiation balance between global and reflected solar radiation.
- **SI unit** of **solar radiation** is **watts/m^2**

- 1 watt = **1 joule/second**
- **CGS unit** of **solar radiation** is **Calories/cm^2/min**
- 697.93 W/m^2 = 1 cal/cm^2/min
- **Lux** is oldest unit of solar radiation
- 10,000 lux = 3.47 Mega Joules
- **Photosynthetic active radiation (PAR)** is measured in **Einstein units.**
- 1 Einstein unit = 1 mole of photons
- **Total incoming radiation** measured by **pyranometer.**
- **Diffused radiation** measured by **shading pyranometer.**
- **Reflected radiation** is measured by **albedometer.**
- **Net radiation** is measured by **net radiometer.**
- **Photosynthetically active radiation** is measured by **quantum sensor.**
- **Direct solar radiation** is measured by **pyrheliometers.**
- **Pyrgeometer** is used to measure **terrestrial radiation.**
- **Sunshine hours** recorded by **sunshine recorder.**
- Height of sunshine recorder from ground surface is **3.08 m.**
- **Cambell stokes sunshine recorder** is used to measure **sunshine hours** in India.
- Height of Stevenson screen from ground surface is **1.22 m.**
- Duration of the day and night are **equal** all over the earth on **March 21** which is called **vernal or spring equinox.**
- From March 21, the day length increases gradually in the northern hemisphere till June 21, which is called the **summer solstice.**
- From June 21 onwards, day length decreases in the northern hemisphere till September 23, which is called the **autumn equinox.**
- Day and night are equal all over the world, with the sun right over the **equator.**
- From September 23, sun moves southward and and the days continue to get shorter and shorter in the northern hemisphere till December 21, which is called the **winter solstice.**

- **Solar radiation** in narrow wave bands is measured by **Spectroradiometer.**
- **Infrared thermometer** measures **temperature of canopy without contact.**
- **Infrared thermometer** senses radiation in the range of 8-14 micro meters wave band (**infrared region**).
- **Infrared thermometer** is used to estimate **water status** of plants and also **to schedule irrigation.**
- **Temperature** is the degree of hotness or coldness of a substance determined by its molecular activity.
- Temperature is measured by **thermometer.**
- **Depth of water table** is measured by **Piezometer.**
- **Conduction** is transfer of heat by molecular activity.
- **Convection** is process of **heat transfer** within **liquids** and **gases** resulting from the motion of fluid.
- **Convection** is **faster** than **conduction.**
- **Radiation** is transfer of energy by **electromagnetic waves** moving at the **speed of light.**
- **Conduction** and **convection** requires **medium**, whereas **radiation** does **not require medium.**
- X-rays are **short.**
- Radio waves are **long.**
- On an average cloudy day **43%** solar radiation **absorbed by earth, 22% by atmosphere** and **35% reflected** into space from earth.
- **Reflected solar radiation** is unchanged in character.
- Solar radiation absorbed by earth or atmosphere is converted into **thermal energy.**
- Solar radiation is more at 12 noon, whereas **highest temperature** is noticed **after 2 P.M.**
- At **equator** seasonal temperature variation is **less.**
- Seasonal variation in temperature is more at **higher latitudes.**
- **Isotherms** are the lines that connect points of equal **temperature.**
- **Vertical temperature** variations influence **cloud formation, condensation** and **precipitation.**
- **Lapse rate** is vertical temperature decrease or gradient.

- Normal lapse rate is **6.5°C per km** or **3.5°F per 1000 feet.**
- **Adiabatic lapse rate** is rate at which temperature changes as air rises or falls.
- **Dry adiabatic lapse rate** is **10°C per km.**
- At some altitudes there is abrupt increase instead of fall of temperature is called **inversion.** This occurs when air near ground cools off faster than above air.
- **Thermal conductivity** is the quantity of heat flowing in unit time through a unit cross section of soil in response to a specified temperature gradient.
- Unit of thermal conductivity is **Watts/m depth of soil/°K temperature gradient.**
- Thermal conductivity depends on **texture, moisture and organic matter content** of soil.
- Thermal conductivity **decreases** with increase in porosity.
- When soil is ploughed, it increases soil porosity and **reduces** thermal conductivity.
- Thermal conductivity **increases** with increase in moisture content.
- Soil organic matter **lowers** thermal conductivity.
- Thermal conductivity **higher** in **sandy soils** than clay soils due to **less porosity** in **sandy soils** compared to clay soils.
- Temperature is measured in Celsius, Fahrenheit or Kelvin scales.
- In Fahrenheit scale **melting point** of water is **32°F.**
- In Fahrenheit scale **boiling point** of water is **210°F.**
- In Celsius scale **melting point** of water is **0°C.**
- In Celsius scale **boiling point** of water is **100°C.**
- **Absolute temperature** is measured by **Kelvin scale.**
- Absolute zero means **0°K.**
- At **absolute zero (0°K)** there will be no activity of molecules in a substance.
- **Melting point** of water in Kelvin scale is **273°K.**
- Formulae for conversion of different temperature scales

  $C = (F-32)5/9$

  $F = (9C/5) + 32$

  $K = C + 273$

- **Maximum thermometer** is used to measure **highest temperature** of a day.
- **Maximum thermometer** is set in the **morning time**.
- **Minimum thermometer** is used to measure **lowest temperature** of a day.
- **Minimum thermometer** is set in the **evening time**.
- **Thermocouple** is used to measure soil temperature.
- **Thermograph** is used to record **air temperature continuously**.
- **Aneroid barometer** and **barograph** are used for measuring **atmospheric pressure**.
- Standard international unit of pressure is **Pascal.**
- **One Pascal** is equal to force of **one Newton m^{-2}**.
- **Ten bars** is equivalent to the S.I. unit **Mega Pascal (MPa)**.
- **Wind velocity** is measured by **anemometer**.
- **Density of gases** is measured by **aerometer.**
- **Specific gravity of liquids** is measured by **hydrometer.**
- **Pycnometer is used to measure specific gravity of liquids.**
- Direction **from which** wind blows is called **windward side**.
- Direction **towards which** wind blows is called **leeward side**.
- Wind direction is measured by **windvane**.
- **Absolute humidity** is the absolute or actual quantity of water vapour by **weight** present in a given **volume** of air.

$$\text{Absolute humidity} = \frac{\text{Weight of water vapour (g)}}{\text{Volume of air}}$$

- Unit of absolute humidity is **g/m^3**.
- **Specific humidity** is the **weight** of water vapour per **unit weight** of air (including water vapour).

$$\text{Specific humidity} = \frac{\text{Weight of water vapour (g)}}{\text{Weight of the air including water vapour (kg)}}$$

- Unit of specific humidity is **g/kg**.
- Absolute and specific humidity are difficult to measure.
- Absolute humidity changes with change in **temperature**.
- Absolute and specific humidity have less effect on crop growth.

- **Relative humidity** is the ratio of amount of water vapour present in the air and the amount of water vapour required for saturation at a particular temperature and pressure.

$$\text{Relative humidity (RH)} = \frac{\text{Water vapour present in the air}}{\text{Water vapour required for saturation}} \times 100$$

- Relative humidity is expressed as **Percentage or ratio**.
- **Relative humidity** is widely used in agriculture compared to absolute and specific humidity.
- RH 90% means still 10% water vapour is required for saturation.
- If RH is low, evaporation and transpiration will be high.
- **Vapour pressure deficit (VPD)** is the difference between saturation vapour pressure and actual vapour pressure.
- Vapour pressure deficit is expressed in **bars or pascals**.
- When VPD is around or less than 1.5kpa air is said to be humid.
- When vapour pressure deficit is more than 2.5kpa then air is said to be dry.
- **Relative humidity** is measured by **hygrometers or psychrometers**.
- **Asmann's psychrometer** is used to measure relative humidity in **crop canopy**.
- **Hair hygrometer** is used to measure relative humidity **inside rooms**.
- **Hygrograph** is used to measure humidity continuously.
- **Cresocograph** is used for continuous recording of **plant growth.**
- **Evaporation** is measured by **evaporimeter/atmometer/atmidometer**.
- Evaporation is measured by using United States Weather Bureau (USWB) open pan evaporimeter, sunken screen evaporimeter, can evaporimeter and portable evaporimeter.
- **USWB open pan evaporimeter** is most widely used for measuring evaporation.
- Evaporation is expressed as **mm/day**.
- **USWB open pan evaporimeter** consists of cylindrical vessel of **25 cm height** and **122 cm diameter**.

- **Portable evaporimeter** is used to measure evaporation for very short period.
- **Piche atmometer** is a porous paper wick atmometer for measuring evaporative rate of water.
- **Lysimeter** is used to measure **evapo-transpiration**.
- Falling of any type of condensed moisture to ground surface is called **precipitation**.
- **Rainfall** is precipitation in the form of liquid drops **larger than 0.5mm** in diameter.
- Size of ordinary rain drop varies from **0.5 to 4mm** diameter.
- Rainfall is measured by **rain gauge** or **pluviograph**.
- **Automatic rain gauges** are used to measure rainfall continuously.
- Drizzle is rain of very light intensity composed of fine droplets **less than 0.5mm** in diameter barely reaching the ground.
- In mist water droplets evaporate completely before reaching the ground.
- **Glaze** or **freezing rain** is formed when rain falls on any material on ground having subfreezing temperatures and freezes into sheet or coating of ice.
- Rime is **freezing fog**. Thick, frostly deposit is formed when objects with subfreezing temperatures encounter fog.
- **Snow** is formed by sublimation of water vapour at subfreezing temperatures.
- **Snow** is solid precipitation in the form of ice crystals or flakes.
- When temperature of air falls below a certain limit before any water vapour is condensed, water vapour passes directly from vapour state to solid state.
- **Sleet** is also solid precipitation in the form of small particles of clear ice which are originally formed as rain drops and later frozen as they fall through a layer of cold air.
- Hail consists of **hard rounded pellets of ice** and compact snow.
- Hail is similar to sleet but larger in size.
- Hails falls from **cumulo nimbus clouds** along **with thunder storms**.

- In Hail formation rain water drops moves upward instead of falling due to strong vertical air currents, and due to freezing temperatures at higher altitude water becomes ice and falls to ground.
- Clouds are classified based on **height**, **shape**, **colour**, **transmission** or **reflection** of light.
- Basic cloud forms are
  1. Cirrus (feathery or fibrous)
  2. Stratus (stratified or in layers)
  3. Cumulus (in heaps)
- If a basic cloud form occurs **above** its **normal height** of **1950m**, then the cloud will be thin and the word **'alto'** should be **prefixed** to its form.
- If any cloud is **associated with rain**, then the word **'nimbus'** is **prefixed** or suffixed to the basic form.
- According to 1956 International Cloud Atlas of world meteorological Department, clouds are classified into **10 characteristic forms.**
- Cloud cover is measured in **Okta** units.
- Clouds which are present at **highest height** are **cirrus clouds.**
- Height of cirrus cloud – **5 to 13 km**
- **Cirrus clouds** appear as bright red or orange before sunrise and after sunset.
- Cirrus clouds comprise of thin crystals or needles of ice, not droplets of water.
- **Cirro-cumulus** clouds are often arranged in **bands** or fused into **waves** or **ripples** resembling those **of sand on sea shore.**
- **Cirro stratus** clouds are responsible for **hallows** and also **milky white appearance** of sky.
- **Alto-stratus** clouds give good amount of **rainfall** in **middle** and **high latitudes.**
- **Stratus** clouds have **no** particular **structure** or form.
- **Nimbo-stratus** clouds are associated with **steady precipitation** in the form of rain or snow.
- **Cumulous** clouds are **flat based**, with pronounced **vertical thickness** and extends upwards as **dome or cauliflower shaped.**

- **Cumulous** clouds are prominent in **summer** season.
- **Cumulo-nimbus** clouds are tremendous towering clouds with a vertical range of **3 to 8 km** from **base to top**.
- **Cumulo-nimbus** clouds forms **thunderstorms**.
- **Low pressure areas** near **equator** are called **doldrums**.
- Due to the rotation of earth, air in the polar region swung to temperate regions resulting in low pressure in polar region called as **polar calms**.
- On earth **doldrums** and **polar calms** are the two low pressure areas.
- Latitudinal belt between **30 to 35°** of both **south and north** are called **horse latitudes**.
- Air currents at the upper layers of equator and poles meet at **horse latitudes** leading to high pressure.
- Due to high temperature at equator air moves upward and creates low pressure area at equator.
- Air from lower layers of atmosphere move from both south and north latitudes to fill the low pressure belt.
- This type of air movements occurring throughout the year are known as **trade winds** or **tropical easterlies**.
- **Trade winds** have same course or track year after year.
- Due to high pressure in upper layers of equator air moves towards south or north in the upper layers. These winds are called **anti-trade winds**.
- Direction of antitrade winds is **opposite** to trade winds.
- **Wind movement** in **trade winds** occurs in the **lower layers** of atmosphere.
- **Wind movement** in **anti trade winds** occurs in **upper layers** of atmosphere.
- Word **monsoon** is derived from **Arabic** term **'Mausam'** meaning **'Season'**.
- Course of trade winds changes during a year due to local factors like **topography, oceans** etc.
- Trade winds with changed direction are called **monsoon winds**.
- **Monsoon winds** change direction with **season**.

- India experiences **south-west monsoon** winds and **north-east monsoon winds**.
- **India** is **situated** in the **north-east trade wind zone** and these trade winds continue throughout the year.
- South east trade winds start from south of equator, while traveling over Indian ocean they absorb large amounts of moisture and while crossing equator they are caught up suddenly in the air circulation over India and deflected as south-west winds.
- **South west monsoon** enter into **Kerala** around **June 1st** every year.
- **South coastal Andhra Pradesh** and **Tamil Nadu** gets sufficient amount of rainfall from **North-East monsoon**.
- South west monsoon or rainy or monsoon period is from **June to September**.
- **60% of total rainfall** of the year is received during **south west monsoon period**.
- **Tropical** climate prevails during **south west monsoon period** *i.e.*, warm, humid climate.
- North-east monsoon or post rainy season or post monsoon period is from **October to December**.
- **33% of annual rainfall** is received during **north east monsoon period**.
- Cyclones are called by different names in different countries

  North America - Hurricane

  Typhoon - Eastern Asia, Philippines

  Baquio - China

  Cyclone - India, Australia
- Cyclones generally originate in water **warmer than 27°C**.
- Centre of cyclone is known as **eye**.
- Intensive **low pressure areas** with more or less circular shape are called **cyclones**.
- **Indian Meteorological Department** was started in **Pune** in **1875**.
- Observed weather conditions are marked in brief coded form as a synopsis of this conditions and this type of report is known as **synoptic report**.

- In synoptic charts or weather charts observations recorded at scheduled times are charted on outline map of India using international code of signals and observations.
- Short range weather forecasts are for a **day or two**.
- **Short range weather** forecasts are useful for irrigation engineers, mariners, aviation engineers and farmers.
- Medium range forecasts are for a period of **3 to 4 days** to **two weeks.**
- **Long range forecasts** are for periods of **more than four weeks**.
- **Long range forecasts** are useful for **choosing crop patterns**.
- Application of foreign material to clouds to induce precipitation is called **cloud seeding**.
- **Silver iodide** is used for seeding **cold clouds**.
- **Sodium chloride (common salt)** is used for seeding **warm clouds**.
- Soil temperature is increased by planting crops on the **sunny wall of furrows**.
- **Decandole** is the first person to attempt classification of climate.
- **Decandole** classified climate based on **vegetation**.
- **Koppen** was the **first person** to classify climate based on **weather elements**.
- **Trolls** climate classification is suitable for **agriculture purpose**.
- **Koppen's** and **Thornthwaite's** classifications are **most widely accepted**.
- **Koppen** has taken **annual** and **monthly means of temperature** and **precipitation** for classification of climate.
- In **tropical climate** even the **coolest month** has **average temperature more than 18°C**.
- In **temperate climate** average temperature of **coolest month** is in the range of **18°c to -3°C**.
- In **cold climates** average temperature of **coolest month** is **less than -3°C**.
- In **polar climate** average temperature of **warmest month** is **less than 10°C**.
- **Koppen** classified climate from **A to E**.

- Depending on the form of precipitation climate is classified into rainy or snow climate.
- If **annual rainfall** is **less than evaporation** then it is called **dry climate**.
- In **Tropical rainy climate (A)** average temperature of **coolest month greater than 18°C**, precipitation in the form of **rain**, rainfall is more than evaporation.
- In **Tropical dry climate (B)** average temperature of **coolest month** is **more than 18°C**, rainfall is less than evaporation.
- **Tropical dry climate (B)** is divided into **Arid** climate (BA) and **Semiarid** (BS) climate.
- In **mild temperate rainy climate (C)** average temperature of **coolest month** is in the range of **18°C to -3°C.**
- In **Cold snow climate (D)** average temperature of **coolest month** is **less than -3°C**, precipitation in the form of **snow.**
- In **Polar climate (E)** average temperature of **warmest month** is **less than 10°C.**
- **Polar climate (E)** is sub divided into **Tundra and Ice cap.**
- These classifications (A to E) are again divided into four letter classification. Second letter after capital letter related to seasonal rainfall, third letter refers to annual temperature and fourth letter relates to specific characteristics.

  E.g. BSmha

  i.e., Tropical dry climate (B), semiarid (S), rainfall received during monsoon season (m), average annual temperature is more than 18°C (h) and with a long hot summer (a).
- Most of **south India** comes under above group.
- **Thornthwaite** classified climate based on **PE index**, **TE index** and **seasonal distribution of rainfall.**
- Precipitation of effectiveness(PE) index = $\frac{P}{E} \times 100$

P = Annual Precipitation

E = Annual evaporation

- Based on PE index climate is classified into 5 groups.

SYMBOL	HUMIDITY PROVINCE	VEGETATION	P.E.INDEX
A	WET	RAIN FOREST	128 and above
B	HUMID	FOREST	64-127
C	SUB-HUMID	GRASSLAND	32-63
D	SEMIARID	STEPPE	16-31
E	ARID	DESERT	<16

- **Steppe** is **dry**, **grassy**, **tree less**, **uncultivated area**.
- Temperature effective (TE) index = $\sum_{i=1}^{12}\left(\frac{T-32}{4}\right)$
- T = mean monthly temperature in ^{o}F.
- Based on **TE index climate** is divided into **six temperature provinces**.

SYMBOL	TEMPERATURE PROVINCE	TE INDEX
A'	TROPICAL	128 and above
B'	MESOTHERMAL	64-127
C'	MICROTHERMAL	32-63
D'	TAIGA	16-31
E'	TUNDRA	1-15
F'	FROST	0

- **Seasonal distribution of** rainfall also included in thornthwaite classification.

Symbol	Seasonal Distribution
R	Rainfall adequate in all seasons
S	Rainfall deficit in summer
W	Rainfall deficit in winter
D	Deficit in all seasons

- **South India climate** can be grouped under **DA's** in **Thornthwaite classification** which means **semiarid tropical** with **rainfall deficit in summer.**
- **Troll** classified climate based on **temperature** and **humid months**.
- In **tropical region** mean monthly temperature of **coolest month** is **more than 18°C.**
- **Tropical region** is divided into **five groups** based on **number of humid months**.
- In a **humid month** monthly **precipitation exceeds** monthly **potential evapotranspiration.**
- Classification of tropical region by Troll, 1965

Symbol	Type of climate	Type of vegetation	Number of humid months
V1	Tropical rainy climate	Evergreen forest	12-9.5
V2	Tropical humid summer	Evergreen forest	9.5-7.0
V2a	Tropical humid winter	Half deciduous	9.5-7.0
V3	Tropical wet dry	Rain forest dry wood	7.0-4.5
V4	Tropical dry climate	Thorny,succulent,wood	4.5-2.0
V4a	Tropical dry climate with humid months in water	-	4.5-2.0
V5	Tropical semi-desert and desert climate	-	<2.0

- Main **drawback of Troll's** classification is **continuity of humid months** is **not considered.**
- ICRISAT revised Troll's classification and developed modified Troll's classification.
- According to **ICRISAT** classification **88 per cent of geographical area** of India is **under tropics.**

- **Dry semiarid tropics** constitute **57 per cent of geographical area** of **India**.
- Climatic regions based on modified Troll's Classification

Climate	Number of humid months	Per cent of geographical area of India
Arid	<2.0	17.00
Semiarid-dry	2.0-4.5	57.17
Semiarid-wet	4.5-7.0	12.31
Humid	>7.0	1.10

- **AICRP on Dryland Agriculture** classified climate based on **moisture deficit index.**

$$MDI = \frac{P\text{-}PET}{PET} \times 100$$

P = Annual precipitation (cm)

PET = Potential evapotranspiration

Type of climate	MDI
Sub humid	0 to -33.3
Semi arid	-33.3 to -66.6
Arid	>-66.6

- If the rainfall exceeds twice the normal deviation at a particular place, that year is said to be a **wet year.**
- **Planning commission** divided India into **15 agro-climatic zones** based on **rainfall, temperature, soil, topography, cropping, farming systems** and **water resources.**
- **Western plateau and hills zone** is the **largest agro-climatic zone.**
- **Western Himalayan zone** comprising of three distinct subzones of **Jammu and Kashmir, Himachal Pradesh** and **Uttar Pradesh hills** are characterized by **skeletal soils of cold region, mountain meadow soils, podsolic soils, hilly brown soils.** Lands are having **steep slopes with undulating terrain.**

- **Eastern Himalayan zone** is characterized by **high rainfall** and **forest cover.**
- **Shifting cultivation** is practiced in nearly **one-third** of **cultivated area** in **Eastern Himalayan Zone.**
- **Lower gangetic plains** zone consists of districts of **West Bengal**, soils are mostly **alluvial** and **prone to floods.**
- **Middle gangetic plains** comprising of districts of **UP and Bihar** has a **cropping intensity of 142%** and **39 per cent** of gross cropped area is **irrigated.**
- In **upper gangetic plains** zone consisting of districts of **UP**, irrigation is through **canals and tube wells.**
- **Trans-gangetic plains zone** consisting of **Punjab, Haryana, Union territories of Delhi and Chandigarh** and **Sriganganagar district of Rajasthan** are characterized by **highest irrigated area**, **high cropping intensity** and **high ground water utilization.**
- **Eastern Plateau and hills zone** comprising of **eastern Madhya Pradesh**, **southern Bengal** and **inland Odisha** is characterized by **shallow and medium deep soils**, **undulating topography**, slope of **1 to 10%** and irrigation through **tanks** and **tube wells.**
- **Western plateau and hills zone** comprising of most of **Maharashtra**, part of **MP**, one district of **Rajasthan** is characterized by 65% net sown area,**11% forests**,**12.4% irrigated area** with **canals** being the main source.
- **Southern plateau and hills** zone comprising of **Andhra Pradesh**, **Karnataka** and **Tamil Nadu** characterized by cropping intensity of **111%** and **dry land farming** is adopted in **81% area.**
- **East coast plains and hills** comprise of **east coast of Tamil Nadu**, **Andhra Pradesh** and **Odisha** characterized by **alluvial soils** and **coastal sands** and irrigation is through **canals and tanks.**
- **Gujarat plains and hills zone** comprising of 19 districts of Gujarat characterized by **arid climate** with **low rainfall**, only 32.5 per cent area is irrigated mainly through **wells and tube wells.**
- **Western dry zone** comprises of nine districts of **Rajasthan** characterized by **hot sandy desert, erratic rainfall, high evaporation, scanty vegetation. Famine** and **drought** are **common features** of this region.

- **Island zone** comprising of island territories of **Andaman and Nicobar** and **Lakshadweep** are **equatorial** with a **rainfall** of **3000mm**, is largely a forest zone with undulated lands.
- India has a coastline of **8129 km**.

INFLUENCE OF CLIMATE ON CROPS

- More than **70 per cent** of the solar radiation absorbed by plants is converted into heat.
- A portion of solar radiation, up to **28 per cent** in terms of energy, is used in **photosynthesis**.
- Radiation up to **0.25 µm (ultraviolet)** is harmful to most plants.
- Solar radiation in the region of **0.30 to 0.55 µm** has photoperiodic effect and from **0.40 to 0.70 µm**, it is most effective in photosynthesis.
- Above **0.74 µm**, it has practically no effect on photosynthesis, its main effect is **thermal**.
- **Near infrared radiation** has influence on seed germination and dormancy of seeds.

Type of radiation	Spectral region (µm)
Ultraviolet	0.3-0.4
Photosynthetically active radiation	0.4-0.7
Near infrared radiation	0.7-4.0
Long wave radiation	4.0-100.0

- **Chlorophyll formation** is promoted by light in the region of **0.300 to 0.338 µm**.
- **Blue light** even at very low light intensities cause inclination of wheat leaf.
- With higher light intensities, leaves become **horizontal**.
- Plants tend to grow prostrate or develop rosette form under high light intensity.
- Interception and utilization of solar radiation can be increased by proper management practices, such as **adjustment of row spacing, plant population** and **selection of the most advantageous time for planting**.

- Light interception **increases** with increase in **leaf area index**.
- As solar radiation enters the crop canopy, its quantity is gradually **decreased** due to interception or attenuation by the crop.
- The amount of solar radiation present in any layer of the crop can be calculated by the formula

$$I = I_0 \, e^{-KLAI}$$

Where I = light intensity at a point, I_0 = light intensity on top of the canopy, LAI = Leaf Area Index, K= extinction coefficient, e = exponential constant

- The extinction coefficient or rate at which light is being attenuated with increase in depth into canopy is dependent on the crop.
- Extinction coefficient in rice is **0.65**, **0.84** in maize and **0.70** in sorghum.
- In groundnut, low light intensity during **peak flowering** reduced number of flowers per plant.
- Flowers opened during **cloudy period** do not produce pegs.
- Low light intensity at **pegging and pod filling** reduces peg and pod number.
- In cereals, number of tillers **increase** with increase in light intensity.
- Low light intensity during **flowering** increases spikelet sterility in cereals.
- The low light intensity from **panicle initiation to grain formation** is critical but **flowering to grain formation** is more critical.
- Low light during ripening reduces yield due to lesser number of filled grains per panicle and lower grain number.
- Reduction in grain yield of rice in wet season compared to dry season is attributed to **solar radiation**.
- Dry matter production **increases** in proportion to the amount of intercepted radiation; but yield may or may not.
- Most plants are influenced by **relative length of day and night**, especially for floral initiation.
- The **duration of the night or complete darkness** is more important than the daylight for floral initiation. This effect of light on plants is known as photoperiodism.

- Long-day plants require comparatively **long days (usually more than 14 hours)** for floral initiation.
- Long-day plants put forth **more vegetative growth** when **days are short**.
- Temperate crops like **wheat, barley, oats** belong to **long day plants**.
- In short-day plants flower initiation takes place when the days are **short (less than 10 hours)** or when the dark period is long.
- Most of the tropical crops like **rice, sorghum, maize** etc. are **short-day plants**.
- Crops that have an absolute requirement for a given day length will remain vegetative for an indefinite period as long as they are not exposed to floral inductive day length.
- **Cocklebur** is a **qualitative short-day plant**.
- Quantitative short day plants initiate flowering even in long-days but initiation of flowering is delayed by a few days to months.
- Most of the **tropical crops** are **quantitative short-day plants**.
- **Day-neutral plants** do not require either long or short dark periods. Photoperiod does not have much influence for phasic changes for these plants.
- **Cotton, sunflower and buckwheat** are **day-neutral**.
- Shorter the days, more rapid is initiation of flowering in **short-day plants**.
- Longer the days, more rapid is the initiation of flowering in **long-day plants**.
- Alternate high and low light intensity influences photoperiodism.
- Low light intensity following high light intensity, is more effective on photoperiodism than high light intensity following low light intensity.
- **Day length** is a function of **latitude and position of the sun**.
- At **equator** both day and night are **equal** in length.
- At the time of **equinoxes**, the length of the day is practically the same at all **latitudes**.
- **Day length** changes due to **position of the sun** during different months.

- In **northern latitude**, day length starts increasing from January onwards and reaches a peak in June and subsequently decreases up to December.
- The photoperiodic effect is realized only when **optimum temperature** prevails.
- Because of the phasic changes taking place due to the influence of both temperature and photoperiod, it is better to calculate **photothermal units (PTU)** instead of heat units for accurate prediction of flowering and maturity.
- The optimum date of sowing can be arrived by estimating **PTU** from climatological data.
- Rice requires **2,200 PTU** for high yield.
- By calculating PTU for different dates of sowing, the best date of sowing can be determined.
- Number of leaves produced is less with decrease and increase in photoperiod with short and long day plants respectively.
- Tillering and plant height **decrease** under extreme photoperiod.
- Leaf number **increases** with increase in temperature.
- Increase in duration of light (for long-day plants) and temperature decreases different stages of crop, especially during vegetative phase.
- A short-day plant, when exposed to short-days earlier, produces less number of leaves thus source is less.
- If short-day plants are subjected to short days at very late stage, more foliage is developed and increases duration of the crop without increasing the yield.
- In **rice, wheat** etc. source is not limited but yield potential is less due to less number of storage organs.
- In sink-limited crops, amount of solar radiation in sufficient quantities is necessary during the period of formation of storage organs *i.e.*, from **panicle initiation to flowering**.
- In some crops, source is limited, hence solar radiation is critical during **grain-filling stage**, low solar radiation during this period causes large number of unfilled grains.

- **Mean temperature** is average of maximum and minimum temperature.
- For each species of plants, there are upper (maximum) and lower (minimum) limits of temperature at which growth is nil or negligible and optimum temperature at which growth is maximum.
- Most of the crop plants grow best at **15 to 30°C**.
- Many crop plants die at a temperature of **45 to 55°C**.
- The minimum, maximum and optimum temperatures of a crop are known as **cardinal temperatures.**
- The crops which grow best in cool weather period are called **cool season crops** and are generally grown in **winter season (November to February)**.
- Most of the cool season crops cease to grow at an average temperature of **30 to 38°C.**
- Cool season crops are **wheat, barley, potato, oats** etc.
- Cool season crops are called **temperate crops** because they are mostly grown in **temperate regions**.
- The cardinal temperatures for cool season crops are

  Maximum temperature: **30-38°C**

  Minimum temperature: **0 to 5°C**

  Optimum temperature: **25 to 30°C**
- Warm season crops are **rice, sorghum, maize, sugarcane, pearl millet, groundnut, redgram, cowpea** etc.
- Warm season crops are also called **tropical crops**.
- **Tropical crops** are generally grown in monsoon season and some also in summer season.
- The cardinal temperatures of warm season crops are

  Maximum temperature: **45-50°C**

  Minimum temperature: **15-20°C**

  Optimum temperature: **30-38°C**
- The rates of biochemical processes are affected mainly by **temperature**.
- Any chemical reaction **increases** with increase in temperature.

- The rate of reaction may **double** or even be more for every **10°C** increase in temperature. This rate of increase in reaction for every 10°C in temperature is called **quotient 10 or Q_{10}.**

$$Q_{10} = \frac{\text{Rate of reaction at } (t+10)\ ^{\circ}C}{\text{Rate of reaction at } t^{\circ}C}$$

- The **heat unit or growing degree-day** concept was proposed to explain the relationship between **growth duration** and **temperature.**
- Growing degree-day concept assumes a **direct and linear relationship** between **growth** and **temperature.**
- A **degree-day or a heat unit** is the mean temperature above base temperature.

$$\text{Growing Degree-days (GDD)} = \sum_{i=1}^{n}\left(\frac{T_{max} + T_{min}}{2}\right) - T_b$$

- **Base temperature (T_b)** is the lowest temperature at which there is no growth.
- Base temperature of wheat is **4.5°C.**
- Base temperature of wheat, maize and pearl millet is **10.0°C.**
- Degree-days are useful for predicting harvesting dates and to select optimum date of planting.
- **Day and night length** is one of the basic factors controlling the period of vegetative growth for photosensitive varieties of crops.
- Mere accumulation of heat units do not predict developmental stages and maturity in **photosensitive varieties**. Therefore, photothermal units are proposed, wherein the degree-days are multiplied by **length of night in case of short-day plants** and **length of the day for long-day plants.**
- Flowering is hastened as the length of night increases in short-day plants, while flowering is delayed as the length of night increases in long-day plants.
- PTU can be expressed by the equation

$$\text{PTU} = \sum_{i=1}^{n} (\text{GDD} \times \text{length of night or day})$$

- High temperature **increases** amino acid concentration in roots and shoots.
- Low temperature stress results in accumulation of **abscisic acid**.
- Abscisic acid production and breakdown of complex products are important mechanisms of temperature stress.
- If the rainfall received is more than **2.5 mm** on any particular day, it is called a **rainy day**.

Chapter 7

Soil Environment and its Modification

- **Soil fertility** is the status or the inherent capacity of the soil to supply nutrients to plants in adequate amounts and in suitable proportions.
- According to modern usage, **soil fertility** is the capacity of the soil to produce crops of economic value and to maintain health of the soil without deterioration.
- **Soil productivity** is the capacity of the soil to produce crops with specific systems of management and is expressed in terms of yields.
- **All productive soils are fertile**, **but all fertile soils need not be productive** due to some problems like waterlogging, saline or alkaline condition, adverse climate etc.
- Under above conditions, crop growth is restricted though the soil has sufficient amount of nutrients.
- Soil physical environment is controlled by soil characters like **texture**, **structure**, **aeration**, **water**, **mechanical resistance** and **depth of soil**.
- **Soil texture** refers to the relative proportions of sand, silt and clay.
- Rock fragments **larger than 2 cm** in diameter are called **stones**.
- Materials between **2 cm and 2 mm** diameter are called **gravel**.
- Soil mineral matter **smaller than 2 mm** in diameter is called **fine earth**.
- Sand, silt and clay together constitute **fine earth**.
- Sand particles of **0.2 to 2 mm** in diameter are classified as **coarse sand**.
- Sand particles of **0.02 to 0.2 mm** in diameter called as **fine sand**.
- Sand particles are small pieces of **unweathered** rock fragments.

- Unless sand particles are coated with **clay or silt**, they do not exhibit properties such as plasticity, cohesion, stickyness, moisture and nutrient retention etc.
- Because of large size of sand particles **macropores** exist between them which facilitate free movement of air and water.
- Size of silt particles are in the range of **0.02 to 0.002 mm**.
- Because of an adhering film of clay, silt particles exhibit some plasticity, cohesion, adhesion and adsorption.
- Silt particles can hold more amount of water than sand but less than clay.
- Sand and silt particles are approximately **spherical** and **cubical** in shape.
- **Clay** fraction controls most of the soil physical and chemical properties.
- Clay particles are **less than 0.002 mm** in diameter.
- **Clay particles** have highest surface area since surface area is **inversely** related to size.
- Clay particles can adsorb and retain water and nutrients.
- Some clays swell on wetting and shrink on drying.
- Clay exhibit properties like **flocculation**, **deflocculation** and **plasticity**.
- Clay behaves like a **weak acid** which is neutralized by bases such as **calcium and magnesium ions**, thus serving as storehouse for several nutrients.
- Classification of soil particles based on **international system**

Particle	**Diameter (mm)**
Stone	>20
Gravel	2-20
Fine earth	<2
Coarse sand	0.2 -2
Fine sand	0.2- 0.02
Silt	0.02-0.002
Clay	<0.002

- **Soil texture** is classified based on the proportion of predominant size fractions of sand, silt and clay.
- If soil contains more than 80% silt fraction, it is called as **silty soil**.
- If soil contains more than 85% sand fraction, it is called **sandy soil**.
- If soil contains 40% clay, it is called as **clay soil**.
- If sand, silt and clay are in **sizeable** proportion, then the soil is called as **loamy soil**.
- Silty clay soil means a soil in which clay characteristics are outstanding and which also contains sufficient silt.
- Textural class of a soil can be known from **textural triangle**.
- If the soil contains 60% sand, 30% silt and 10% clay then texture is **sandy loam**.
- **Soil texture** is a **permanent feature** of soil and its change over years is negligible.
- Soil texture can be changed by **adding sand** or **silt** or **clay** as an amendment to improve physical condition.
- **Tank silt** is added to sandy soil to improve the water holding and nutrient retention capacities.
- **Sand** is added to heavy clay soil to improve **internal drainage**.
- Application of rice husks at 4.5 t/ha decreased soil bulk density, increased total porosity, decreased penetration resistance, improved saturated hydraulic conductivity.
- Bulk density of mineral soils varies from 1.4-1.8.
- Particle density of mineral soils varies from 2.5 – 2.7.
- **White grub** damage is less in crops grown in **clay soil** compared to loamy and sandy soils.
- Soil texture influences soil physical and chemical properties like water holding capacity, nutrient retention, nutrient fixation, nutrient availability, drainage, strength, compressibility and thermal regime.
- **Clay soils** have a high capacity to adsorb and retain nutrients and moisture.

- **Clay soils** are difficult to handle in tillage operations.
- **Loamy soils** exhibit properties intermediate between sand and clay soils.
- **Loamy soils** are considered best for agricultural production, because they retain more water and nutrients than sandy soils and have better drainage, aeration and tillage properties than clay soils.
- Suitability of a soil to a particular crop depends on **texture** in addition to **soil depth**, **depth of water table**, **salinity** and **alkalinity**.
- Rice, cotton, sorghum, coriander are grown on **heavy textured** soils which include clay loam, silty clay loam, silty clay and clay.
- **Medium textured** soils like loams, silt loams, silts and sandy loams are suitable for **most of the crops**.
- Sandy, loamy sand, sandy loam and sandy clay are **light-textured** soils and these are suitable for **groundnut**, **potato**, **tobacco**, **pearl millet** and **leguminous fodder crops**.
- Primary soil particles *viz.*, sand, silt and clay are usually grouped together in the form of aggregates.
- The arrangement of primary particles and their aggregates into certain defined patterns is called **soil structure**.
- Natural aggregates are called **fragments**.
- Artificially formed soil mass is called **clod**.
- Stable aggregates are those that resist break down by disruptive forces such as water and wind.
- Fine clay particles *i.e.*, colloids, flock or group together due to **cohesion** and form a cluster.
- Sand and silt particles stick to the clay cluster, thus forming an aggregate amount and nature of colloidal clay influences aggregate formation.
- **Calcium and hydrogen** ions bring about better aggregation than magnesium and potassium ions.
- Wetting of clay particles with a liquid like water is required to form aggregates because water molecules show dipole movement.

- **Sesquioxides *i.e.*, iron and aluminium oxides**, act as cementing agents for binding sand and silt particles to form aggregates. A part of the iron in solution acts as a flocculating agent and remaining acts as a cementing agent
- Aggregates formed with **sesquioxides** are more stable than those formed by silicate clays.
- **Humic and fulvic acids** produced during decomposition of organic matter are also sticky in nature and help in aggregate formation.
- **Colloidal organic matter** is more effective in forming aggregates than clay.
- Clay is adsorbed on humus forming clay-humus complex and it helps in forming stable aggregates.
- Fungi and actinomycetes produce sticky materials which are helpful in forming aggregates.
- Microbial products capable of bounding soil aggregates are **polysaccharides**, **hemicelluloses** and several other natural polymers.
- Above materials are attached to clay surfaces by means of cation bridges, hydrogen bonding, vander waal forces and anion adsorption mechanism.
- Soil structure types are single grained, massive and aggregated.
- When particles are unattached to each other as in **sandy soils**, it is called **single grained structure**.
- When soil is tightly packed in large cohesive blocks, as in the case of **clay**, the structure is called **massive**.
- Between the above two extremes, an intermediate condition in which the soil particles are associated in **quasi-stable small clods** are known as **aggregates or peds**.
- **Aggregate** structure is generally the most desirable condition for plant growth especially in the critical early stages of germination and seedling establishment.
- Diameter of macroaggregates is **more than 250 μm**.
- Diameter of microaggregates is **less than 250 μm**.

- **Shapes of soil structure**

Platy Structure	Prismatic/Columnar	Blocky	Spherical or Spheroidal
Horizontally layered, thin and flat aggregates resembling thin leaves in a bundle	Vertically oriented pillars, often six sided and up to 15 cm in diameter	Cube like blocks of soil up to 10 cm in size, some times angular with well defined planar faces	Rounded aggregates not larger than 2 cm diameter
Occurs in **recently deposited clay soils**	This structure occurs in **B horizon of clayey soils**, particularly in **semi-arid regions**	This structure occurs in upper part of **B horizon**	Often found in loose condition in **A horizon**
	When **tops are flat**, vertical aggregates are called **prismatic**		These units are called granules and when porous, they are called crumbs
	When **tops are rounded**, vertical aggregates are called **columnar**		

- Aggregates of **B horizon** are bigger due to weight of the top-layers and less shrinkage and expansion activity as there are **less** fluctuations of soil moisture.
- Profiles in **semi-arid** region contain **granulated A horizon** with a **prismatic B horizon**.
- In **humid temperate** regions, **A horizon** contains **granulated aggregates** while **B horizons have platy or blocky aggregates.**
- Water is held around soil particles in thin layers due to **adhesion** and **cohesion**.
- Water is held with greater force (***i.e.*, 10,000 bars**) near the particle surface.
- As the thickness of water layer increases, the force with which it is held is **reduced**.

- When the soil particles are holding water with less than **0.3 to 0.1 bar** force, water is lost into deeper layers due to **gravitational pull**.
- When pure water is held in hypothetical place where no force is acting on it, its capacity to do work is **zero**.
- When water is held by soil particles or if it contains salts or due to gravitational force, its ability to do work or its potential is restricted. Therefore, water potential in soils is always **negative**.
- Water potential of soil is expressed in **bars** or **mega pascals**.
- Soil water, held between **-0.3 to -15 bars**, is considered as available water.
- Soil water moves from higher potential to lower potential.
- **Specific heat** is the heat in calories required to raise the temperature of one gram of a substance to **1°C**.
- Specific heat of water is **1.0 cal/g**.
- Specific heat of organic matter is **0.5 cal/g**.
- Specific heat of soil is **0.2 cal/g**.
- If one calorie of heat raises the temperature of water by 1°C, it increases organic matter temperature by 2°C and soil temperature by 5°C.
- Specific heat of soil **increases** with increase in **moisture content**.
- Flow of temperature in the soil is expressed as **thermal conductivity**.
- Thermal conductivity **increases** with water content and **decreases** with porosity.
- In moist soils, with higher thermal conductivity, heat flows into lower layers and surface temperatures are therefore low.
- Tillage improves **porosity** and **decreases** thermal conductivity resulting in **higher** surface temperature.
- Latent heat of vaporisation for water is **580 calories**.
- Dark coloured soils get warmed up quicker than light coloured soils, since dark coloured soils reflect back less radiation to atmosphere and thereby absorb more heat.
- Sandy soils warm up **quicker** than clay soils, since clay soils have more water holding capacity.

- Optimum soil temperature for germination of different crops are
    - Winter cereals : 15-18°C
    - Mustard : 18-23°C
    - Maize: 32°C
    - Sorghum, sugarcane and cotton: 30°C
- Crops such as **maize or sorghum** need high soil temperature for active seedling growth.
- No microbial activity is noticed **below 5°** or **above 50°C** with optimum between **25°C and 35°C.**
- Nutrient availability is higher at **optimum temperature**.
- **Field air capacity** is the fractional volume of air in a soil at field capacity.
- In sandy soils field air capacity is **25% or more**, loamy soils **15 to 20%, clay soils < 10%.**
- **Carbon dioxide** content and **relative humidity** are higher and **oxygen** is less in soil air compared to atmospheric air.
- CO_2 content in atmospheric air is **0.03%.**
- CO_2 content in soil air is **0.25%.**
- Growth of most crops is affected and stops when soil oxygen content reaches **below 2%.**
- Root growth is **decreased** due to decrease in oxygen and increase in concentration of CO_2.
- Germination is inhibited in the absence of **oxygen**.
- **Potato, tobacco, cotton, linseed, tea** and **legumes** need **higher** level of oxygen in soil air compared to other crops.
- Cereals except rice are **intermediate** in oxygen requirement.
- **Rice** can tolerate very low level or even complete absence of oxygen in the soil.
- Nutrient and water uptake are **reduced** when the oxygen content of soil is less as it affects activity and **permeability** of roots.
- Volume of soil not occupied by soil particles is known as **pore space**.
- Pore space is occupied by air or water or both.
- Plant roots exist and grow in pore space.

- **Pore space** directly controls the amount of water and air in the soil and thus **indirectly** controls plant growth and crop production.
- Diameter of micropores is **2 to 20 μm**.
- Diameter of macropores is **200mm to 0.3mm**.
- Amount of pore space depends on **particle size**, **texture**, **structure and biological activity**.
- Clay soils have **less** macropores compared to sandy soils.
- Total pore space in clay soils is **50-60%**, loamy soils is **30-50%**, sandy soils is **20-30%**.
- Sandy soils contain **25,000 pores/m^2**.
- Clay soils contain **25 million pores/m^2**.
- Vertical section of the soil to expose the layers is called **soil profile**.
- Upper layer of soil is usually higher in organic matter and darker in colour than the layers below.
- Upper layer of soil is called **A horizon or top soil**.
- Middle part of the profile usually contains **more clay**. This layer is called **B horizon or subsoil**.
- A and B horizons together are referred to as **solum or true soil**.
- Crops feed mostly in the **top soil** and to a very less extent in subsoil.
- **C horizon** commonly referred to as **parent material**, occurs beneath the solum and extends downward **up to bedrock**.
- All crops suffer due to shallow water table except **rice**.
- **Soil strength or soil mechanical resistance** indicates the resistance offered by the soil to root penetration.
- Soil strength or soil mechanical resistance is measured with **cone penetrometer** and expressed as **kg/cm^2 or bars**.
- Factors responsible for soil colour are **parent material**, **soil organic matter**, **presence of minerals**.
- **Red sand stone** gives rise to red soil.
- Soil organic matter in surface soil imparts **dark brown** to **black colour**.

- Presence of certain minerals in soils like **titamin** compounds impart darker colour.
- Iron compounds like **haematite**, give **red** and **limonite yellow** colour.
- Preponderance of silica or lime results in **whitish** or **grayish tinge** to the soil.
- Accumulation of salts makes soils **white** or **black**, depending on the type of salts.
- If soil is **well drained** as in **lateritic soil**, **ferric** compounds of iron are commonly formed and they give **red colour** to the soil.
- If drainage is poor, soil colour is **greenish** or **bluish** in waterlogged soils.
- In subsoil layers, colour variegation or mottling of soil is due to alternate **oxidizing** and **reducing conditions** due to fluctuations in water table.
- Dark brown soils indicate high **organic matter** and **fertility**.
- **Red** colour shows good aeration.
- White colour of soil indicates **accumulation of salts**.
- Nutrient transformation and its availability in soils depends on **pH**, **clay minerals**, **cation and anion exchange capacity**.
- **pH** is defined as the negative logarithm of hydrogen ion activity.
- pH influences rate of nutrient release through its influence on **decomposition**, **cation exchange capacity** and **solubility of materials**.
- Important source of nitrogen and sulphur is **organic matter**.
- Decomposition of organic matter is **slowest at pH below 6** and **fastest between 6 to 8**.
- Availability of phosphorus is high within a pH range of **6.5 to 7.5** due to higher solubility of phosphorus compounds.
- At low pH, phosphorus is precipitated as **Fe and Al phosphates**.
- At high pH, **calcium phosphate** is formed which is less soluble.
- Metallic cations such as Fe, Mn, Cu, Zn and also B precipitate at **high** pH, hence their availability is less in **alkaline soils**.
- Availability of K and B are influenced by pH through its effect on **cation exchange capacity**.

- At lower pH, H^+ ions replace K and leaching of K occurs.
- At high pH, **potassium** compounds are converted into **non-exchangeable form** and thus availability is reduced.
- **Boron** is leached out at **low** pH.
- Optimum pH range for availability of different nutrients

Nutrient	Optimum pH range
N	6.0-8.0
P	6.5-8.5
K	6.0-7.5
S	6.0 and above
Ca and Mg	7.0-8.5
Fe	6.0 and below
Mn	5.0-6.5
B, Cu, Zn	5.0-7.0
Mo	7.0 and above

- Soil with pH **above 8.5** is alkaline with high sodium content which deflocculates soil colloids. It results in destruction of soil structure and movement of water and air are impaired in the soil.
- **Rice** and **tea** prefer acidic soil reaction and most of the other crops prefer **neutral pH**.
- pH preference of rice is **4.0 to 6.0**.
- pH preference of tea is **4.0 to 6.0**.
- Crops tolerant to acidity – **paddy, potato, tea, millets**
  Semi tolerant – **Bengal gram, maize, sorghum, peas, wheat, barley**
  Sensitive to acidity – **Redgram, soybean, cotton, oats**
- Within a pH range of 5 to 7, the acidity of soils is due to exchangeable hydrogen ions.
- At pH **< 5.0**, H^+ ions replace **Al^{3+}** from the lattice of clay mineral.
- Aluminium released is hydrolysed with liberation of H^+ ions. Iron behaves similarly and contributes to acidity.
- On soils with low CEC and in high rainfall regions, leaching of bases occurs resulting in reduction of pH.
- Addition of acid forming fertilizers increases **acidity**.

- KCL is an **acid** forming fertilizer.
- During the decomposition of organic matter, several acids are formed which increase the acidity.
- In acid sulphate soils, pH is low due to formation of **sulphuric acid** by oxidation of sulphur and sulphides.
- Acid soils can be converted into neutral soils by addition of **lime**.
- Liming materials are **oxides, hydroxides** and **carbonates of calcium and magnesium**.
- Application of lime at full lime requirement increased soil pH and reduces **aluminium content**.
- Continuous submergence **reduces** aluminium content below toxic levels compared to alternate submergence or irrigation regions at saturation.
- Availability of **P and Fe** is **high** under continuous submergence compared to alternate submergences or at saturation.
- Soils with pH higher than 7 are called **alkaline soils.**
- High base saturation other than H^+ ions especially of **sodium** and presence of **free carbonates of Ca and Na** are the main reasons for alkalinity.
- **Exchangeable sodium** has higher effect on pH than of Ca and Mg since sodium hydroxide is a **stronger base**.
- Hydrolysis of carbonates of Ca and Mg release hydroxyl ions which increase pH.
- Presence of excess salts also **increases** pH.
- Classification of alkaline soils

Soil class	EC (dS/m)	ESP	pH
Saline	>4	<15	<8.5
Saline-alkali	>4	>15	<8.5
Alkali	<4	>15	8.5-10

- Modified classification of alkaline soils

Soil class	EC (dS/m)	SAR	pH
Saline	>2	-	-
Saline-sodic	>2	>15	>8.5
Sodic	-	>15	-

- **Electrical conductivity (EC)** of soil is defined as the reciprocal of the electrical resistance of the extract of the soil which is one centimeter long and a cross-sectional area of one square centimeter.
- **EC** is generally expressed as **dS/m** at **25°C** and is used to express the **salinity** of the soil.
- **Exchangeable Sodium Percentage (ESP)** is defined as the degree of saturation of the soil exchange complex with **sodium**.

$$ESP = \frac{\text{Exchangeable sodium}\left(\text{C mol kg}^{-1}\right)}{\text{Cation exchange capacity}\left(\text{C mol kg}^{-1}\right)} \times 100$$

- In saline soils, **excess salt** is the main cause for high pH of the soil.
- Saline soils contain neutral soluble salts sufficient to interfere seriously with plant growth. These soils are also called as **white alkali or solon chalk**.
- Excess salts can be removed by **leaching** with rain or irrigation water. Free drainage is provided to leach the salts beyond the root zone of crops.
- **Leaching requirement (LR)** is that fraction of water that must be leached through the soil root zone depth to control the salinity at a specified level.

$$LR = \frac{\text{Electrical conductivity of applied water (ECa)}}{\text{Electrical conductivity of drainage water (ECd)}}$$

- Reclamation of alkali soils requires removal of a part or most of the exchangeable sodium and its replaceable by the more favourable **calcium ion** in the root zone.
- Chemical amendments for reclaiming alkali soils are
  - ✓ Soluble salts like gypsum ($CaSO_4.2H_2O$), Calcium chloride, phosphogypsum.
  - ✓ Sparingly soluble calcium salts like calcite, calcium carbonate.
  - ✓ Acids or acid formers like sulphuric acid, iron sulphate, aluminium sulphate, lime sulphur, pyrites etc.
  - ✓ Quantity of an amendment required for improvement of an alkali soil depends on the amount of exchangeable sodium which in turn depends on soil pH.

✓ Calcium present in the gypsum replaces sodium from the exchange complex.

✓ When exchangeable complex has sufficient calcium, **flocculation** occurs resulting in aggregation which in turn improves movement of water and air.

Amendment	Gypsum equivalent
Gypsum	1.00
Calcium chloride	0.85
Sulphur	0.19
Sulphuric acid	0.57
Iron sulphate	1.62
Aluminium sulphate	1.29

- **Sodium adsorption ratio (SAR)** indicates comparative concentrations of Na^+, Ca^{2+} and Mg^{2+} in soil solution.

$$SAR = \frac{Na^+}{\sqrt{Ca^2 + Mg^{2+}/2}}$$

Where Na^+, Ca^{2+} and Mg^{2+} are concentrations (C mol kg^{-1}) of sodium and magnesium ions in soil solution.

- Surface of sodic soils is usually black due to deposition of dispersed humus and hence the name **black alkali**.
- A **mineral** is a naturally occurring inorganic substance with a definite chemical composition and distinct physical characters.
- A mineral that forms the original component of a rock is known as **primary mineral**.
- **Primary mineral** is generally **anhydrous** (without water molecule in its composition) and is originally formed by cooling and solidification of molten mass.
- **Feldspar, hornblende, mica** etc. are some of the primary minerals.
- **Secondary mineral** is a mineral that has been formed as a result of subsequent changes in rocks.
- Secondary mineral is **hydrous** and is formed due to **weathering or metamorphosis** of primary mineral.

- Examples of secondary minerals are **kaolinite, montmorillonite, illite, limonite, gibbsite, dolomite, calcite, apatite, gypsum and pyrites**.
- **Hydrated aluminosilicate secondary minerals** with particle size **less than 0.002 mm** in diameter are clay minerals.
- **Clay minerals** together with **organic matter** constitute the colloidal fraction of the soil which is the active seat of physical and chemical properties of soil.
- Colloids are particles of size **less than 0.0002 mm** in diameter.
- Individual particle of a colloid is called **micelle**.
- Most of the clay minerals that are **less than 0.0002 mm** in diameter and also humus exhibit colloidal properties.
- **Humus** is an organic colloid.
- Inorganic colloids may be either **silicate** or **non-silicate** clay minerals.
- **Kaolinite**, **montmorillonite** and **illite** are silicate clay minerals.
- Depending on the number of **silica** and **alumina** layers silicate clay minerals are classified as 1:1 and 2:1 clay minerals.

Kaolinite group	Montmorillonite group	Illite group
Each crystal unit consists of one sheet each of silica and alumina, so called as 1:1 type clay minerals	Each crystal unit consists of two sheets of silica and one sheet of alumina, so called as 2:1 type clay minerals	Belongs to 2:1 type
Two sheets are held together by oxygen atoms which are mutually shared by Si and Al atoms of their respective sheets	Sheets of a unit are held loosely by weak vander Waal's forces	Micelles are held by K^+ ions more tightly than oxygen linkages as in montmorillonite
Units are held together rigidly by hydrogen bonding	Units are held loosely by very weak oxygen to oxygen linkages	

Due to strong bonding between crystal units, the distance between two units is fixed and no expansion ordinarily occurs between the units when wetted	These are easily expandable allowing water molecules and cations in between these units	Less expandable than montmorillonite
Cations and water do not enter between structural units of the micelle or colloids		
Effective surface area of kaolinite is restricted to its outer surface	In addition to external surfaces, the movement of water and cations between crystal units exposes a very large internal surface area which greatly exceeds the external surface area	
Cation exchange capacity is less due to its low surface area	Higher CEC, plasticity, shrinkage and swelling properties	
Size of kaolinite units range from 0.1 to 5.0 µm in width	0.1 to 1 µm in width	
Kaolinite clay minerals are bigger than other clay minerals	Montmorillonite crystals are much smaller than kaolinite micelle	

- CEC of clay minerals

Clay mineral	CEC (me/100g)
Kaolinite (1:1)	3-15
Montmorillonite (2:1)	80-120
Vermiculite (2:1)	100-120
Illite (2:1)	20-50

Mineral	Occurence
Kaolinite	Per humid regions
Montmorillonite	Semi arid and arid regions with black cotton soils
Vermiculite	Moderate leaching zones
Illite & Chlorite	Semi arid zone with high potash environment

- Non silicate clay minerals are **hydrous oxides of iron** and **aluminium** and **allophanes**.
- Hydrous oxides of **iron** and **aluminium** are colloids present in red and yellow soils of tropical and sub-tropical regions.
- Hydrous oxides of iron and aluminium are oxides of iron and aluminum with different number of water molecules, depending on the clay mineral.
- **Gaethite ($Fe_2O_3.H_2O$)** is an iron oxide with one water molecule.
- **Gibbsite ($Al_2O_3.3H_2O$)** is a hydrous aluminium oxide with three water molecules in its structure.
- Hydrous oxides of iron and aluminium micelles also carry **negative charges**, but less than those of kaolinite.
- Most hydrous oxides are not sticky and lesser in plasticity and cohesiveness than **silicate clay minerals**.
- Soil dominated by **hydrous oxides** has much better physical condition.
- Amorphous mineral matter in soils is called **allophanes** which are a combination of silica and sesquioxides.
- Approximate composition of allophanes is **$Al_2O_3.2SiO_2.H_2O$**.
- Allophanes have high cation and anion exchange capacities.
- **Humus** is an organic soil colloid.
- **Humus** is a product of decomposition of plant and animal residues which is fairly stable, amorphous and brown to black in colour.
- On equal weight basis, organic colloids exhibit **five to seven** times higher adsorption of water and cations than inorganic colloids.
- Charges of humus colloids are **p^H dependent**.
- Under strongly acidic conditions, **hydrogen** is tightly bound and not easily replaceable by other cations.
- Organic soil colloids exhibit **low** negative charge.

- With increase in p^H, hydrogen from carboxyl group followed by hydrogen from phenolic group, ionize and are replaced by Ca, Mg and other cations in humus.
- **Cation exchange capacity** is a very important property of the soil from plant nutrition point of view.
- Most clay micelles have a **crystalline** structure while humus micelles are **amorphous**.
- Negative charges on clay micelles are due to **isomorphic substitution**, **ionization of hydroxyl groups** and **exposed carboxyl and hydroxyl groups**.
- **Isomorphic substitution** of silica or alumina atom by an atom of similar geometry, but of low charge results in higher negative charge.
- Negative charges on humus micelles are due to exposed **carboxyl (COOH)** and **hydroxyl (OH)** groups.
- Due to the presence of **negative** charges cations are adsorbed on surface of the micelles.
- **Divalent** cations are more strongly adsorbed than monovalent cations.
- Cations that are adsorbed on the surface of micelles are capable of exchanging with those in solution.
- Process of exchange of cations between solid and liquid phases is called **cation exchange**.
- Cations are held over the micelle in two layers and it is known as **electrical double layer**.
- Quantity of cations is expressed in **milli equivalents**.
- **One gram** of hydrogen is one equivalent weight because the atomic weight of hydrogen is considered as one.
- One milli equivalent of hydrogen is **one-thousandth of a gram of hydrogen** or one milligram equivalent weight, which is shortened to **milli equivalent**.
- **Equivalent weight** of an element is its atomic weight divided by its charge.
- Atomic weight of potassium (K^+) is **39** and its charge is **one**.
- **39** grams of potassium (K^+) will displace **one** gram of H^+.
- Equivalent weight of potassium (K^+) is **39**.

- Calcium (Ca^{2+}) has an atomic weight of **40** and charge of **2**.
- Equivalent weight of Ca^{2+} is 40/2 or **20**.
- **CEC** of soils influences the capacity of the soil to hold nutrients such as Ca, Mg, NH_4^+ etc. and the quantity of a nutrient required to change its relative level in soils.
- Percentage of bases in the total cations (except hydrogen) present on the exchange complex is called **base saturation**.
- Hydrogen is a cation, but it is **acidic** and not basic like Ca, Mg, K, Na.
- **Per cent base saturation** indicates the proportion of basic cations in CEC.
- Availability of nutrients increases with their **saturation** per cent.
- **Anion exchange capacity** is less in magnitude compared to **CEC**.
- When plant absorbs cations, roots release **H^+ ions** in exchange resulting in decrease in soil pH.
- If anions are absorbed, **OH^- ions** are released into the soil solution increasing pH.
- Small increase in H^+ or OH^- concentration does not reflect on soil pH due to **buffering capacity** of soil.
- **CEC** is the principal buffering mechanism in soil.
- Some of the exchangeable cations **are basic (Ca^{2+}, Mg^{2+} etc.)** and others are **acidic (H^+, Al^{3+})**.
- Only **active** portion of the H^+ ions are measured in the pH.
- **Apatite** mineral contains **phosphorus**.
- **Mica** and **feldspars** contain potassium.
- Minerals containing calcium are **dolomite, calcite, calcium carbonate, gypsum** etc.
- **Dolomite** is a source of **magnesium**.
- **Manganite** and **pyrolusite** minerals are source of **manganese**.
- **Olivine** is a source of **molybdenum**.
- **Sphalerite** is a source of **zinc**.
- On mineralization, organic matter releases **ammonium** and **nitrate**.
- Optimum soil moisture for mineralization is **50 to 70 per cent water holding capacity** of soils.

- Mineralization is **temperature** dependent process and rate of mineralization is more at **high** temperatures.
- Immediately after application of urea, it is hydrolysed in the presence of **urease** and forms **ammonium carbonate**.
- **Ammonium carbonate** is an **unstable** compound and decomposes into **ammonium** and **carbon dioxide**.
- Ammonium is adsorbed on the clay complex, a portion is absorbed by the crop and around **11%** is lost as volatilization.
- Sine urea is soluble, leaching losses occur under **lowland** conditions.
- Mixing urea with soil and incubating for 24 to 48 hours results in conversion of urea into **ammonical ion** and adsorbed on complex **reducing** leaching losses.
- Incubating urea with soil is applicable only to **acid and neutral** rice soil.
- Incubating urea with soil increases volatilization in **alkaline** soils.
- Volatilization losses range from **0.1 to 20.0** per cent.
- Volatilization losses can be reduced by **incorporation of fertilizers** or **by placement**.
- Loss of nutrients beyond root zone along with water is known as **leaching**.
- **Nitrate** forms of nitrogenous fertilizers are subjected to higher leaching losses compared to other forms.
- Leaching losses with **ammonical** fertilizers are less as ammonium ions are adsorbed on clay complex.
- Leaching losses of fertilizers are **more** in submerged soils and in soils with less CEC.
- Nitrates present in the soil are converted into **elemental nitrogen** and is lost into the atmosphere.
- Denitrification losses are more in **submerged** soils.
- Fixation of ammonium is due to trapping of these ions within crystal lattice of **montmorillonite, illite** and **vermiculite** minerals.
- The above minerals fix more ammonium when the soil is dry due to contraction of these minerals.

- Amount of nitrogen fixed ranges from **4 to 54** per cent of total N content.
- Mineralization is faster in **aerobic** soils and is carried out by **fungi, actinomycetes and bacteria**.
- When large quantities of organic matter is added to the soils, the microorganisms utilize **available nitrogen** in the soils for their multiplication.
- Temporary locking up of nitrogen in microorganisms is called **immobilization**.
- **Immobilization** is reverse process of mineralization.
- Inorganic phosphorus is **more** in soil than organic phosphorus.
- Inorganic forms of soil phosphorus are **Ca-P, Fe-P and Al-P**.
- Dominant form of phosphorus in vertisols is **Ca-P**.
- Dominant form of phosphorus in alfisols is **Fe-P**.
- In Indian soils, Ca-P is around **40 to 50 per cent** of total phosphorus in neutral and alkaline soils and **more than 50 per cent** in alkaline soils.
- Fe-P and Al-P are **less than 10 per cent** in these soils.
- Phosphorus in soil solution is in the form of **primary and secondary orthophosphates ($H_2PO_4^-$ and HPO_4^{2-})**.
- **Primary orthophosphate ($H_2PO_4^-$)** is more in **acid** soils.
- **Secondary orthophosphate (HPO_4^{2-})** is more in **alkaline** soils.
- Phosphorus in soil solution depends on **rate of decomposition of organic matter** and **rate of reaction with inorganic fraction**.
- Organic and inorganic phosphorus is in equilibrium with **phosphorus in soil solution**.
- Fixation of phosphorus is by **adsorption**, **isomorphous substitution** and **double decomposition**.
- Fixation of phosphorus is influenced by **pH**, **nature and amount of clay, free oxides of Fe and Al, calcium carbonate** and **organic matter**.
- Acidic soils fix **more** phosphates than neutral, alkaline and calcareous soils.
- At pH **2 to 5**, fixation is mainly by formation of **insoluble Fe and Al phosphates** as Fe and Al are more in acid soils.

- Within the pH range of **4.5 to 7.5**, phosphate is fixed on clay particles by replacing two hydroxyl ions from aluminium in clay with one ion of primary orthophosphate and by forming clay phosphate linkage.
- Within the pH range of **6 to 10**, phosphate is precipitated as **phosphates of calcium or magnesium** as calcium and magnesium are more in alkaline range.
- Phosphorus fixation is more when the **clay** content is high.
- Vermiculite and smectite clay fixes **more** phosphorus than kaolinite.
- Black soils have higher fixing capacity than red soils.
- Presence of **oxides of Fe & Al** results in formation of sparingly soluble phosphate.
- Phosphate fixation is high in soils with high **$CaCO_3$**.
- Presence of **FYM** shortens period of 'P' fixation and promotes its availability.
- Application of **poultry manure** decreases phosphorus availability initially, increases rapidly and attains steady state after 20 days.
- Crop production on **red soils** is largely limited by low availability of **phosphorus**, which is attributed to adsorption of phosphate by minerals including Fe and Al oxides and Kaolinite.
- Water soluble potassium is present in the soil solution as **K^+ ion**. It is in equilibrium with exchangeable K.
- Fixed, exchangeable and soluble potassium are in dynamic equilibrium in soil.
- Unavailable K or fixed K in mica and feldspars made available slowly through weathering process.
- **Iron** is most abundant metal element in earth crust.
- Iron occurs as oxides, hydroxides, phosphates in primary and secondary minerals.
- Iron deficiency occurs in **calcareous** soils and soils with **high phosphorus**.
- Available and exchangeable iron **decreases** with increase in pH as it is inversely related to solubility of iron.
- Higher concentration of **phosphorus** causes deposition of iron on root surfaces or just inside the root, possibly as **iron phosphate**.

- Iron is oxidized in the **rhizosphere**.
- **Grasses** have **more** oxidizing power than legumes.
- Iron availability is **reduced** with oxidation.
- Iron availability is higher in **submerged** soils due to reduction of **insoluble ferric** compounds to **soluble ferrous** compounds.
- **Organic matter** improves availability of iron.
- **Zinc in earth surface is mainly found as sphalerite a sulphide mineral.**
- Zinc also exists as a constituent of organic matter.
- Zinc transformations are mainly influenced by pH.
- Within 24 hours after application of fertilizers only 2% soluble zinc is present in soil solution in soils with pH above 7.0.
- Adsorption of zinc on clay complex and organic matter is **high** at higher pH.
- Zinc availability is more in **acid soils**.
- Zinc availability **reduced** with higher level of phosphates due to low solubility of zinc phosphate.
- Zinc availability **reduced** with high organic matter as zinc is strongly adsorbed on **humus**.
- **Zinc deficiency** is common in **calcareous** soils due to adsorption of zinc or carbonates of Ca & Mg and formation of insoluble carbonates.
- **The primary minerals of manganese are present chiefly as oxides and to some extent as carbonates and silicates.**
- Secondary minerals of manganese are **pyrolusite** and **manganite**.
- Manganese in the soil is generally considered to exist in **divalent** **(Mn^{2+}), trivalent (Mn_2O_3) and tetravalent (MnO_2)** forms in equilibrium.
- Availability of manganese **increases** in acid soils as in the case of iron.
- In acid soils, the available manganese is up to **16 per cent** of total manganese content of soils, while in alkaline soils it seldom exceeds **one percent**.
- Manganese availability is **more** in **submerged soil** due to **reduction of insoluble manganic** compounds to **soluble manganous** compounds.

- **Tri and tetra-valent** forms of Mn are present under high pH and oxidizing conditions.
- **Calcium carbonate** decreases manganese availability due to strong binding of **Mn^{2+}** on calcium carbonate.
- Organic matter **decreases** the availability of manganese.
- Copper in earth crust occurs mainly as sulphides and most abundant mineral of copper is **chalcopyrite ($CuFeS_2$)**.
- Solubility of copper fertilizers **decreases** with a rise in soil pH. It is due to adsorption of Cu^{2+} on soil colloids and due to precipitation as **copper hydroxides**.
- Copper is fixed strongly on **organic matter**.
- Molybdenum is present in soil as **MoO_4^{2-}**.
- Unlike other micronutrients, **molybdenum** availability is high at **high pH**.
- Oxides of Fe and Al **increase** the adsorption of molybdenum.
- Higher level of **P fertilizers** increases availability of **molybdenum**, but **sulphur** reduces it.
- Higher soil moisture **increases** molybdenum availability due to **decrease in ferric iron** which is responsible for adsorption.
- Organic matter increases availability of **Fe and B**, but reduces availability of **Mn, Zn and Cu**.
- **Acidity** increases the availability of Fe, Mn and Cu.
- **Alkalinity** increases the availability of **Mo**.
- In calcareous soils the availability of **Zn and Mn** decreases.
- **Submergence** increases the availability of **Fe, Mn and Mo**.
- Based on the temperature requirement, microorganisms are grouped into **psychrophiles (< 10°C)**, **mesophiles (20-40°C)** and **thermophiles (>40°C)**.
- **Actinomycetes** dies under anerobic conditions.
- The optimum moisture for aerobic bacteria is **50 to 75** per cent water holding capacity.
- Actinomycetes predominates in **dry regions**.
- Most microflora of the soil are **mesophiles** and grow well at **15 to 45°C** with optimum being **37°C**.
- Direct sunlight is injurious to most microflora.

- **Bacteria** grows well within pH range of **6.5 to 8.0**.
- **Fungi** prefer **acidic** pH range (**4.5 to 6.5**).
- **Actinomycetes** prefer **slightly alkaline** conditions.
- Fungi involved in decomposition of cellulose are ***Penicillium, Trichoderma, Aspergillus*** *and* ***Fusarium***.
- Lignin is decomposed by **Basidiomycetes** fungi.
- **Protein** is decomposed by fungal species like ***Fusaria, Aspergillus, Mucor*** and ***Citromycetes***.
- Mycorrhizae that live inside roots (endotrophic) are ***Phoma and Rhizoctonia***.
- The ectotrophic mycorrhizae which develop on root surfaces are ***Amanita and Boletus***.
- Rhizobium is a **heterotrophic**, **aerobic** bacteria.
- The *Rhizobium* present in the root nodules are known as bacteroids and each host cell contains several bacteroids.
- Though *Rhizobium* is aerobic, **nitrogenase** enzyme functions only in the absence of oxygen.
- The host cells that contain bacteroids produce a reddish protein called **leghaemoglobin**.
- **Leghaemoglobin** has high affinity for oxygen and even the low level of oxygen present around the host cell is absorbed.
- **There are some actinomycetes which fix nitrogen on non-leguminous plants.**
- ***Casuarina alder*** lives in association with ***Casuarina*** and fixes atmospheric nitrogen.
- Free living bacteria capable of fixing atmospheric nitrogen are ***Azotobacter chroococcum, A.vinelandi*** *and* ***Clostridium pasteurianum***.
- *Azotobacter* is a **heterotrophic** bacteria.
- *Clostridium* is an **anaerobic** bacteria.
- ***Azospirillum*** fixes atmospheric nitrogen in **grasses**.
- Nitrification ceases below **pH 5.0**, the optimum being **6.5 to 7.5**.
- The optimum temperature for nitrification is **30°C to 35°C**.
- The important denitrifying bacteria are ***Pseudomonas*** and ***Bacillus***.

- The optimum C:N:P ratio is **100:10:1** and if the C:P ratio is more than **100:1**, immobilization of phosphorus occurs.
- The C:S ratio of **50:1** is critical.
- The pH of most acid and alkaline soils converges between **6 and 7** within 2 to 3 weeks after flooding.
- Hydrates of ferric oxide are reduced to ferrous compounds within two to three weeks after submergence. As a result, the soil colour changes from brown to grey.
- **Manganese** is more rapidly reduced and rendered soluble than **iron** compounds.
- **Actonomycetes** and **fungi** are absent in submerged soils.
- Availability of **zinc** is reduced under **flooded conditions** due to precipitation as zinc hydroxide ($Zn(OH)_2$) or as zinc carbonate ($ZnCO_3$) due to high concentration of carbon dioxide.

Chapter 8

Problematic Soils and Management

- More than 50% of net cultivated area falls in the category of problem soils.
- Wind erosion occurs in **arid and semiarid areas** devoid of vegetation where wind velocity is high.

Highly permeable coarse textured soils:

- Productivity of coarse textured sandy and loamy sand soils is low due to its exceptional permeability which permits percolation of water and nutrients and does not encourage high level of costly inputs.
- Occurs in larger areas of **Rajasthan, Haryana and Gujarat**.
- Soil compaction and clay mixing should be done to improve them.

Slowly permeable soils:

- These soils associated with black clay soil. Occurs in **MP, Maharashtra, AP, Gujarat and TN**.
- Problems of these soils are linked with topography and annual rainfall.

Crusting soils:

- Crusting of alluvial soils is serious problem all over country especially in **Haryana, Punjab, Rajasthan, Bihar and West Bengal**.
- Formation of soil crust involved breakdown of soil aggregates by the impact of raindrops, dispersion of soil water to form soil suspension and then resedimentation.
- Application of FYM or green manuring will improve them.

Red chalka soils:

- Red sandy loam soils “chalka” cover large area in **Andhra Pradesh**.
- Becomes very hard on drying, so crop growth adversely affected.

- Incorporation of slow decomposing crop residues and other inorganic materials such as powdered groundnut shell, paddy husk each at 50q/ha helps in favourable crop growth by reducing hardness of the soil.

Based on chemical nature:

Salt affected soils:

- Soils containing excess soluble salts in the root zone which adversely affect growth and yield of crop plants are called **salt affected soils**.
- In India salt affected soils covers **7 mha**.

  UP-1.29 mha, Gujarat – 1.21 mha, West Bengal – 0.85 mha, Rajasthan – 0.72 mha, Punjab – 0.69 mha
- Salt affected soils are categorized into three groups
  1. Saline soils
  2. Alkali soils (sodic) soils
  3. Saline alkali soils

Saline soils:

EC> 4 dS/m, pH < 8.5, ESP < 15

- They have excessive salt concentration in soils which adversely affect the plant growth mainly due to increased **osmotic pressure** which causes **physiological drought**.
- Predominant salts are **Cl^- and SO_4^{2-} of Na^+, Mg^{2+}**
- There is imbalance of available plant nutrients leading to toxicity or deficiency.
- Excess soluble salts should be reduced upto moderate levels (6 dS/m in 0-30 cm depth) by leaching with good quality water.
- Leaching requirement calculated according to intensity of problem and quality of leaching water.
- Leaching is the process of displacing the saline soil solution from the root zone with water of lower salt concentration

$$\text{Leaching requirement} = \frac{Ddw}{Diw} = \frac{ECiw}{ECdw}$$

Ddw = Depth of drainage water

Diw = Depth of irrigation water

ECiw = EC of irrigation water

ECdw = EC of drainage water

- Provision of drainage is of utmost importance in the case of saline soils resulting in lowering water table, reducing salt content and increasing crop yields.
- Mulching helps to reduce soil salinity. Mulching reduces upward movement of salt due to decline in evaporation losses.
- Addition of organic matter improves physical condition of the soil and more water holding capacity keeps salts in diluted form.
- **Barley, cotton, sugarbeet** – tolerant to salinity

  Wheat, rice, oats, maize, sorghum, potato – medium tolerance

  Legumes, Beans, groundnut – sensitive

Alkali soils:

- EC< 4 dS/m, pH > 8.5, ESP > 15
- Excessive exchangeable Na, high pH, lack of nutrients Ca, N, Zn and poor physical conditions, coupled with poor aeration are chief causes for low productivity.
- Soil colour becomes black due to dispersion of clay and organic matter
- Water infiltration rate becomes very low resulting in stagnation of water
- Soil becomes **cloddy and hard at drying.**
- Heavy irrigation is applied after the addition of gypsum to facilitate the leaching of soluble slats of Na.
- In order to replace excessive amount of Na, application of **Ca** is essential.
- Several amendments such as **gypsum, S, H_2SO_4, $CaCl_2$, $FeSO_4$, iron pyrites, $Al_2(SO_4)_3$** are available but gypsum is most popular.

Saline-alkali soils:

EC >4 dS/m, pH > 8.5, ESP >15

- These soils have mixture of characteristics of both saline and alkali soils.

- Soils showing high salinity and ESP should be reclaimed for both but first for salinity and later for excessive exchangeable Na.
- Tolerance of crops to exchangeable sodium

  Tolerant – **Rice, Sugarbeet, Dhaincha**

  Medium tolerant – **Wheat, Barley, Oats, Millets**

  Sensitive – **Legumes, Maize, Groundnut**

Acid soils:

- Blue litmus paper turns red in contact with moist acid soil.
- These soils high in exchangeable **Al^{3+} and H^+**, with pH < 5.5 and responds to lime application.
- Exchangeable Al^{3+} derived from breakdown of soil clay minerals.
- Soils with organic matter more than 15% show acidic condition because of considerable exchangeable H^+ in addition to exchangeable Al^{3+}.
- The greatest inhibition effect of an increasing Al^{3+} concentration in soil solution is on the absorption of Ca^{2+} irrespective of plant type and absorption of Mg^{2+} and K^+ is also inhibited.
- These soils normally belong to laterite and lateritic, red and yellow group rich in Kaolinitic clay minerals with low CEC.
- They have **low organic matter, N, P and MgO**.
- Acid soils cover a large area of about 4.5 mha in **Assam, Tripura, Manipur, West Bengal, Bihar, Odisha, Karnataka, Tamil Nadu, Himachal Pradesh, Kerala**.
- Principal factors which influence lime requirement are **pH, amount and type of clay, CEC, buffering capacity of soil**.
- **Paddy, Potato, Tea, Millets** – tolerant to acidity

  Semi tolerant – Bengal gram, Maize, Sorghum, Peas, Wheat, Barley

  Sensitive – Arhar, Soybean, Cotton, Oats

Chapter 9

Tillage

- **Jethro Tull** is considered as father of tillage.
- **Jethro Tull** proposed a theory that plants absorb minute particles of soils.
- **Tillage** is the physical manipulation of soil to result in good tilth for better germination and subsequent growth of crops.
- **Tilth** is a physical condition of the soil resulting from tillage.
- **Tilth** indicates **size distribution of aggregates** and **mellowness or friability** of soil.
- Relative proportion of different sized soil aggregates is known as **size distribution** of soil aggregates.
- Higher percent of **larger aggregates > 5mm diameter** are necessary for **irrigated agriculture.**
- Higher percent of **smaller aggregates of 1-2 mm diameter** are desirable for **dry land agriculture.**
- Size distribution of aggregates depends on **soil type**, **soil moisture content at** which **ploughing** is done and subsequent cultivation.
- **Mellowness or friability** is that property of soil by which the clods when dry become more **crumbly.**
- Seed bed should be **fine** for **small seeded crops** and **moderate** for bold **seeded crops.**
- Summer deep ploughing improves soil structure due to **alternate drying and cooling**.
- **Frequent harrowing** results in destruction of soil structure.
- Tillage at improper moisture damages soil structure and leads to development of **hard pans**.
- Tillage hastens organic matter decomposition by improving soil aeration which helps in multiplication of microorganisms.

- Degradation of herbicides, pesticides and allelopathic chemicals **increases** under tillage.
- Roots occupy only a **tenth of soil mass.**
- Crop residues and farmyard manure decomposition **increases** when incorporated in the soil.
- Air filled spaces between soil particles constitute **pore space**.
- With tillage pore space is **increased**.
- When soil is in **good tilth**, **capillary and non capillary pores** would be **roughly equal**.
- Soils with **crumbly and granular clods** are considered as soils with **good structure**.
- When soil is subjected to tillage at **optimum soil moisture**, **crumb structure** is delayed.
- Soil aggregates of **1-5 mm size** are favourable for growth of the plants.
- Bulk density of tilled soil is **less** than untilled soil.
- **Organic matter** is mainly responsible for **dark brown to dark grey** colour of soil.
- Tillage **increases** oxidation and decomposition of organic matter resulting in fading of colour.
- **Roughness** is a measure of **micro-elevations** and **depressions** caused by furrows and ridges, clods and depression.
- **Random roughness** indicates elevation and depressions of the field without a pattern.
- **Tillage** creates optimum temperature for seed germination and seedling establishment.
- Tillage loosens the soil surface and **decreases** thermal conductivity and heat capacity.
- **Preparatory cultivation** is carried out before sowing the crop.
- **After cultivation** is practiced after sowing the crop.
- Tillage operations that are carried out from the time of harvest of a crop to sowing of next crop is known as **preparatory cultivation.**
- Preparatory cultivation includes **primary tillage**, **secondary tillage** and **layout of seed bed**.

- **Ploughing** is opening of compacted soil with the help of different ploughs.
- Ploughing is mainly done to open the hard soil.
- **Optimum** range of **soil moisture** for effective ploughing is **25 to 50% depletion of available soil moisture.**
- **Light soils** can be ploughed in wide range of soil moisture conditions while the range is narrow for **heavy soils**.
- Depth of ploughing depends on the **effective root zone depth** of the crops.
- Crops with **taproot system** require greater depth of soil, while **fibrous, shallow rooted crops** require shallow ploughing.
- In heavy soils **3 to 5 ploughings** are needed.
- In light soils **1 to 3 ploughings** are required.
- Country plough is used for multiple purposes.
- **Disc plough** is used for cutting of creeping or spreading grass and inversion.
- **Tractor drawn mould board** plough used for deep ploughing and inversion.
- **Animal drawn mould board plough** is used for incorporation of manures, fertilizers and plant residues.
- 1 cm of surface soil over one hectare of land weighs about **150 t.**
- In western countries deep ploughing is *50cm* depth for rainfed conditions *70cm* for irrigated conditions
- According to **CRIDA, shallow ploughing: 5-6 cm**
  medium deep ploughing: 15-20 cm
  deep ploughing: 25-30 cm
- A deep tillage of **25-30cm depth** is necessary for deep rooted crops like **pigeonpea**.
- Moderate deep tillage of **15-20 cm** is required for **maize**.
- Residual effect of deep tillage is marginal.
- It is advisable to go for deep ploughing only for **long duration, deep rooted crops**.
- Cotton roots grow to a depth of **2m** in **deep alluvial soil** without any pans.

- When hard pans are present, cotton roots grow only up to **15-20cm**.
- **Subsoiling** is breaking the hard pan without inversion and with less disturbance of top soil.
- **Chisel ploughs** are used to break **hard pans** present even at **60-70 cm**.
- Effect of subsoiling does not last long.
- To avoid closing of subsoil furrow, **vertical mulching** is adopted.
- Tillage operations carried out throughout the year are known as **year round tillage**.
- For wheat, soybean, pearl millet, groundnut, castor **flat leveled seed bed** is prepared.
- For **maize, vegetables** field has to be laid out into **ridges and furrows.**
- Sugarcane is planted in **furrows or trenches**.
- Crops like **tobacco, tomato, chillies** are planted with **equal inter and intra-row** spacing to **facilitate two-way intercultivation**.
- **Setline planting** is adopted in **Gujarat** for sowing **cotton** and **groundnut**.
- In **setline planting** every year seed rows are in the same place, since the seed lines are set permanently at wider spacings.
- In setline planting **inter-row space** is not cultivated.
- Tillage operations carried out in the standing crop are called **after tillage**.
- **After cultivation** includes **side dressing of fertilizers**, **earthing up** and **intercultivation**.
- Earthing up is carried out with **country plough** or **ridge plough**.
- **Earthing up** provides **extra support against lodging** in **sugarcane**, **more soil volume** for better growth of **tubers like potato**, facilitates **irrigation in vegetables**.
- Intercultivation serve as moisture conservation measure by closing deep cracks in black soils.
- **Ploughs** are used for primary tillage.
- **Cultivators, harrows, plank** and **rollers** are used for secondary tillage.

- Concept of **minimum tillage** was started in **USA**.
- Reason for introducing minimum tillage was high cost of tillage due to steep rise in **oil prices in 1974**.
- **Minimum tillage** aims at reducing tillage to the minimum.
- Seed germination is **lower** with minimum tillage.
- In minimum tillage **more nitrogen** has to be added as rate of decomposition of organic matter is **slow.**
- In minimum tillage **nodulation** is affected in some leguminous crops like **peas** and **broad bean**.
- **Zero tillage** is an extreme form of **minimum tillage**.
- Zero tillage is also known as **no-till.**
- In **zero tillage**, **primary tillage** completely **avoided** and **secondary tillage** is restricted to seed bed preparation in **row zone** only.
- Zero tillage is resorted to soils subjected to wind and water erosion.
- Organic matter content **increases** in zero tilled soils due to **less mineralization**.
- Large population of **perennial weeds** appears in zero tilled plots.
- Continuous adoption of zero-tillage reduced the infestation of *Phalaris minor* to a great extent.
- Successful examples of zero tillage in India are

  Rice followed by wheat in North India

  Rice followed by maize in coastal Andhra Pradesh

  Rice followed by black gram in Andhra Pradesh.
- Traditional methods of tillage are developed in **temperate moist climates** increases soil erosion when used indiscriminately in **arid land cultivation**.
- **Dust bowl of central United States** created due to ploughing original **prairie lands** for growing cereals with clean tillage methods.
- In **stubble mulch tillage**, soil protected at all times whether by growing a crop or by residues left on the surface during fallow periods.

- **Stubble mulch farming** is the year round system of managing plant residues with implements that undercut residue, loosen the soil and kill weeds.
- Unlike other tillage operations, **puddling aims at destroying soil structure.**
- Soils with bulk density **less than 1.0** are considered as **problematic soils** as puddling with animal drawn implements is difficult.

Chapter 10

Seeds and Sowing

- Seeds are used for **multiplication** purpose.
- Grains are used for **consumption** purpose.
- Sugarcane is planted with stem cuttings known as **setts**.
- Forage grasses like **napier grass**, **guinea grass**, **para grass** etc. are mainly propagated by **stem cuttings** or **rooted slips**.
- **Rooted slips** are basal two or three internodes of the stem with a few roots.
- **Tubers** are used as seed material in **potato**.
- **Grafting, budding** and **layering methods** are used for the propagation of horticultural crops.
- Good quality seed is of prime importance in agriculture.
- Cultivar is a contraction for cultivated variety.
- Cultivar is synonymous with variety.
- A **variety** is a subdivision of a species with some special characteristics.
- A **cultivar** is a unique population of plants, artificially maintained by human efforts.
- A **synthetic cultivar** is composed of plants produced by combining a number of genetically distinct but phenotypically similar lines which have been allowed to cross-pollinate at random.
- A **hybrid line** is the F_1 generation of the two inbred lines.
- **Breeders seed** originates with the **sponsoring plant breeder or institution** and provides initial source of all other classes of certified seeds.
- **Foundation seed** is the **progeny of breeders seed** and is so handled to maintain the highest standard of genetic identity and purity.

- **Foundation seed** is produced under **direct supervision of technical persons.**
- **Registered seed** is the **progeny of foundation seed** or sometimes from **breeders seed.**
- Registered seed is produced under specified standards approved by the certifying agency.
- **Certified seed** is the **progeny of registered seed**, sometimes of **breeders or foundation seed** which is produced in **largest volume** and distributed to growers.

Type of Pollination	Crop	Isolation distance		
		Foundation seed	Registered seed	Certified seed
Self pollinated	Rice, wheat, barley, oats, groundnut, soybean, cowpea	Fields should be separated by a definite boundary	-	-
Self pollinated with certain amount of cross pollination	Cotton (Upland type)	30 m from cultivars which differ markedly	-	-
	Cotton (Egyptian type)	400m	400m	200m
	Tomato	60m	30m	9m
Cross pollination by insects	Millets	400m	400m	200m
	Onion	1600m	800m	400m
Cross pollination by wind	Grasses	273m	91m	50m

- Separation of different cultivars is needed in production of **self-pollinated plants** to prevent mechanical mixing of seed during harvest. Minimum distance usually specified between plots is **3m.**
- **Viability** and **vigour** are important characters of seed quality.
- **Viability** can be expressed by the germination percentage which indicates the number of seedlings produced by a given number of seeds.

- Low germination percentage, low germination rate and low vigour are often associated.
- **Vigour** is indicated by the **higher germination percentage**, **high germination rate** and **quicker seedling growth**.
- **Germination percentage** is the number of seeds germinated to number of seeds planted and is expressed as percentage.
- Germination rate is expressed in two ways
  1. Number of days required to produce a given germination percentage
  2. Average number of days required for radical or plumule to emerge
- Moisture content at harvest is in the range of **25-35%** for most of the seeds.
- After harvest seeds are sun dried for **2-3 days**.
- When the outside temperature is more than **40°C**, seeds should be dried under **shade** to maintain viability.
- Seed vigour tests may be categorized as quick tests, standard germination and stress type germination tests.
- **Quick tests** can be performed within 24 hours.
- Standard germination and stress type germination tests require **7 to 12 day**s.
- **Calcium assay** is included as a quick method to assess quality since it is a critical nutrient for seed groundnuts.
- **Tetrazolium** and **electrical conductivity** tests both evaluate aspects of tissue integrity.
- Standard germination test is indicative of seed vigour with **> 85% germination** considered strong vigour.
- **Accelerated aging** and **cold germination tests** are stress type tests that are good indicators of seed strength.
- Onion is propagated by **bulbs**.
- Gladiolus is propagated by **corms**.
- Potato is propagated by **tubers**.
- **Sweet potato** and **Dahlia** are propagated by **tuberous roots**.
- **Rhizome** is a specialized stem.
- **Sugarcane, banana** and **many grasses** have rhizome structures.

- Soil moisture in the range of **50% available moisture** to **field capacity** is sufficient to ensure **good germination of seeds** though **80% of soil moisture at field capacity** gives **best germination**.
- Soil temperature of **10°C for temperate crops** and **20°C for tropical crops** is the **minimum** requirement for germination.
- Establishment of crop is difficult under **zero tillage** and in **problematic soils** like saline and alkaline soils.
- When soil sodicity is high **transplanting** gives better establishment of rice than drilling.
- Germination in wheat in saline soils with EC 13 dS/m can be improved by soaking seeds for 24 hours in **gibberellic acid solution (200 mg/l)**.
- Soaking of seeds in **thiamin solution (200 mg/l)** reduces adverse effects of salinity on germination and seedling growth.
- In **SRI** method **10 days** age rice seedlings are transplanted.
- In other methods **65 days** aged rice seedlings are also transplanted.
- In general, **younger** the **seedlings**, **better** is the **establishment** and **yield of crop**.
- Sowing very early in the season may not be advantageous.
- Sowing rainfed groundnut in **June** may result in failure of the crop if there is prolonged dry spell from the second week of June to second week of July.
- However, in certain situations early sowing increases the yield.
- Advancing sowing of rabi sorghum from November to **September-October**, increases the yields considerably as more moisture would be available for early sown crop.
- The **optimum time of sowing** for **tall varieties of wheat** was **October**, for **dwarf varieties** it was **second or third week of November**.
- **Rainfed sorghum** yields are reduced due to delay in sowing beyond **June**.
- In rainfed groundnut, sowing beyond **July** reduced the yields of all varieties at Tirupati.
- Delayed sowing of redgram and soybean reduced yields due to early induction of flowering, unfavorable temperature and rainfall.
- Most of the tropical plants are **short-day plants**.

- Day length **starts falling** from **July onwards**, but the reduction in day length is **steep from October** onwards.
- Flowering is induced in **short-day** crops earlier due to **absolute short days** or **relative reduction in day length**.
- If sowings are delayed, there is very little time for **vegetative growth** leading to reduction in yield.
- **Late sown** crops are exposed to increased population of pests and diseases.
- Late sown sorghum is subjected to severe attack of **shoot borer**.
- Optimum time of sowing for most of **tropical crops** is immediately after the onset of monsoon *i.e.,* **June or July**.
- Optimum time of sowing for **temperate crops** like wheat and barley is from **last week of October** to **first fortnight of January**.
- Optimum time of sowing for most of **summer crops** is **first fortnight of January**.

DEPTH OF SOWING

- Uneven depth of sowing results in uneven crop stand.
- Shallow or deep sowing results in lesser plant population as all seeds do not germinate.
- Weed problem becomes severe under uneven plant population with large gaps.
- Optimum depth of sowing depends on size of **seed**, **seed reserve**, **coleoptile length** and **soil moisture**.
- Crops with **bigger sized seeds** like **groundnut**, **castor**, **sunflower** etc. can be sown even up to a depth of **6cm**.
- **Small sized seeds** like **tobacco**, **ragi**, **gingelly** have to be sown **as shallow as possible**.
- If seeds are sown too shallow, the surface soil dries up quickly and germination may not occur due to lack of moisture.
- Shallow sized seeds which are sown shallow should be watered frequently to ensure good emergence of crop.
- The **thumb rule** to sow seeds to a depth approximately **3 to 4 times their diameter**.
- Optimum depth of sowing for most of the **field crops** ranges between **3 cm to 5 cm**.
- For small seeds like **gingelly**, **finger millet** and **pearl millet** optimum depth of planting is **2 cm to 3cm**.

- Very small seeds like **tobacco** are placed at a depth of **1 cm** by broadcasting on the soil surface and mixing them by raking.
- Traditional tall varieties of wheat have **long** coleoptiles and Mexican varieties have **short** coleoptiles.
- Traditional tall varieties of wheat are sown **deep** in the soil with seed drill.
- **Mexican** varieties do not emerge when they are sown deep.
- Mexican wheat give higher yields compared to tall varieties only when they are sown at a depth of **4cm**.

METHODS OF ESTABLISHING THE CROP

- **Broadcasting** is the most primitive method of sowing crops.
- In **broadcasting** seeds are spread uniformly over well prepared land and are covered by ploughing or planking.
- In broadcasting method seeds fall at different depths leading to uneven crop stand.
- It is common to observe plants from seedling stage to flowering in crops that are sown by **broadcasting**.
- Intercultivation is difficult in **broadcasting** as seeds fall randomly.
- **Broadcasting** is followed in **fodder crops** or crops where seeds are cheap or crops which can easily establish and suppress weeds.
- In **drilling method** seeds are sown in lines with seed drills.
- **Drilling** facilitates uniform depth of sowing resulting in uniform crop stand.
- Weeds can be controlled economically by inter-cultivation in line sown crops.
- In planting method, crops with bigger sized seeds and which need wider spacing like cotton, maize, potato, sugarcane etc. seeds or seed material is placed in the soil by manual labour or by machine.
- In transplanting method **thumb rule** for **optimum age of seedlings** is one week for **every month of total duration crop**.
- The depth of transplanting should be as **shallow** as possible for getting more **number of tillers** in tillering crops.
- Transplanting of rice seedlings more than **2 cm deep** results in poor tillering.

TYPE OF SOWING

- **Dry sowing** is adopted in **black soils** where sowing operations are difficult to carry out once rains commence.
- Seeds are sown in dry soil around **7 to 10** days before the anticipated receipts of sowing rains.
- **Wet sowing** is the most common method of sowing crops.
- Minimum amount of rainfall necessary for taking up sowing is **20mm**.
- Plastic mulch helps in increasing soil temperature by **1 to 5°C**.
- Providing light irrigation (20-40mm) preferably with sprinkler 5 to 7 days after sowing helps in good establishment of winter sown groundnut in south India, by increasing soil moisture and by marginally raising soil temperature.
- In olden days cotton seeds are rubbed with paste made of **wet dung and earth** and then dried to facilitate in sowing seeds.
- Fluff on cotton seeds can also be removed by treating the seeds with **concentrated sulphuric acid** for two minutes.
- Earth or sand is mixed with seeds of **ragi, gingelly, tobacco** etc. before sowing as seeds are minute to facilitate in **sowing**.

BREAKING DORMANCY

- **Scarification** is the process of breaking, scratching, mechanically altering or softening the seed coats to make them permeable to water and gases.
- In hot water treatment seeds are dropped in water of **75° to 100°C**.
- In acid treatment, **concentrated sulphuric acid** twice the volume of seed is added.
- Duration of acid treatment varies from **10 minutes to six hours or more** depending on the seed coat of plant species.
- In leaching method germination inhibitors are removed by soaking seeds in running water or by placing them in frequent changes of water.
- Length of leaching time is **12 to 24 hours**.
- Treating the seeds with **gibberellic acid (GA_3) of 500 ppm** for a period of 12 hours breaks the dormancy.

- **Cytokinins** and **ethylene** are also used to break dormancy.
- In **priming** seeds are soaked in water for **24 to 48 hours** to induce incipient germination.
- **American cotton** is sown after soaking the seeds in water for **12 to 24 hours.**
- Safe duration of soaking seeds is **24 hours** for **maize and rice, 12 hours for wheat** and **10 hours for chickpea.**

1000 SEED WEIGHT OF DIFFERENT CROPS

Crop	Test Weight/Seed Index (g)
Rice	20-30
Wheat	36-50
Barley	35-40
Pearlmillet	5-9
Grain Sorghum	25-30
Finger millet	1.0 – 4.5
Chickpea(Desi)	140-259
Chickpea (Kabuli)	260–450
Pigeonpea	45-105
Lentil	17-38
Blackgram	36-49
Greengram	20-70
Soybean	80-150
Cowpea	100-250
Horsegram	25-41
Groundnut	200-250
Rapeseed and mustard	3-5
Sunflower	40-50
Safflower	10-70
Castor	100-150
Linseed	4-8
Sesame	2.85-4.06
Niger	3-5
Tobacco	0.05-0.12
Cotton (Seed Index or 100 seed weight)	7-10

Chapter 11

Plant Population

- Establishment of **optimum plant population** is essential to get **maximum yield**.
- In crops grown on stored soil moisture under rainfed conditions, population should not be high to deplete most of the moisture before crop matures and not low to leave moisture unutilized.
- Under conditions of sufficient soil moisture and nutrients, **higher** population is necessary to utilize other growth factors efficiently.
- If soil moisture and nutrients are not limiting, yield of crop is limited by **solar radiation**.
- Level of plant population should be such that **maximum solar radiation** is intercepted.
- Full yield potential of individual plant is achieved at **wider spacing**.
- Yield per plant **decreases** gradually as plant population per unit area is increased, but yield per unit area is **increased** due to efficient utilization of resources.
- Maximum yield per unit area is obtained when individual plants are subjected to **severe competition**.
- Plant height **increases** with increase in plant population due to competition for **light**.
- Sometimes moderate increase in plant population may not increase but **decrease** plant height due to competition for **water** and **nutrients** but not for light.
- Increase in plant height due to higher plant population is advantageous for better light interception due to exposure of individual leaves at wider vertical interval.
- Leaf thickness **increases** with increase in plant density.
- Leaf orientation is altered due to **population pressure**.
- Leaves are erect, narrow and are managed at **longer vertical intervals** under **high plant densities**.

- Drymatter production per unit area **increases** with increase in plant population up to a limit when the reduction in the growth of a plant is more than compensated by increase in the number of plants per unit area.
- In **indeterminate plants** at higher plant density yield reduces due to reduction in **number of ears**.
- In determinate plants at higher plant density yield reduces due to reduction in **size of ears or panicles**.
- Highly branching or tillering plants behave as **indeterminate** plants, and yield reduction is due to reduction in number of ears, pods etc.
- In non tillering or non-branching plants reduced yield is due to reduction in size of ears.
- Under very high population levels, plants become **barren**.
- **Holliday** suggested two types of response curves, **asymptotic** and **parabolic** to quantify the relationship between **plant population** and **yield**.

ASYMPTOTIC RESPONSE

- In **fodder crops** where **entire dry matter** is the **economic product** or in **tobacco** where most of the dry matter is economic product, response to increasing plant density is **asymptotic**.
- In **asymptotic response** with **increase in plant population after a limit**, yield or dry matter does not decreases instead it **remains constant**.
- For **fodder crops**, dense stands are recommended to get maximum yield.
- Dense stands in fodder crops provides **lean stems** and more **leafy fodder**.
- Asymptotic curve is expressed as follows

$$Y = Ap + \frac{1}{1 + Abp}$$

Y = Yield of dry matter/unit area

A = Apparent maximum yield per plant

P = number of plants per unit area

b = linear regression coefficient

- Maximum yield obtained in particular situation when the plants are widely spaced with practically no competition is denoted as **A or apparent maximum yield per plant.**
- The term $\frac{1}{1+Abp}$ represents maxima in which maximum plant yield (A) is reduced by increasing competition resulting from greater plant density.

PARABOLIC RESPONSE:

- In **crops** where **economic yield** is a **fraction of total dry matter**, relationship between plant population and yield is expressed by **parabolic curve.**
- In **parabolic response**, yield increases with increase in plant population, then reaches maximum. With further increase in population yield decreases unlike asymptotic curve.
- Parabolic response can be fitted to **quadratic equation.**

$$Y = a + bp + cp^2$$

Y = Yield/unit area

P = plant population

a, b and c = regression coefficients

- Drawback in representing parabolic response as quadratic equation is yield does not fall suddenly with increase in plant population, there is a plateau for some range of plant population depending on elasticity of plants.
- Disadvantage of quadratic function can be overcome by **square root function**

$$Y = a + bp + c\sqrt{p}$$

- As density increases, the amount of dry matter in vegetative parts **increases.**
- **Economic yield** increases with increase in plant population up to a point and subsequently decreases with increase in plant population.
- **Biological yield** increases with increase in plant population up to a point and with further increase in plant population no additional biological yield can be obtained.
- Most important factors that influence optimum plant population are **day length** and **temperature**.

- **Photosensitive varieties** respond to day length resulting in change in size of the plant.
- Red gram plants sown as **winter** crop will have half the size of those grown in monsoon crops.
- Optimum population of monsoon season red gram is **55,000 plants/ha**, whereas for winter crop it is **3.33 lakhs/ha**.
- In winter as low temperature retards rate of growth, **higher population** is established for quicker ground cover.
- In **sorghum**, when climate is **favourable** during pre-anthesis period, optimum plant population is **two lakh plants/ha**, when climate is not congenial for growth during pre-anthesis it is **four lakh plants/ha**.
- In **non tillering plants like maize**, higher the fertility more should be the plant population to get higher yield.
- Increasing plant population increases the proportion of ears or fruits in the upper layer of canopy which facilitates ease in harvesting.
- **Cotton** sown with a **closer spacing**, produces mostly **sympodial branches** and most of the bolls appear in the top layer of the canopy.
- With higher plant population, rice panicles appear in the upper layer of the canopy
- **Plant geometry** refers to the shape of plant.
- **Crop geometry** refers to the shape of space available for individual plants.
- **Crop geometry** is altered by changing inter and intra-row spacing.
- **Square** arrangement of plants will be more **efficient** in the utilization of light, water and nutrients available to the individual plants than in rectangular arrangement.
- In wheat, decreasing inter-row spacing below the standard 15-12 cm *i.e.*, reducing rectangularity, generally increases yield slightly.
- In crops like **tobacco**, intercultivation in both directions is possible in **square planting** and helps in effective control of weeds.

- Groundnut sown with a spacing of 30 x 10 cm gave **higher yield** than same amount of population in square planting.
- Pod yield is reduced either by increasing rectangularity or approaching towards square planting.
- Skipping of every alternate row is known as **skip row planting**.
- When one row is skipped, the population is adjusted by decreased intra-row spacing, it is known as **paired-row planting**.
- **Skip row** planting is generally resorted to introduce an intercrop.
- Gap filling is not advantageous for **short duration crops**.

Chapter 12

Soil Fertility and Nutrient Management

- **AB Stewart** laid the foundations of soil fertility research in India.
- **Lawes** was the first person to manufacture a fertilizer, he manufactured **SSP**.
- First fertilizer factory setup in India at **Ranipur** in the year **1906**.
- Quantity of plant nutrients depleted annually from Indian soils is **8-10 MT of $N+P_2O_5+K_2O$.**
- In recent soil sample analysis in India **43% deficient in Zinc**, **33% deficient in B**, **15% deficient in Iron**, **6% deficient in Manganese**, **4% deficient in Copper**.
- Nutrient deficiencies are found to be in the order **N = P > Zn = S > B > K = Fe > Mn > Cu**.
- **Mineral nutrient** refers to inorganic ion obtained from the soil and required for plant growth.
- The process of absorption, translocation and assimilation of nutrients by the plants is known as **mineral nutrition**.
- Plants need **16** elements for their growth and completion of life cycle.
- **Ni** is the nutrient considered essential for plant growth in addition to 16 nutrients.
- In addition, four elements *viz.*, **sodium**, **cobalt**, **vanadium** and **silicon** are absorbed by some plants for special purposes.
- All these essential elements are not required for all plants, but all have been found essential for one plant or the other.
- All carbon atoms and most of the oxygen atoms are derived from **carbon dioxide** which is assimilated principally in photosynthesis.
- Approximately **one-third of oxygen atoms** in organic material in higher plants are derived from soil water and **two-thirds** from carbon dioxide of the atmosphere.
- **C, H, O** are not minerals.

- Rest of the elements are absorbed from the soil and these are are called mineral elements since they are derived from minerals.
- **Arnon and stout (1939)** proposed criteria of essentiality which was refined by **Arnon (1954)**.
- Criteria of essentiality of an element are
  1. Plants cannot complete vegetative or reproductive stage of life cycle due to its deficiency.
  2. When this deficiency can be corrected or prevented only by supplying this element.
  3. When the element is directly involved in the metabolism of the plant.
- According to criteria of essentiality, **sodium** is considered as **non-essential**.
- However, **sodium** increases yield of several crops like **sugarbeets, turnips and celery.**
- **Nicholas (1961)** proposed the term **functional nutrient** for any mineral element that functions in plant metabolism whether or not its action is specific.
- **Sodium**, **cobalt**, **vanadium** and **silicon** are also considered as functional nutrients in addition to 16 essential elements.
- Number of functional nutrients is **20**.

Element	**Essentiality established by scientist**
Nitrogen	Theodore de Saussure in 1804
P,K,Ca,Mg	C.Sprengel in 1839
Boron	K.Warington in 1923
Sulphur	Sachs Knop in 1857
Iron	Gris in 1844
Manganese	Mc Hargue in 1922
Molybdenum	Arnon & Stout in 1939
Zinc	Sommer and Lipman in 1926
Copper	Sommer, Lipman, Mc Kinney in 1931
Sodium	Brownell and Wod
Cobalt	Ahmad and Evans
Silicon	Lewin
Chlorine	Broyer, Carlton, Johnson and Stout

- **C, H** and **O** which constitute **96 per cent** of total dry matter of plants are considered as **basic nutrients**.
- **C** and **O** constitute **45 per cent** each of the total dry matter.
- Nutrients required in large quantities are known as **macronutrients (N, P, K, Ca, Mg and S)**.
- **N, P and K** are called **primary nutrients**.
- **Ca, Mg and S** are known as **secondary nutrients**.
- **Secondary nutrients** are inadvertently applied to the soils through N, P and K fertilizers which contain these nutrients.
- Nutrients which are required in small quantities are known as **micronutrients or trace elements (Fe, Zn, Cu, B, Mo and Cl)**.
- **Micronutrients** are very efficient and minute quantities produce optimum effects.
- **N, P, S, B, Mo and Cl** are **non-metals**.

FUNCTIONS OF NUTRIENTS

- **C, H** and **O** are the elements that provide **basic structure** to the plant.
- **N, S and P** are useful in **energy storage, transfer** and **bonding**.
- N, S and P are accessory structural elements which are more active and vital for living tissues.
- **K, Ca and Mg** are necessary for **charge balance**. They act as **regulators and carriers**.
- **Fe, Mn, Zn, Cu, B, Mo and Cl** are involved in **enzyme activation** and **electron transport**. They act as **catalysers and activators.**
- Basic nutrients **C, H and O** are constituents of **carbohydrates** and several **biochemical compounds**.
- **Nitrogen** is a constituent of **proteins**, **enzymes**, **hormones**, **vitamins**, **alkaloids**, **chlorophyll** etc.
- **Phosphorus** is a constituent of **sugar phosphates**, **nucleotides**, **nucleic acids, coenzymes** and **phospholipids.**
- Process of anabolism and catabolism of carbohydrates proceed when organic compounds are esterised with **phosphoric acid**.
- **Potassium** is not a constituent of any organic compound.
- **Potassium** is required as a cofactor for 40 or more enzymes.

- **Potassium** controls movement of **stomata** and maintains **electroneutrality** of plant cells.
- **Sulphur** is a constituent of several **aminoacids and fatty acids**.
- **Calcium** is a constituent of cell wall as **calcium pectate**.
- **Calcium** is required as a cofactor in **hydrolysis of ATP and phospholipids**.
- **Magnesium** is a constituent of **chlorophyll**.
- **Magnesium** is required in several enzymes involved in **phosphate transfer**.
- **Iron** is a constituent of various enzymes like **cytochrome**, **catalase** and plays the part of a vital catalyst in the plant.
- **Iron** is a key element in various **redox reactions** of respiration, photosynthesis and **reduction of nitrates and sulphates**.
- **Manganese** is a constituent of several cation activated enzymes like **decarboxylases, kinases, oxidases** etc.
- Manganese is essential for the **formation of chlorophyll**, **reduction of nitrates** and **for respiration**.
- **Copper and Zinc** are involved in cation activated enzymes.
- Boron helps in **carbohydrate** transport.
- **Boron** is necessary for the **germination of pollen**, formation of flowers and fruits and for the **absorption of cations**.
- **Molybdenum** is required for the **assimilation of nitrates** as well as for the **fixation of atmospheric nitrogen**.
- **Chlorine** is involved in reaction relating to **oxygen evolution**.
- **Co, Se** are the elements that need to be applied to **forage crops** from the viewpoint of animal nutrition.
- **Cobalt** is essential for the synthesis of vitamin $\mathbf{B_{12}}$.

NUTRIENT MOBILITY IN SOILS

- In case of **immobile nutrients**, roots have to reach the area of nutrient availability and **forage volume is limited to root surface**.
- For highly **mobile nutrients**, entire volume of the root zone is forage area.

- Mobile nutrients are **highly** soluble and they are **not adsorbed** on clay complex. *e.g.*, NO_3^-, SO_4^{2-}, BO_3^{2-}, Cl^-, Mn^{2+}
- **Less mobile nutrients** are also soluble, but they are **adsorbed** on clay complex and so their mobility is reduced *e.g.*, NH_4^+, K^+, Ca^+, Mg^{2+}, Cu^{2+}
- **Immobile nutrient ions** are **highly reactive** and get fixed in the soil *e.g.*, $H_2PO_4^-$, HPO_4^{2-}, Zn^{2+}
- Nutrients are transported to plant roots by **mass flow and diffusion**.
- **Mass flow** is movement of nutrient ions and salts along **with moving water**.
- In mass flow movement of nutrients reaching the root is dependent on the **rate of water flow**.
- **Diffusion** occurs when there is concentration gradient of nutrients between the root surface and surrounding soil solution.
- In **contact exchange theory** a close contact between root surfaces and soil colloids allows a direct exchange of H^+ released from the plant roots with cations from soil colloids.
- Importance of contact exchange in nutrient transport is less than with soil solution movement.
- Labile pool of nutrients in the soil represents **quantity factor**.
- Nutrient concentration of the soil solution represents **intensity factor**.
- Nutrient absorption by plant roots directly depends on the **concentration of the soil solution (intensity factor)** which in turn is regulated by the **labile pool (quantity factor)**.
- Many elements in their **most oxidized state** are favored in absorption.
- **Fe and Mn** are more available in their **reduced form**.

MOBILITY IN PLANTS

- N, P and K - Highly mobile
- **Zinc** is **moderately mobile** in plants and deficiency symptoms appear in **middle leaves**.
- S, Fe, Mn, Cu, Mo and Cl – less mobile
- Ca and B – Immobile

- A mobile nutrient in plant moves to the growing points in case of deficiency, so deficiency symptoms appear on **lower leaves**.
- Cell wall is **differentially permeable** and selectively absorbs particular cations and anions.
- Among the cations and anions, **cations** have competitive advantage.
- But three anions **NO_3^-, $H_2PO_4^-$ and SO_4^{2-}** are taken in large quantities.
- Entry of inorganic materials into xylem occurs at the **root tips**.
- Absorption of nutrients is primarily by **root hair cells**.
- Each root hair may be effective for absorption just for a few days.
- In **passive absorption** nutrients enter the plants along with **transpiration stream without** the use of **energy**.
- **Active absorption** is the absorption of nutrients from soil solution containing low concentration of nutrients compared to plant sap, **by expending energy**.
- A portion of absorbed nitrate nitrogen (NO_3-N) is reduced to **ammonical nitrogen (NH_4-N) and glutamine** in roots. These compounds along with remaining portion of NO_3-N passes through the **symplast (living connection between cells)** and enters the xylem.
- **Nitrate reduction** takes place in **leaves**.
- Reduced compounds enter phloem vessels and are translocated to growing points like young leaves, roots, fruits etc.
- Metabolic transformation of inorganic plant nutrients into organic plant constituents is known as **assimilation**.
- A fraction of absorbed nutrients may be stored in **vacuoles** without being assimilated.
- Plants absorb nitrogen mostly as **NO_3^- and NH_4^+**.
- **Nitrate assimilation** is mainly carried out in **leaves** and a small fraction in **roots**.
- Nitrate in plants is transformed into ammonia in two steps. First, nitrate is reduced to nitrite by **nitrate reductase enzyme** and the reducing power is supplied by **NADH**.
- **Molybdenum** is a constituent of **nitrate reductase**.
- Deficiency of **molybdenum** blocks **nitrate assimilation** resulting in **nitrate accumulation**.

- Deficiency of **molybdenum** causes **nitrogen deficiency symptoms** in addition to molybdenum deficiency symptoms.
- Second, nitrite is reduced to ammonia in presence of **nitrite reductase enzyme**. **Nitrite reduction** occurs in **chloroplasts in leaves** and reducing power is supplied by **respiration**. A portion of energy released during light reaction of photosynthesis is used for the reduction of nitrite to ammonia.
- Nitrite reduction occurs in dark also both in root and leaf and the reducing power is supplied by respiration.
- **C_4** plants assimilate **nitrate** more **efficiently** than C_3 plants.
- Presence of ammonia in plants is due to reduction of nitrates, absorption of ammonical nitrogen, breakdown of proteins, break down of urea absorbed by plants and due to nitrogen fixation.
- Ammonia is assimilated rapidly in plants.
- **Glutamic acid** combines with **ammonia** to form **glutamine**.
- **Glutamine** combines with **alpha ketoglutaric acid** to form two molecules of **glutamic acid** which is an amino acid.
- **Glutamic acid** is used as base material for the synthesis of other aminoacids and this process is known as **transamination**.
- Most of the ammonia absorbed by plants is transformed into **glutamine** in root cells and transported to leaves where it combines with **alpha ketoglutaric acid** to form **glutamic acid**.
- Assimilation of **sulphates** takes place in **chloroplasts**.
- Sulphate ion reacts with ATP and is activated and is reduced to sulphite.
- Sulphite is reduced to sulphide with the help of the enzyme **ferrodoxin** which in turn is incorporated into **cysteine**, a **sulphur containing aminoacid**.
- **Straight fertilizers** are those which supply **only one primary plant** nutrient, namely nitrogen or phosphorus or potassium.

  e.g., urea, ammonium sulphate, potassium chloride, potassium sulphate
- **Complex fertilizers** contain **two or three primary plant nutrients** of which two primary nutrients are in chemical composition.

  e.g., DAP, nitrophosphates, ammonium phosphate

- **Mixed fertilizers** are physical mixtures of **straight fertilizers.** They contain two or three primary plant nutrients.
- **Low analysis fertilizers** contain **less than 25 per cent** of primary nutrients.

  e.g., SSP (16%P_2O_5), Chilean nitrate or sodium nitrate (16% N)
- In **high analysis fertilizers** total content of primary nutrients is above **25 per cent.**

  e.g., urea (46%N), anhydrous ammonia (82.2% N), ammonium phosphate (20% N + 20% P_2O_5) and DAP (18% N + 46% P_2O_5)
- SSP is in **powder** form.
- Ammonium sulphate is in **crystal** form.
- Urea, DAP and superphosphate occurs as **prills.**
- When the nitrogenous, phosphatic, potassic and other fertilizer materials are completely dissolved in water, these are called **clear liquid** fertilizers.
- **Suspension liquid** fertilizers are those in which some of the fertilizer materials are suspended as fine particles.
- Fertilizers which leave an acid residue in the soil are called **acid forming fertilizers.**
- Amount of **calcium carbonate** required to neutralize the acid residue of a fertilizer is called as its **equivalent acidity.**

Fertilizer	**Acid equivalent**
Ammonium chloride	128
Ammonium sulphate	110
Ammonium sulphate nitrate	93
Ammonium phosphate	86
Urea	80

- Fertilizers which leave **alkaline residue** in the soil are called **alkaline -forming fertilizers** or **basic fertilizers.**

Fertilizer	**Equivalent basicity**
Calcium cyanide	63
Sodium nitrate	29
Dicalcium phosphate	25
Calcium nitrate	21

- **Fertilizer grade** refers to the guaranteed minimum percentage of N, P_2O_5 and K_2O contained in fertilizer material.

  e.g., 28-28-0 indicates 100 kg of fertilizer material contains 28 kg N, 28 kg P_2O_5 and no potash. Each individual fertilizer contain same quantity of nutrients.

NUTRIENT DEFICIENCY SYMPTOMS

- When nutrient is not present in sufficient quantity, plant growth is affected. Plants may not show visual symptoms up to a certain level of nutrient content, but growth is affected and this situation is known as **hidden hunger**.
- Deficiency symptoms of mobile nutrients like **N, P, K, Mg** and **Mo** appear on lower leaves or older leaves.
- In **K and Mo** deficiency dead spots occur.
- In **N, P and Mg** deficiency there are **no dead spots**.
- In **Mg deficiency** veins remain **green**.
- In **N deficiency** veins are **yellow**.
- Deficiency symptoms of less mobile elements like **S, Fe, Mn and Cu** appear on **new leaves**.
- In **Fe and Mn deficiency** veins are **green**.
- In **S and Cu deficiency** veins are **yellow**.
- Deficiency symptoms of immobile nutrients like **Ca and B** appear on **terminal buds**.
- **Chlorine deficiency** is less common in crops.

Nutrient	Deficiency symptoms
N	1) **Uniform yellowing** of leaves including veins 2) Leaves become **stiff and erect** in cereals 3) **Leaf may detach** after a little forceful pull in extreme deficiency in dicotyledonous crops 4) **Cereal crops** show characteristic **'V' shaped yellowing** at the tip of lower leaves
P	1) Leaves are **small**, erect, **unusually dark green** with a greenish red, **greenish brown or purplish tinge** 2) Rear side of leaf develops **bronzy appearance**

Mg	1) **Causes yellowing** but differs from nitrogen 2) **Yellowing** takes place **between veins** and **veins remain green** 3) Leaf is not erect 4) **Leaf detaches very easily** and may be shed by blowing wind 5) Necrosis occurs in extreme cases only in the margins
Mo	1) **Translucent spots** of **irregular shape** in between the veins of leaves 2) Spots are light green, yellow or brown in colour 3) **Affected spots are impregnated with resinous gum** which exudes from rear side of the leaf from the reddish brown spots
Fe	**1) Veins remain green** 2) Principal veins remain conspicuously green and other portions of the leaf turn **yellow tending towards whiteness** 3) Under severe deficiency, most part of the leaf becomes white
Mn	1) **Veins** remain **green** 2) Principal veins as well as smaller veins are green 3) **Interveinal portion** is **yellowish**, not tending towards whiteness 4) Dead spots appear at later stage 5) **Chequered appearance** of the leaf
S	1) Leaf becomes **yellowish** 2) Looks like **nitrogen deficient leaf** 3) Leaf is small 4) Veins are paler than interveinal portion 5) **No dead spots** appear 6) Plant does not lose lower leaves as in the case of N deficiency
Cu	1) **Leaf is yellowish tending towards whiteness** 2) In extreme deficiency, chlorosis of veins occur and leaf loses lustre 3) Leaf is unable to retain its turgidity hence wilting occurs 4) Leaf detaches due to **water soaked** conditions of the base of petiole

Ca	1) Bud leaf becomes chlorotic white with the **base remaining green** 2) About **one-third chlorotic portion of the tip hooks downward** and becomes brittle 3) Death of terminal bud occurs in extreme cases
B	1) **Yellowing or chlorosis** which starts from the **base to tip** 2) Tip becomes very much elongated into a **whip like structure** and becomes **brownish or blackish brown** 3) Death of terminal bud occurs in extreme cases
Zn	**1)** Leaves become narrow and small. **Lamina becomes chlorotic, veins remain green** 2) Dead spots develop all over the leaf including veins, tips and margins 3) In cereals **deficiency** appears **on 2-4 leaves** from the top during vegetative stage 4) Plants appear **bushy** due to **reduced internodal elongation** 5) **Panicle fails to emerge** completely or emerges partially

- Indicator plants are also used as a diagnostic tool for plant nutrient deficiencies.

Deficient nutrient	Indicator plant
N	Cauliflower, cabbage
P	Rapeseed
K	Potato
Ca	Cauliflower, cabbage
Mg	Potato
Fe	Sugarbeet
Mn	Sugarbeet, oat, potato
B	Sugarbeet

TOXICITY SYMPTOMS

Nutrient	Symptoms
Nitrogen	1) Excess nitrogen causes **delay in maturity** 2) Excess nitrogen **increases succulency** 3) Excess nitrogen causes **lodging and abortion of flowers**
Phosphorus	1) Causes **deficiency of iron and zinc** 2) In maize leaves develop **purple colouration** and plant growth is stunted 3) In cotton leaves become dark green in colour, maturity of bolls delayed and stem turns red
Iron	**1) Tiny brown spots** appear on the **lower leaves** of rice starting from **tips and spreading towards bases** 2) Leaves usually remain green 3) In extreme case, entire leaf turns purplish brown in colour
Manganese	1) Plant is stunted and tillering is often limited 2) **Brown spots** develop on the veins of leaf blade and leaf sheath, especially on lower leaves 3) Manganese toxicity occurs in **lowland rice**
Boron	1) **Chlorosis occurs at the tips of the older leaves**, especially along the margins 2) **Large, dark brown, elliptical spots** appear subsequently 3) Leaves ultimately turn brown and dry up

NITROGEN

- Nitrogen constitutes about **78%** of the atmospheric gases.
- Most of the N in soil is in **organic form (95 to 99%)**.
- Total N in Indian soils vary from **0.02 to 0.1%**.
- Value of total N in hill soils vary from **0.01 to 0.319%**.
- Only about **1.5 to 3.5%** of the organic N of soil mineralizes annually.
- Soils in India except those in the hills are generally low in **organic matter and total N** due to **high temperatures**.

- In mineralization process, organic N in soil organic matter is converted into plant-usable **inorganic forms (ammonium and nitrate)**.
- Inorganic forms of N in soil include **ammonium**, **nitrate**, **exchangeable ammonium** and **fixed ammonium**.
- In well-aerated soils **nitrate-N** is the dominant form.
- Under anaerobic conditions **ammonium** is the dominant form.
- Nitrogen is taken up by crop plants as **nitrate (NO_3^-) or ammonium (NH_4^+) ions**.
- Most crop plants will equally take nitrate and ammonium.
- **Rice** is reported to prefer **ammonium** than nitrates.
- In rice **ammonical** and **amide fertilizers** are applied.
- Wheat prefer more **ammonium** at early growth stages and **nitrate** at later growth stages.
- Nitrogen interacts **positively** with all plant nutrients.
- **Haber and Bosch** first synthesized ammonia from N and H.
- Ammonia synthesis by **Haber-Bosch** process is carried out at a temperature of **1000 to 1200°C** and at **200 to 100** atmospheres pressure.
- Industrial fixation (fertilizer nitrogen) by Haber-Bosch process is estimated at about **150 million tonnes** per year by 2015.
- Global estimates of biological nitrogen fixation (BNF) are at **175 million tonnes** per year.
- Anhydrous (**without water**) ammonia contains **82% N**.
- **Ammonia** is the most reduced form of reactive nitrogen and most abundant alkaline constituent in the atmosphere.
- **Urea** was the first organic compound to be synthesized from inorganic materials.
- Urea was first separated from urine by **Roulle in 1773**, hence the name urea.
- In India, the first urea plant was set up in **1959** at **Sindri in Bihar**.
- About 80% of fertilizer N is consumed as **urea**.
- Nitrogen content in urea super granules is **46%**.
- **Urea** is used as a substitute for **protein** in animal feed.

- The permissible limit of biuret in urea is **1.5%** as per Fertilizer Control Order.
- Highest permissible concentration of urea in the spray solution for foliar spray is **3%** beyond which the leaves get scorched.
- Plant leaves turn **yellow** due to N deficiency, because N is an important component of **chlorophyll**.
- Cereals remove **20-27 kg N, 8-18 kg P_2O_5** and **20-40 kg K_2O** per tonne of grain harvested.
- For producing each tonne (1000 kg) of wheat, the crop removes **25 kg N/ha**.
- Nitrogen content in rice grains is **lesser** than wheat grains.
- The first nitrogen fertilizer used was **sodium nitrate** containing **16% N.**
- **Sodium nitrate** also known as **nitrate of soda or Chilean nitrate** is considered as the first natural mineral containing fixed N and the only natural source of nitrate N.
- Ammonium nitrate contains **32 to 37.5 % N.**
- **Ammonium nitrate** is hygroscopic.
- In calcareous soils, losses from **ammonium nitrate** are much less than from **ammonium sulphate** and **urea.**
- Ammonium sulphate contains **20.5% N.**
- **Organic N content** of soil **increases** steadily with the application of **ammonium sulphate.**
- Ammonium sulphate nitrate contains **26% N.**
- Ammonium sulphate nitrate is an **acid** forming fertilizer.
- Ammonium chloride (NH_4Cl) contains about **26% N** and is equally effective as **ammonium sulphate** for rice.
- Potassium nitrate contains **13.8% N** and **36.5 % K.**
- Calcium nitrate contains **15.5 % N** and **19.5 % Ca.**
- Calcium ammonium nitrate (CAN) is produced by mixing **Ammonium nitrate** and **calcium carbonate.**
- CAN is produced in two grades containing **20.5% N** and **25% N.**
- In **CAN** half of the nitrogen is in **nitrate form** and half of the nitrogen is in **ammonical form.**
- CAN is a **neutral** fertilizer.

- For **alkaline soils**, **acid forming** fertilizers and **calcium** containing fertilizers are preferred.
- During mineralization, **ammonium** is converted into **nitrate** by **Nitrosomonas** bacteria.
- In rice, percolation losses are **60 to 70 per cent** of total water requirement.
- Nitrogen fertilizers are **highly** soluble in water, therefore subjected to **leaching**.
- Nitrates are subjected to **leaching** and **nitrification** losses in submerged soils.
- **Leaching** of N in the form of **NO_3^-** beyond soil profile is one of the major loss mechanisms that can be as high as 80% depending on the soil properties and water and nutrient-management practices.
- To reduce leaching losses **solubility** of nitrogen fertilizers is **reduced**.
- Inherently less soluble nitrogen fertilizers are **Isobutylidene diurea (IBDU) – 32.2% N**, **Crotonilidene diurea – 32.5% N.**
- **Sulphur coated urea**, **shellack coated urea**, **neem coated urea** are barrier coated nitrogen fertilizers.
- **Borax**, **gypsum and nimin coatings** reduce the rate of N release from prilled urea in lowland rice. Borax is effective and increases the productivity of rice.
- A major portion of N fertilizer applied to soil is lost through **volatilization** as **gaseous ammonia**.
- Loss of N due to ammonia volatilization from agricultural field in India is estimated at **4.1 million tonnes**.
- **Denitrification** is sequential reduction of NO_3^- to N_2 by denitrifying bacteria under **anaerobic** conditions.
- Loss of N due to denitrification from agricultural field in India is estimated at **3.1 million tonnes**.
- On an average, denitrification losses reported in India ranged from **10 to 30** and **5 to 10 kg N/ha** in **rice** and **wheat** respectively.
- Denitrification is controlled by **soil moisture, redox potential (Eh), temperature, pH** and **substrate (NO_3, NO_2, NO and N_2O) concentrations**.
- N losses due to denitrification are likely to be most under **alternate flooding and drying** as obtained under aerobic rice systems.

- Agriculture sector contributes **more than 80%** of total anthropogenic NH_3 emission to the atmosphere.
- Application of N fertilizer in soil contributes **more than 25%** of the total NH_3 emission from agriculture.
- Current crop removal of N in India is estimated at **9.8 million tonnes**.
- Apparent recovery of fertilizer N applied to rice in India is **30-40%.**
- Recovery efficiency of fertilizer N in crop production is about **30-60%.**
- Deep placement of fertilizer N **increases** its use efficiency.
- **Nitrification inhibitors** are chemicals that inhibit or retard oxidation of ammonium to nitrate N.
- Examples of nitrification inhibitors are
  - ✓ N-Serve or nitrapyrin (2-chloro-6-(trichloromethyl) pyridine)
  - ✓ DCD(dicyandiamide)
  - ✓ AM(2-amino-4-chloro-6-methyl pyrimidine)
  - ✓ CMP(1-carbamoyle-3-methylpyrazole)
  - ✓ Terrazole (etridiazole)
  - ✓ CP(2-cyanimino-4-hydroxy-6-methyl pyrimidine)
  - ✓ AT/ATc (4 aminotriazole)
  - ✓ ST(sulphatiazole or sodium thiosulphate)
  - ✓ ATS(ammonium thiosulphate)
  - ✓ ZPTA(thiosulphoryl triamide)
  - ✓ Neem extractives (containing epinimbin, deacetylnimbin, azadirachtin)
- **Nitrapyrin, AM** and **DCD** are the most widely used nitrification inhibitors.
- Growing of crops especially **maize** increases the release of inorganic N - forms.
- Loss of **nitrate** nitrogen from the soil is less in the presence of **maize**.
- **Urease inhibitors** reduce the rate of hydrolysis of urea to ammonium and can reduce loss of N due to ammonia volatilization when urea is surface applied.

- Examples of urease inhibitors are **phenyl phosphorodiamide (PPDA), aminothiosulphate, hydroquinone, phosphoric triamide, cyclohexyl phosphoric triamide, thiophosphoryl triamide, N-(n-butyl) thiophosphoric triamide**.
- Adoption of best management practices improves nitrogen use efficiency.

Classification of Nitrogen fertilizers

NITRATE FERTILIZERS	AMMONICAL FERTILIZERS	NITRATE AND AMMONICAL FERTILISERS	AMIDE FERTILIZERS
e.g., Sodium nitrate ($NaNO_3$)-16% N Calcium nitrate [$Ca(NO_3)_2$] 15.5% N 19.5% Ca	Ammonium sulphate [$(NH_4)_2SO_4$]-20% N Ammonium Chloride [NH_4Cl]-24 to 26% N Anhydrous ammonia [NH_3]-82% N	Ammonium nitrate [NH_4NO_3] 33 to 34 % N Calcium ammonium nitrate [$CaNH_4NO_3$] 20% N	Urea [$CO(NH_2)_2$] 46% N Calcium Cyanide [$CaCN_2$] 21% N
Highly mobile in soil	Easily available to plants as they are readily soluble in water	Nitrate nitrogen is readily available to plants for rapid growth and ammonical nitrogen is available at later stage of crop growth	Contain nitrogen in the form of amide
Suitable for top dressing	-	-	Known as organic fertilizers since they contain carbon atoms
Highly soluble and subjected to leaching	Leaching losses are less as ammonium ions are adsorbed on clay complex	Leaching losses are less	Though plants take nitrogen in amide form it is converted into ammonical and nitrate form in the soil which plants generally utilize
Subjected to denitrification in water logged soils	These fertilizers are well suited to submerged soils	-	
Increase alkalinity as they are basic in their residual effect	Reduce alkalinity as they are acidic in their residual effect	Acidic in nature	

PHOSPHORUS

- Phosphorus was first discovered by **Brandt** in 1669.
- It has oxidation states ranging from **-3 to +5**.
- **Phosphorus** is a component of **genetic material (nucleic acids)** and **energy currency (ATP)** of plants.
- Unlike N and K, P is taken up in **smaller** quantities by the plants.
- Phosphorus is the tenth most abundant element and constitutes about **0.12%** of the earth's crust.
- Soils usually contain **0.013-0.155%** P and the insoluble phosphate compounds constitute **95-99%** of the total P.
- Phosphorus is present in soil in three fractions
  a) Insoluble inorganic fraction
  b) Organic fraction
  c) Soluble P
- **Soluble P** is the only fraction that can be absorbed by the plants.
- Soluble P fraction varies from **0.001 mg/litre to 1.0 mg/litre** depending on the soil pH, quantity and type of fertilizer P added, organic matter content and other soil properties.
- **Primary orthophosphate ($H_2PO_4^-$)** and **secondary orthophosphate (HPO_4^{2-})** are the main forms of plant P absorption.
- Organic P constitutes about **30 to 65%** of the total P in soils.
- **Fine textured clay and clay loam soil** contain a higher proportion of P in the organic form than the coarse textured sandy soils.
- **Phytate** is the primary storage form of **P** in plant.
- Inorganic p fraction forms about **35-75%** of the total soil P.
- With the increase in soil acidity, the solubility of Fe and Al phosphates **increases**.
- **Apatite ($Ca_{10}(PO_4)_6(OHFCl)_2$)** is the main form of mineral P present in the parent material.
- Soils with high **Fe and Al sesquioxides** hold the phosphate ions strongly.
- In calcareous soils, P can be adsorbed on the **$CaCO_3$ surface** by replacement of the CO_3^{2-}.

- **Heavy-textured clay soils** had **higher** phosphate sorption than light-textured soils.
- **Heavy textured clay** soils need an additional dose of P fertilizers.
- With an increase in time, the P gets converted to insoluble compounds of **Fe, Al and Ca phosphates** and is referred to as **'phosphate ageing'**.
- **Mineralization** is the process of conversion of organic, unavailable P fractions into inorganic available form.
- Mineralization is brought about by the enzymes **phosphatases (phosphomonoesterases, phosphodiesterases and inorganic pyrophosphatase)** produced by microorganisms like *Bacillus megaterium, B. subtilis, Serratia spp. Proteus spp., Arthrobacter spp., Streptomyces spp. Penicillium spp., Rhizobium spp., and Cunninghamella spp.*
- **Immobilization** refers to assimilation of the P into the organic cell constituents leading to unavailability of the P for crop uptake.
- Ratio of **C:P <200** results in net mineralization.
- **C:P >300** results in net immobilization.
- Conversion of Fe^{3+} bound P to **Fe^{2+} P** form makes P more available to the plant.
- Flooded crops such as **rice** respond less to P compared to the upland crops.
- In general, P availability to plants follows the trend: **$H_2PO_4^-$ > HPO_4^{2-} > PO_4^{3-}**
- At pH **7.2** monovalent ($H_2PO_4^-$) and divalent (HPO_4^{2-}) forms of orthophosphate are present in **equal** proportions.
- Below pH **6**, soil P becomes tightly bound with the Fe and Al oxides and precipitated as **$FePO_4$ and $AlPO_4$**.
- With increase in pH, activity of Fe and Al **decreases** and **increases** the available P.
- At soil pH > **7.5**, P gets precipitated as **Ca and Mg phosphates** and available P decreases.
- P availability is at a maximum at **near neutral soil pH**, when the adsorption is minimal.
- **Liming** is considered as a management strategy to make P more available by replacing the fixed P in acidic soils.

- Over-liming can result in precipitation of new, positively charged hydroxyl Al surfaces, increasing P adsorption and reducing P availability.
- Application of organic manure or acidifying materials such as pyrites is an option for **alkaline** soils.
- Soils with greater content of di and tri-valent cations have **greater** P-fixation capacity than the mono-valent cations.
- Ammonium ions **increase** the P uptake by plants as a co-transport ion.
- Ammonium ions **reduce** the pH and makes more P available to the plants.
- Anions present in the soil compete for adsorption on the soil surface.
- Among the anions, **sulphate** offers competition to P fixation.
- Tendency to fix is greater for $\mathbf{PO_4^{3-}}$ anion than for the SO_4^{2-}.
- Nitrate and chloride anions are weakly held and do not offer any competition. Soils saturated with these anions, will be displaced and P fixed making it less available to plants.
- Soils with **finer** texture are **more** prone to fixation than the coarse-textured ones, as the amount of P fixed is a function of clay content.
- Greater the amount of **clay**, greater quantities of P will be fixed in soils.
- Soils with a predominance of **kaolinitic** clay minerals show higher P fixation than the smectitic/montmorillonite clays.
- **Kaolinite clays** predominant in the **Alfisols** have less surface area for P adsorption than the **smectites of Vertisols.**
- Application of nitrogenous fertilizers in **ammonical** form makes P more available to the plants on **calcareous** soils because of the acidic conditions created in the soil microsites.
- **Phosphorus** is actively involved in **energy-transfer** processes in plants.
- **Phosphorus** stimulates early root growth and development and helps in early establishment of seedlings.
- **Phosphorus** improves the activity of **rhizobia** and formation of **root nodules** and helps in **N fixation.**
- P is an essential structural component of **nucleic acids** and plays a vital role in plant **reproduction** and **seed formation.**

- **P** is an essential constituent of **phospholipids** which are components of cell membranes and help maintain structural integrity.
- **P** is a component of Vitamin B complex, **niacin**.
- **Phosphorus** imparts strength to straw of cereals and decreases the tendency of plants to **lodge**.
- Phosphorus is **mobile** in plants, so deficiency symptoms first appear on **older leaves**.
- **Smaller** leaves with more **dark green** than normal and **purple cast** with drying tips indicate typical **P-deficiency** symptoms.
- Inadequate P slows down **carbohydrate** utilization imparting dark green colour to leaves.
- Accumulation of **polysaccharides** in P-deficient plants is accompanied by over production of **anthocyanins**, imparting **red/purple** colour to the leaves.
- P absorption by the roots is mainly through **diffusion (in potassium also)**.
- **Diffusion** contributes to more than **90%** of the total P absorbed by the crop plants.
- A small portion of the total P is absorbed by roots due to **root interception**.
- **Mass flow** contributes to a small extent **(<5%)** because of low solution P concentration.
- Phosphorus is a major limiting nutrient to crops grown on **lateritic soils** such as the **Ultisols and Oxisols**, as they have very low P content as well as the strong capacity to fix P.
- **Small grain crops** have a **shallow root system** with a limited capacity to explore the soil profile and will respond well to applied P than crops like cotton, tobacco or pigeonpea that have a deeper root system.
- Dependence of crops on phosphorus is in the order **potato** > **wheat > maize > rice, millets > legumes > cotton, jute**.
- Deficiency of both **N and P** are widespread in Indian soils.
- In alkaline soils **ammonium based fertilizers** improve the P availability by their acidifying effects.
- Both N and P are closely involved in the photosynthesis and protein synthesis and N:P **ratio of 10:1** is considered optimum.

- **N x P** interaction is **synergistic** in most non-leguminous crops, often **antagonistic** in grain legumes (pulses and leguminous oilseeds), **positive** in leguminous vegetables (field peas).
- In most field crops **P x S** interaction may be **synergistic** at low to medium application rates. **Antagonistic** effects are observed at high levels of **P (> 60 kg/ha)** or **S (> 40 kg/ha)**.
- **Magnesium** will improve both the uptake and utilization of P.
- **Fe x P** interaction may be **antagonistic**.
- **P x Zn** interaction is **antagonistic**.
- Most of our soils **(80%)** are rated **low to medium** in available P content.
- **Omission plot** technique was developed to identify soils that have little P to produce acceptable yields.
- By the **omission plot** technique, we obtain the soils **indigenous** P supply.
- Omission-plot technique was developed by **Dobermann *et al.***
- Plant rhizosphere is dominated by the fungi ***Pencillium* sps.**
- **Bacteria**, **fungi**, **actinomycetes** and **cynobacteria** can dissolve insoluble inorganic P sources present in the soil and are collectively known as **phosphorus-solubilizing microorganisms (PSM)**.
- Among PSM, **fungi** are the most effective in solubilizing P.
- ***Bacillus*** and ***Pseudomonas*** are phosphorus solubilizing bacteria.
- Symbiotic association between **plant root** and **fungal hyphae** is known as **mycorrhiza**.
- For our country where most of the soils have pH in the neutral to alkaline range, the **Olsen's** extractant is best suited.
- For acid soils prevalent in the North-east, **Brays** extractant is advised.
- Response to phosphorus is greater in **cereals followed by legumes, oilseeds, cotton and jute**.
- P content of the earth's crust is **0.12 %**.
- The fraction of the applied P taken up by the crop fertilized with P fertilizer ranges from **15-30%.**
- **Olsen's** extractant is suitable for both acid as well as alkaline soils for estimation of phosphorus content.

- Arbuscular mycorrhiza is an **obligate** symbiont.
- **Citric** and **malic acids** are the two main organic acids produced by roots under **P deficient** conditions.
- **Soil pH** and **particle size** are the important factors governing the solubilisation of **rock phosphate** applied as fertilizer.
- Soils rich in **clay and sesquioxides** have higher P buffering capacity than sandy soils.

PHOSPHATIC FERTILIZERS

- $P_2O_5 = P \times 2.29$
- $P = P_2O_5 \times 0.43$
- **Rock phosphate** is the basic raw material for the production of the phosphatic fertilizers.
- Phosphatic fertlisers classified into three groups

Water Soluble Phosphoric acid	Citric acid soluble phosphoric acid	Phosphoric acid not soluble in water or citric acid
Available in the form of monocalcium phosphate or ammonium phosphate	These fertilizers contain citrate soluble phosphoric acid or dicalcium phosphate	Contains phosphoric acid which is not soluble in water or citric acid
Examples: 1) Single super phosphate or ordinary super phosphate (16% P_2O_5) 2) Double superphosphate 32% P_2O_5 3) Triple superphospate 46-48% P_2O_5 4) Ammonium phosphate 20% P_2O_5 and 20% N 5) Monoammonium phosphate 48% P_2O_5 and 11% N 6) Ammonium phosphate-sulphate 20% P_2O_5 and 16% N	1) Basic slag (14-18% P_2O_5) 2) Dicalcium phosphate (34-39% P_2O_5)	1) Rock phosphate (20-40% P_2O_5) 2) Raw bone meal (2-2.5% P_2O_5) 3) Steamed bone meal (22% P_2O_5)

Contd....

Water Soluble Phosphoric acid	**Citric acid soluble phosphoric acid**	**Phosphoric acid not soluble in water or citric acid**
Suitable for neutral and alkaline soils	As they are basic in reaction and contain calcium they are suitable for acidic soils	Suitable for strongly acidic or organic soils
Forms insoluble iron and aluminium phosphates in acid soils	They are converted into monocalcium phosphate in acid soil	-
These fertilizers are used when crop requires quick start	-	Availability of phosphorus from these fertilizers can be increased by ploughing in along with green manures
Used for short duration crops like wheat, sorghum, pulses *etc.*	Used for long duration crops like Sugarcane, tapioca, tea, coffee and lowland rice.	Suitable for plantation crops like tea, coffee, rubber, cocoa, coconut *etc.*

- Water-soluble sources of fertilizer P are recommended for crops grown on **alkaline** soils.
- **SSP** was the first P fertilizer manufactured in India.
- Single superphosphate contains **16-22%** P_2O_5 of which **90%** is water soluble.
- **SSP** is a mixture of **monocalcium phosphate** and **calcium sulphate (gypsum)**.
- When SSP is added to soil it is coverted into insoluble **dicalcium phosphate** in alkaline soils.
- In acidic soils SSP is converted into **iron and aluminium phosphates**.
- Enriched compost with super phosphate is the **super-digested compost**.
- Triple super phosphate contains **44-52% P_2O_5**.
- Dicalcium phosphate contains **53% P_2O_5**.
- Monoammonium phosphate contains **12% N** and **61% P_2O_5**.

- DAP is available in two grades **16-48-0** and **18-46-0**.
- **Ammonium phosphate sulphate** contains **16% N and 20% P_2O_5**.
- Nitrophosphate contains P_2O_5, half in water soluble form and half in citrate soluble form.
- **Bone-meal** is suitable for **acid soils** and **long duration crops**.
- **Basic slag** is suitable for **acid** and near **neutral soils**, but not for alkaline soils.
- **Basic slag** contains **14-18 % P_2O_5** of which **80 per cent** is citrate soluble.
- **Rock phosphate** contains **25 - 39 % P_2O_5** and **33-36% Ca**.
- **Phosphocompost** is a cheaper source of P than DAP.
- Phosphocompost/ N-enriched phosphocompost is produced by the use of PSM's namely ***Aspergillus awamori, Pseudomonas striata*** and ***Bacillus megaterium***.

POTASSIUM

- Potassium management in Indian agriculture has been traditionally overlooked because of high fertilizer cost and anomalous crop response to fertilizers in majority of Indian soils.
- Most crops absorb as much or more K than they absorb **N** from the soil.
- About **70-75%** of the K absorbed is retained by **leaves, straw** and **stover** and the rest is found in grains, fruits, nuts etc.
- **Potassium** activates more than **60 enzymes** and is directly or indirectly involved in all major plant growth processes.
- **Potassium** promotes the transport of **photosynthates** to storage organs of crops.
- **Potassium** is essential for the formation and **translocation of sugars** in plants and is of utmost importance for crops like **sugarcane, sugarbeet, sweet potato and other tuber crops**.
- **Potassium** is important in making plants more resistant to **lodging**.
- **Potassium** improves the **quality** of crops and prolongs their shelf-life.

- Soil K exists in 4 forms
  a) Soil solution K **(0.1-0.2%)**
  b) Exchangeable K **(1-2%)**
  c) Fixed or non-exchangeable (1-10%)
  d) Structural or mineral (90-98%)
- Forms of soil K in the order of their availability to plants and microbes are
  Solution > exchangeable > fixed (non-exchangeable) > mineral
- Exchangeable (available) K is generally **<1%** of the non exchangeable K.
- Soil solution K, exchangeable K and non-exchangeable K contribute to plant K uptake.
- Most of the total K in soils is in the mineral form, mainly as K-bearing primary minerals such as **muscovite, biotite** and **feldspars.**
- Mineral K comprises about **98%** of the total K.
- Exchangeable K is generally **higher** in **Vertisols and vertic type soils** and in the **fine-textured alluvial soils** than in red and lateritic soils, acidic alluvial soils with kaolinite as dominant clay mineral, and light textured alluvial soils.
- **Antagonistic** interactions of K may occur between **K and Ca** or **K and Mg.**
- K application resulted in **reduced** uptake of Fe, B and Mo and **increased** the utilization of Zn, Cu and Mn.
- **Potassium** application is known to correct **Fe toxicity** in rice grown on Fe-rich acid soils, as it improves metabolic activity and Fe excluding power of plant roots.
- Increasing level of K supply **decreases** the Fe content in paddy.
- **Low soil temperature** reduces available soil K and its absorption by plants.
- Leaching losses are a problem in **sandy** soils in high-rainfall areas, under such conditions **split** application of K is a possible solution.
- **Canada** has the largest reserves of K.
- **Germany** dominated world potash market for 75 years.
- **Langbeinite** contains **Mg** and **S** in addition to K.

- Deficiency of K is seen on **leaf-margins**.
- For optimum growth, the **N:K ratio** in straw in cereal crops should be between **1.1 and 1.4**.
- All the food grain crops require more **potash** than nitrogen for production of 1 tonne of grain.
- $K_2O = K \times 1.2$
- $K = K_2O \times 0.83$
- Potassic fertilizers are grouped in two forms chloride form and non chloride form.
- Potassium chloride belongs to the first group.
- Potassium sulphate, potassium magnesium sulphate, potassium nitrate etc. belong to the second group.
- **Potassium chloride** is unsuitable for **sugar crops**, **tobacco** and **potato**.
- **Potassium chloride** or **muriate of potash** is the most common and cheap fertilizer among potassic fertilizers.
- KCl contains **58-60 % K_2O**.
- KCl is suitable for most of the crops **except sugarcane, sugarbeet, potato and tobacco**.
- In **sugar crops**, accumulation of sugar is affected due to **chloride ion** present in the fertilizers.
- Higher content of **chloride** in tobacco leaf **reduces** its burning quality.
- KCl or muriate of potash is suitable for **acidic and heavy soils** but not for alkaline soils.
- Potassium sulphate contains **48-50% K_2O** and **17.5 % Sulphur**.
- **Potassium sulphate** can be safely applied to any crop including sugarcane, sugar beet and tobacco.
- Potassium magnesium sulphate is a double salt of potassium sulphate and magnesium sulphate and contains 22 % K_2O and 11% Mg and 22% S.
- **Potassium nitrate** or **salt petre** or **nitre** contains **13 % N** and **44% K_2O**.
- Potassium polyphosphate contains 56% P_2O_5 and 24% K_2O.

SULPHUR

- **Sulphur** is regarded as the fourth major nutrient.
- **Sulphur** requirements of crops are very similar to that of **phosphorus** needs.
- Indian soils are deficient in **nitrogen, phosphorus, potassium, sulphur** and **zinc**.
- **42 %** of soil samples have been found S deficient in India.
- Sulphur occurs as sulphides in **igneous and sedimentary rocks**.
- Major source of sulphur under natural conditions is **organic matter**.
- More than 90% of total sulphur in soil is present in organic matter under **temperate** conditions, but inorganic sulphates are also important in tropics and sub-tropics.
- Total sulphur in upper layer of the cultivated soils may vary from **50 to 300 ppm (mg/kg soil)**.
- Available S can constitute **1-15%** of total soil S.
- Soil testing less than **10 ppm** available S (10 mg S/kg soil) or **20 kg S/ha** are considered to be low/deficient in sulphur.
- Total sulphur content may be more than **1000 ppm** in saline and acid sulphate soils.
- Sulphur content is more in **surface** soils than in sub soils.
- Among Indian soils, only **30%** of the total S in soil may be in organic form but in Mollisols of tarai (foot-hill) region, it may be around **70%**.
- Sulphur in the soil is associated with organic carbon in a fixed C:S ratio of about **140:1**.
- Sulphur is taken up by the plants in the ionic form of SO_4^{2-}.
- Deficiency of sulphur is generally noticed on the **younger** leaves of the plant.
- Sulphur is constituent of sulphur-bearing aminoacids such as **cysteine, cystine** and **methionine**.
- The two major reasons for increase in deficiency of S in Indian agriculture are **intensification of agriculture** and **increased crop production** due to use of high yielding varieties.

- Sometimes, the plant level of sulphur falls below the critical level and plant does not show any deficiency symptoms. This is also known as **hidden hunger** which affects crop yield adversely.
- Atomic number of sulphur is **16** and atomic weight is **32**.
- Suitable extractant for extracting available sulphur from soil is **0.15 % $CaCl_2$** or **500 ppm solution of KH_2PO_4**.
- The biochemical reaction of S is mediated by autotrophic bacteria belongs to genus ***Thiobacillus***.
- Less oxidized forms of sulphur are **Sulphite (SO_3^{2-}), thiosulphate ($S_2O_3^{2-}$)** and **elemental S**.
- Three important sulphur containing fertilizers are **SSP, Ammonium sulphate** and **Ammonium phosphate sulphate**.
- General recommendation of S in cereals is **20-40** kg/ha and oilseeds is **20-50** kg/ha.
- For tubers and fodders the rate of sulphur requirement range from **25 to 60** kg/ha.
- To overcome sulphur deficiency in standing crop, fertilizer such as **ammonium sulphate** can be effective because top dressing of N is also required.
- Gypsum is a source of **Ca** and **S** nutrients.
- In assessing quality parameters, application of S improves **protein** content of the plant.
- Number of sulphur deficient districts in the country are **300**.
- Mineralization is the process of conversion of organic S to **sulphate S**.
- Sulphur is necessary for **chlorophyll** formation.
- Application of Sulphur improves **sugar recovery** in sugarcane.
- **Sulphur** is very important for oilseed crops.
- Deficiency symptoms of sulphur appear first and become more severe on **younger** leaves. Whole plant generally appears low pale green or pale yellow but the youngest leaves appear the most pale.
- Due to **sulphur** deficiency shoot growth is restricted, maturity in cereals is retarded and fruits remain light green and do not mature fully.
- Due to **sulphur** deficiency nodulation in legumes may be poor thereby reducing the **N-fixation**.

- Indicator plant species for sulphur deficiencies are **Lucerne, clover and raya**.
- Most crop plants contain sulphur in the range of **0.2 – 0.4%** on dry-matter basis.
- Generally, the sulphur content is found in the order of

  cruciferous oilseeds > other oilseeds > cruciferous/legume forages > pulses > cereals
- Crop response to sulphur in terms of kg yield increase per kg sulphur was in the order of **cereals > oilseeds > pulses.**
- The most promising fertilizer containing elemental sulphur is **bentonite-sulphur** containing **90% S**.
- Elemental S - containing sources like **pyrites** and **bentonite** sulphur should be added 3-4 weeks before planting as elemental sulphur has first to be converted to plant usable sulphate form.
- Ammonium sulphate contains **24% S** and **20.6 % N**.
- SSP contains **11-12%** sulphur.
- Phosphogypsum contains **16-20% S** and **23% Ca**.
- Pressmud contains **2.3%** S.
- Zinc sulphate monohydrate contains **35% Zn** and **18% S**.
- Zinc sulphate heptahydrate contains **21% Zn** and **10% S**.
- Ferrous sulphate contains **19% Fe** and **10.5% S**.
- Sulphur use efficiency is **8-12%**.
- Gypsum contains **29.2 % Ca** and **18.6 % S**.
- SSP contains **19.5% Ca**, **12.5% S**, **16%** P_2O_5.
- Copper sulphate contains **21% Cu** and **11.4% S**.
- Elemental sulphur contains **100% S**.

CALCIUM AND MAGNESIUM

- In plants, **calcium** is present as **calcium pectate** which is a constituent of the **middle lamellae** of the cell-walls.
- Calcium is considered essential for the growth of **meristematic** tissues and to the functioning of the **root tips**.
- Calcium is absorbed by plants as Ca^{2+} **ion**. This takes place from the soil solution and possibly by **root interception** or **contact exchange** from the exchange sites.

- The only nutrient which might be supplied completely by interception is **calcium**, although the process may provide a significant part of the requirement for Mg, Zn and Mn.
- The quantities of calcium required by the plants can be readily transported to root surfaces by **mass flow** in most soils, except highly leached and unlimed acid soils.
- Quantities of magnesium taken up by plants are usually **less than** calcium and potassium.
- **Anorthite** is primary source of **calcium**.
- **Augite** and **hornblende** also contains **calcium**.
- Among the secondary minerals, **calcite ($CaCO_3$)** is the dominant source of calcium in soils of semi-arid and arid regions.
- **Dolomite ($CaMg(CO_3)_2$)** may also be present in association with calcite and gypsum ($CaSO_4.2H_2O$) in arid regions.
- Usually **Ca** is the cation of the highest concentration in the soil in both soluble and exchangeable forms for soils high in **pH>8.0**.
- Ca^{2+} concentration of the soil solution is frequently about **10 times** greater than that of K^+, its uptake is usually **lower** than that of K^+..
- Capacity of plants for uptake of Ca^{2+} is limited, because it can be absorbed only by **young root tips** in which the cell-walls of the endodermis are still unsuberised.
- Two soil calcium minerals having the maximum solubility are **calcium sulphate** and **calcium carbonate**.
- Calcium sulphate usually occurs only in arid soils where the sulphate concentration in solution exceeds **0.01 mol/L**.
- Calcium is abundant in leaves and its normal concentration ranges from **0.2 to 1.0%**.
- Calcium is well known for its role in **cell division** and **cell elongation**.
- Calcium deficiency leads to diseases such as **bitter pit in apple, blossom end-rot in tomato, black head in celery, internal browning in Brussel's sprout, blossom end-rot of pepper** and **cavity spots in carrots.**
- Plants generally use Ca in amounts **lower** than N and K but **higher** than P.
- Most of the **acid soils** in India are deficient in **calcium**.

- Under **high rainfall** and in soils with **low base saturation**, Ca leach down from the root rhizosphere and the soils become deficient in Ca.
- Soils containing less than **25% of cation-exchange capacity** or **less than 1.5 cmol (p+) Ca** per kg soil considered as Ca-deficient.
- In acid soils, application of Ca through liming increases the availability of P to crops.
- Plants generally take up Mg in **smaller** amounts than Ca.
- For optimum growth, plants require a ratio of exchangeable Ca : Mg very close to **6**.
- Plants grow well and meet their Ca and Mg requirement in soils with Ca:Mg ratios varying from **1:1 to 15:1**.
- Liming materials commonly used for amelioration of acid soils are the **oxides, hydroxides, carbonates** and **silicates of calcium and magnesium**.
- In chlorophyll, **magnesium** as the central atom is bound to **N atoms** of 4 **porphyrin** rings by 2 covalent and 2 co-ordinate bonds.
- Content of magnesium in plant ranges between **0.15 and 1.00%** of the dry matter in leaf tissue.
- Magnesium deficiency results in **interveinal chlorosis** of the leaf, in which only the veins remain green.
- In **cotton**, due to magnesium deficiency lower leaves may develop a **reddish purple cast**, which gradually turns brown and finally becomes necrotic.
- Availability of P is more in soils having pH **6.5-7.5**.
- Calcium in soil mostly moves through the process of **root interception**.
- The liming material commonly used for acid soils is **calcium carbonate**.
- **Dolomite** is source of both **calcium and magnesium**.
- Interaction effect of calcium with phosphorus in acid soils is **synergistic**.
- Calcium content in $CaCO_3$ is **100%.**
- The neutralizing value of CaO is **179**, $Ca(OH)_2$ is **136**, $CaMg(CO_3)_2$ is **109**, $CaCO_3$ is **100**, $CaSiO_3$ is **86**.

- **Magnesium** element dominates the cation-exchange capacity in soils derived from **serpentine rock**.
- **Tetany** disease of cattle is mainly attributed to **magnesium** deficiency.
- The common extractant used in most soil-testing laboratories in India for estimation of calcium and magnesium is **Neutral normal ammonium acetate**.
- **Serpentine ($MgSiO_3$)** contains **26%** Mg.
- Leaching loss of Mg is **lower** than calcium.
- Calcium requirement of dicots is **more** than monocots.
- Presence of high concentration of **K^+**, **NH_4^+** or **Ca^{2+} ion** on soils restricts the uptake of Magnesium.
- **Triethanolamine (TEA)** buffered at **pH 8.25** has been generally used for measurement of **exchange acidity**.
- Over liming leads to **boron** deficiency in **acid soils**.
- Calcium and magnesium are present in soils in three different forms as mineral, exchangeable, solution form.
- Many crops respond to calcium application when the degree of calcium saturation of the CEC falls below **25%**.
- Soil is considered as ideal one when ratios of cations is as follows

  Ca : Mg = 6.5:1

  Ca : K = 13:1

  Mg : K = 2:1

MICRONUTRIENTS

- Organic compounds like **EDTA** (Ethylene Diamine Tetra Acetic acid), **DTPA** (Diethylene Triamine Penta Acetic acid), **Cyclohexane diamine tetra Acetic acid** have the ability to chelate or loosely hold metallic ions in their cyclic structure and these metal-organic complexes are called **metal chelates**.
- Metal chelates are soluble in **water**, but they do not ionize in soil solution. Metal ions, therefore, do not react with soil constituents.

- Chelate forms of nutrients are **more** soluble than those from ordinary salts.
- **Iron, copper, zinc** and **manganese** fertilizers are available in chelated forms.

ZINC

- Nearly **half** of the Indian soils are poor in available Zn.
- Zinc deficiency is less prevalent in the **western states of Rajasthan** and **Gujarat**.
- Zn deficiency was first detected in rice at **Pantnagar, Uttarakhand** in 1965 by **Nene (plant pathologist)** and given the name **Khaira**.
- The solubility of Zn is highly pH dependent and decreases **100-fold** with each unit increase in soil pH.
- Zn deficiency is most prevalent in **calcareous** soil due to
  a) Increase in pH decreases Zn availability
  b) Zn is directly sorbed on carbonates
  c) Calcium carbonate can form insoluble calcium zincate
- Lack of **moisture** leads to Zn deficiency in soil and plants. Thus, more Zn deficiency is reported in **aerobic** rice systems.
- Zn is **relatively immobile** in plants, so deficiency symptoms generally appear on the growing young tissue.
- In **rice** the characteristic symptom of Zn deficiency is **bronzing**.
- Zinc interacts **positively** with N and K and **negatively** with P.
- Zn reacts **antagonistically** with all 3 secondary nutrients (Ca, Mg and S).
- Phosphate application **decreases** the uptake of Zn.
- Zn shows negative interaction with **Fe, Cu and Mn**.
- **Zinc Sulphate** is the most commonly used zinc fertilizer which contains **36% Zn**.
- **Zinc Oxide (ZnO)** contains **50-80% Zn** and is used for seed treatment. It is not soluble in water.
- Soil application of **10-25 kg/ha** zinc sulphate is the most common recommendation.
- For foliar spray **0.5%** solution of **zinc sulphate** mixed with a small quantity of lime is the general recommendation.

- For foliar application, **zinc chelates** are a better source, although they are more expensive. Zn chelates are better for fruit orchards.
- **Zinc sulphate heptahydrate (21% Zn)** is the most popular Zn fertilizer in India.
- Zinc is taken up by crop plants as **Zn^{2+}**.
- Concentration of Zinc in soil solution is **$2x10^{-9}$ M**.
- Zinc removal by a 5 tonnes/ha grain producing rice crop is **200 g/ha**.
- Zinc coated urea was first tested in agronomic experiments at **IARI, New Delhi**.

BORON

- Essentiality of Boron was established by **K. Warington** in **1923**.
- Boron is taken up by most plants as **H_3BO_3**.
- Common soil B mineral is **tourmaline**.
- Maximum toxic element (**Arsenic**) is found in B fertilizer **Colemanite**.
- **Boron** is a **non metal** micronutrient.
- **Boron** is neither a constituent of enzymes nor it directly affects the enzymatic activities in plants.
- **Boron** helps in germination and growth of pollen grains.
- Boron also acts as fuel pump, aiding the transmission of **sugars** from older leaves to new growth areas and root-system.
- Boron helps in uptake of **calcium**.
- Boron moves in plant through **phloem**.
- Boron deficiency causes **cracking** in fruits.
- Average concentration of B in plants is **20ppm**.
- Boron deficiency is wide spread in soils of **humid zone**.
- Boron content is more in **igneous rocks**.
- Maximum B deficiency is reported in soils of **Karnataka**.
- The deficiency of micronutrient **Boron** is prominent in **eastern India**.

- The magnitude of B deficiency in crops is almost similar to that of phosphorus (P) and zinc (Zn) and even more than sulphur (S) deficiency.
- Average boron deficiency in soils of whole India is **42-52%.**
- Wide-spread deficiency of B is found in **calcareous** soils.
- Boron deficiency is widespread when soil had **25% $CaCO_3$**.
- Boron deficiency can be corrected by application of **Granubor.**
- Optimum concentration of Solubor solution for foliar spray on crops is **1 g/L.**
- Borax is the most commonly used boron fertilizer which contains **11% B.**
- Borax is highly soluble in water and is lost by **leaching.**
- To avoid leaching losses of boron, boron frits are developed which contains **2 to 6% B.**
- **Boric acid** and **solubor** are boron fertilizers for foliar application.
- Boric acid contains **17% B.**
- Boron solubility is maximum for **Solubor.**
- General dose of borax penta hydrate **(14.6%)** is **2 kg/ha.**
- Boron is approved for fortification with **DAP.**
- Fortified fertilizers are allowed by **ministry in agriculture.**
- Boron foliar sprays are more beneficial than soil application to **litchi.**
- Boron foliar sprays response can be seen on early growth plus maturity.
- Contribution of irrigation water is important in correcting **B deficiency.**
- Boron toxicity in crops occurs in **salt affected soil.**

IRON, MANGANESE, COPPER, MOLYBDENUM AND CHLORINE MANAGEMENT

- **Ferrous sulphate** is the most commonly used fertilizer which is sprayed on the crop to control **iron chlorosis.**
- When ferrous sulphate is applied to the soil, it is oxidized to **ferric sulphate** which is not readily available to plants.

- To overcome above problem, **iron chelates** are used both for soil and foliar application.
- Iron frits which contain **22 % iron** can be used for **acid soils**.
- Ferrous sulphate contains **19% Fe**.
- Potassium interacts **positively** with Fe.
- **Fe and Mn** reach toxic levels under submergence.
- A **negative** interaction exists between **P and Fe, Mn and Zn**.
- Fe deficiency appears in **younger** leaves, while Mn deficiency appears in **older** leaves.
- DTPA-extractable CDL for Fe in soil is **2.5-4.5 mg**/kg soil.
- CDL for Fe in plant leaves is **30-50 mg**/kg dry matter.
- **Bronzing** disease in rice is due to the toxicity of **Fe**.
- In plants Fe and Mn interact **negatively**.
- Fe should preferably be applied as **foliar spray**.
- With an increase in soil pH from 4 to 8, the concentration of Fe^{3+} ions declines from 10^{-8} to 10^{-20} M.
- The solubility of Fe decreases by **1000 fold** for each unit increase of soil pH in the range of 4-9 compared to 100 fold decreases in the activity of Mn, Cu and Zn.
- Iron exists in Fe^0 (metallic), Fe^{2+} (ferrous), and Fe^{3+} (ferric) forms.
- Under acidic conditions, Fe^0 readily oxidizes to Fe^{2+}, and Fe^{2+} oxidizes to Fe^{3+} as the pH increases above 5.
- Ferric Fe (Fe^{3+}) is reduced to **Fe^{2+}** and is readily available to plants in **acidic soils**, but precipitates in alkaline soils.
- Minimum Fe solubility occurs between **pH 7.5 and 8.5**, which is the pH range of many calcareous soils.
- Iron deficiency, which occurs predominantly in **calcareous and alkaline soils**, is commonly enhanced by low soil temperature and high water or poorly aerated conditions.
- Fe plays a role in the synthesis of **chlorophyll**, **reduction of nitrate and sulphate**, and in **N assimilation**.
- **Interveinal chlorosis** in the young leaves is the characteristic symptom of Fe deficiency and in extreme conditions the entire leaves may turn **white**.
- **Sorghum** is the indicator plant for Fe deficiency in soil.

- Fe deficiency is observed on **neutral to alkaline** soils.
- Fe deficiency is more frequent on **upland** than on submerged soils.
- With the same calcareous soil, **upland** rice may suffer severe iron deficiency, while lowland rice may grow normally.
- Fe toxicity occurs only in **lowland** rice. Fe toxicity is likely to occur in **acid sandy**, **acid latosolic**, and **acid sulphate soils**.
- Iron toxicity also occurs on some organic soils such as **peaty soils**.
- Iron deficiency is reported from **Punjab, Haryana and Himachal Pradesh** in the north and from **Karnataka and Tamil Nadu** in the south.
- In well-drained aerobic conditions under which crops other than rice are grown, Fe occurs in oxidized **ferric (Fe^{3+}) form** which is **insoluble** and availability to crop plants is considerably **reduced**.
- Iron deficiency has been reported from **upland** nurseries and **aerobic** rice systems.
- **Frequent irrigation** of upland rice nurseries can easily overcome **Fe deficiency.**
- Prolonged flooded conditions in rice fields can increase the content of ferrous (Fe^{2+}) iron from **0.1** (under drained conditions) to **500-1000 mg/kg** and may lead to Fe toxicity.
- Crops generally absorb more **iron** than any other micronutrients.
- Among the cereals, **maize** absorb more Fe than rice, wheat, sorghum or pearl millet.
- **Ferrous sulphate heptahydrate ($FeSO_4.7H_2O$)** containing **18-20% Fe**, is the most popular Fe-fertilizer.
- **Soil** application of inorganic Fe sources is highly uneconomical because very high doses of Fe required to correct the deficiency.
- For foliar spray **1-2%** solution of **ferrous sulphate** is recommended.
- Iron chlorosis is observed in upland crops especially **rice, sorghum, groundnut, sugarcane, chickpea** etc. grown in highly calcareous soils.
- **Zn** and **Mo** reduce Fe uptake.
- Both Fe and Zn interact **positively** with N and **inversely** with P.

- Fe and Mn interact **negatively** with each other as well as with several other nutrients, such as P, Zn and Mo.
- The soluble Mn^{2+} content decreased **100-fold** for each unit increase in pH.
- Increase in soil pH **decreases** both the water-soluble and exchangeable Mn content in soils to produce **Mn** deficiency in **alkaline** soils.
- Mn deficiency is very common in **fine-textured** soils in comparison to coarse-textured soils.
- Organic matter improves the availability of Mn particularly in **acid sandy** soils.
- The combination of flooding, organic matter, and high temperatures **increases** Mn^{2+} content in soil.
- In well drained aerobic conditions under which crops other than rice are grown, Mn occurs in **manganic (Mn^{4+}) form**, being **insoluble** form and availability to crop plants is considerably **reduced**.
- Submerged condition in paddy soils, particularly in the presence of a high amount of organic matter, increases Mn concentration in soil solution to even a toxic level.
- **Mn** is essential for splitting the water molecule during photosynthesis.
- Manganese deficiency occurs in young leaves which wither or produce **interveinal chlorosis** with prominent dark green spots along with major veins.
- In case of **Fe deficiency**, veins also become **light yellow or yellow**, which is the only visible difference between iron and Mn deficiency.
- In **manganese** deficiency, the veins remain green with a fine reticulate pattern, with or without necrosis.
- Deficiency of Mn is named as
  a) Marsh spot of peas
  b) Grey speck of oats
  c) Speckled yellows of sugarbeets
  d) Crinkle leaf of cotton
  e) Curly top of cotton

- Mn deficiency is seen in crops grown on **alkaline** soils.
- Mn toxicity in plants is associated with **poorly drained acid** soils.
- Mn deficiency in wheat has been reported in **punjab**.
- Toxicity symptoms of Mn in rice are **interveinal yellowish brown spots, stunted plants** and **reduced tillering**.
- **Silicon** application reduces Mn toxicity.
- **Liming** the soils **reduce** Mn toxicity.
- **Manganese sulphate tetrahydrate ($MnSO_4.4H_2O$) (23-28% Mn)** is the most popular Mn-fertilizer.
- **0.1-1.0%** solution of **manganese sulphate** is required for **foliar spray**.
- Over-liming acid soils may lead to **Cu** deficiency.
- Amount of exchangeable Cu **decreases** as the pH increases.
- DTPA extractable CDL for Cu in soil is **0.2 mg**/kg soil.
- **Copper** is a part of **plastocyanin**.
- Copper sulphate contains **21%** Cu.
- Cu inhibits the uptake of **Zn**.
- Molybdenum is present in the **chloroplast** of leaves.
- **Molybdenum** is a structural component of **nitrogenase** which plays an active role in **nitrogen fixation** by Rhizobium, Azotobacter and some algae and actinomycetes.
- Molybdenum interacts **positively** with P and **negatively** with S and N.
- **Molybdenum** has deficiency symptoms similar to **N**.
- Whiptail disease in cauliflower is due to the deficiency of **Mo**.
- Pale yellow leaves despite high nitrate concentration indicate the deficiency of **Mo**.
- **Chlorine** is involved in production of **oxygen** during photosynthesis.
- **Chlorine** is involved in Hill reaction in **Photosystem II** in photosynthesis.
- Deficiency of secondary nutrient **sulphur** is wide-spread in India.
- The deficiency of micronutrient **Zinc** is widespread in India.

NUTRIENT INTERACTIONS

Antagonistic effects: Excess of one nutrient may induce deficiency of another as expressed below.

- Excess of Ca may induce P deficiency
- Excess of Ca and Mg may depress K uptake
- Excess of Ca may reduce Mg uptake, if ratio is wider than 7:1
- Excess of K^+ and NH_4^+ may reduce Mg uptake
- Excess of N,K and Ca may reduce B toxicity
- Excess of Fe and SO_4^{2-} may accentuate Mo deficiency
- Excess of Cu, Mn and NH_4^+ may depress Mo uptake
- Excess of Cu^{2+}, Fe^{2+} and Mn^{2+} may inhibit Zn^{2+} uptake
- Excess of P induces Zn deficiency
- Excess of N,P,K may induce Cu deficiency
- Excess of Zn and Al induces Cu deficiency
- Excess of P and Mo may cause Fe deficiency
- Excess of NO_3^- - N may cause Fe deficiency

Synergistic effects

- Application of Cl^- containing and acid forming N-fertilizers boost Mo uptake.
- Application of N usually enhances micronutrient uptake and utilization
- Application of Mg increases P uptake
- Application of P increases uptake and translocation of Mo
- Application of NH_4^+ - N improves P uptake
- Application of N and P improves K uptake
- Higher availability of Mg and NO_3^- - N boosts Mo uptake

FERTILIZER DOSE RECOMMENDATION BASED ON DIFFERENT METHODS:

- Diagnosis Recommendation Integration System (DRIS) approach was given by **Beaufils** in 1973.
- DRIS method considers **nutrient ratios** in plants for fertilizer recommendation.

- In DRIS method plant samples are analysed for nutrient content and they are expressed as ratios of nutrients with others.
- DRIS approach is suitable for **long duration** crops, but it is being tested for short duration crops like soybean, wheat etc.
- **Modeling approach** is suitable for recommendation of **nitrogenous** fertilizers where soils are rich in **organic matter** as in temperate regions.
- In soil, mineralization depends on soil **temperature.**
- Soil contribution is estimated by the formula

  $Y = K [(T - 15) \times D]^n$

  Y = amount of mineralized nitrogen

  T = Soil temperature

  K = Coefficient related to potential of mineralized nitrogen

  n= constant relating to the pattern of nitrogen mineralization

  15 = threshold temperature

  D = incubation period
- N use efficiency for applied fertilizers ranges from **30 to 40%.**
- Based on mineralisable N during crop period, the balance amount of nitrogen is supplied to the crop through fertilizer after considering nitrogen use efficiency.
- In soil test based fertilizer recommendation, **full dose** of fertilizers applied for **medium fertility** status, **25% less** fertilizer dose for **high fertility** status and **25% more** fertilizer dose for **low fertility** status.
- By leaf colour chart method, **nitrogen** fertilizers are recommended based on leaf colour to rice.
- Leaf colour is estimated every week on **fully developed new leaf** with leaf colour chart.
- When leaf colour falls below a critical level, a dose of **20 to 30 kg N** is applied.
- When previous crop is legume and without addition of legume residue to the soil, nitrogen dose for succeeding crop is reduced by **25%** and **normal dose** of P and K is applied.
- When previous legume crop is incorporated N dose is reduced by **half** and reduce P and K dose by **25%.**

- When previous crop is cereal and with or without residue incorporation, for the succeeding crop **25% more N** is applied.
- When previous crop is sunflower or castor, for the succeeding crop, **25% more N** is applied.

METHODS OF FERTILIZER APPLICATION

- Application of fertilizer uniformly on the soil surface is known as **broadcasting of fertilizers.**
- **Broadcasting** is the most widely practiced method in India due to ease in application.
- Entire dose of P and K fertilizers applied by broadcasting before sowing.
- Because of **low mobility** in soil P and K fertilizers are **broadcasted and** then **incorporated** in the soil.
- Application of fertilizers in narrow bands beneath and by the side of the crop rows is known as **band placement.**
- Band placement is practiced when
  1) Crop needs initial good start
  2) Soil fertility is low
  3) Fertilizer materials react with soil constituents leading to fixation
  4) Where volatilization losses are high
- In crops like **castor, redgram, cotton** etc. with tap root system, fertilizer band can be **5 cm below** the seed.
- In **cereals and millets**, which produce fibrous root system, it is advantageous to place fertilizers **5 cm away** from the seed row and **5 cm deeper** than the seed placement.
- Placement of fertilizers near the plant either in a hole or in a depression followed by closing or covering with soil is known as **point placement of fertilizers.**
- **Point placement** is adopted for top dressing of nitrogenous fertilizers in **widely spaced crops.**
- **Sub-soil placement** refers to the placement of fertilizers in the subsoil with the help of high power machinery.

- Sub-soil placement is recommended in **humid and sub humid** regions where sub-soils are **acidic**.
- Application of fertilizers with irrigation water is known as **fertigation**.

ORGANIC MANURES

- **Manures** are plants and animal wastes that are used as sources of plant nutrients.
- Bulky organic manures contain small percentage of nutrients and they are applied in **large quantities** *e.g.,* **FYM, compost and green manure**
- **Farm yard manure** refers to the decomposed mixture of dung and urine of farm animals along with litter and left over material from roughages or fodder fed to the cattle.
- FYM contains **0.5 %** N - **0.2 %** P_2O_5 - **0.5%** K_2O
- Cattle urine contains **1%** N – **1.5%** K_2O
- Nitrogen present in urine in the form of **urea** which is subjected to **volatilization** losses.
- During storage nutrients are lost due to **leaching** and **volatilization**.
- Chemical preservatives like **gypsum** and **superphosphate** are added to reduce losses and enrich farm yard manure.
- There is positive correlation between **N content** in FYM and **decomposing rate**.
- Partially rotten farmyard manure has to be applied **three to four weeks** before sowing while well rotten manure can be applied immediately before sowing.
- The entire amount of nutrients present in farm yard manure is not available immediately.
- About **30 per cent** of **nitrogen**, **60 to 70 per cent** of **phosphorus** and **70 per cent** of **potassium** are available to the first crop.
- A mass of rotted organic matter made from waste is called **compost**.
- Compost made from farm waste like **sugarcane trash**, **paddy straw**, **weeds** and other plants and other waste is called **farm compost**.

- Composition of farm compost is **0.5%** N - **0.15%** P_2O_5 - **0.5%** K_2O.
- Compost made from town refuses like **night soil**, **street sweepings** and **dustbin refuse** is called **town compost**.
- **Night soil** is human excreta, both solid and liquid.
- Night soil contains **5.5 %** N - **4.0 %** P_2O_5 -**2.0%** K_2O.
- In the modern system of sanitation adopted in cities and towns, **human excreta** is flushed out **with water** which is called **sewage.**
- Solid portion of sewage is called **sludge**.
- Liquid portion of sewage is called **sewage water**.
- Compost that is prepared with the help of earthworms is called **vermicompost**.
- India has about **3000** species of earthworms.
- **Earthworm** is called as an **ecosystem engineer**.
- The weight of the material passing through the body each day is almost equal to the weight of the earthworm.
- Vermicompost is rich in all essential plant nutrients and contains valuable **vitamins, enzymes and hormones**.
- Vermicompost contains **3%** N – **1%** P_2O_5 – **1.5%** K_2O.
- Human urine contains **1.1 to 1.2%** nitrogen.
- Manure from bullocks will be **richer** in nutrients than from cow producing milk.
- Droppings of sheep and goats are **richer** in nutrients than FYM and compost.
- Sheep and goat manure contains **3%** N-**1%** P_2O_5-**2%** K_2O.
- In **sheep penning**, sheep and goats are kept overnight in the field and urine and faecal matter added to the soil is incorporated to a shallow depth by working blade harrow or cultivator.
- Poultry manure contains **3.03%** N - **2.63%** P_2O_5 -**1.4%** K_2O.
- Edible oilcakes can be safely fed to livestock *e.g.,* **groundnut cake**, **coconut cake** etc.
- **Nonedible oilseeds** are not fit for feeding livestock *e.g.,* **castor cake**, **neem cake**, **mahua cake** etc.
- Decorticated safflower cake contains **7.9%** N.
- Groundnut cake contains **7.3%** N.
- **Raw bone meal** contains **20-25%** P_2O_5.

- **Steamed bone meal** contains **25-30%** P_2O_5.
- The dry, inert powder made from animal blood is **blood meal**.
- The excrement of seabirds, cave-dwelling bats, pinnipeds or birds is known as **bird guano**.
- Paddy straw generally takes about **6-9 weeks** to develop into mature compost, if efficient microbial inovulants containing *T. viride*, *Aspergillus awamori*, *Paecilomyces fusisporus* or *Phanerochaete chrysosporium* are used.
- Composting can be done by mainly two methods **windrow** and **pit** methods.
- Wind-row composting involves placing the mixture of raw materials in long narrow piles called **wind rows**.
- **Bangalore process** of composting was developed by **C.N. Acharya**.
- A majority of the composting processes involve **aerobic** composting.
- **Karnataka** produces the largest amount of rural and urban compost.
- The **Indore process** of composting was developed by **Dr Howard** at the Institute of Plant Industry, Indore.
- **Coimbatore process** was developed by **Dr T.S. Manickam**.
- Compost can be enriched by **rock phosphate, bone meal** and **superphosphate**.
- Green, undecomposed plant material used as manure is called **green manure**.
- **Green manuring** is growing in the field plants usually belonging to **leguminous** family and incorporating into the soil after sufficient growth.
- Plants that are grown for green manure are known as **green manure crops**.
- **Sunhemp**, **dhaincha**, **pillipesara**, **clusterbean** and ***Sesbania rostrata*** are the green manure crops.
- Optimum temperature for decomposition of green manure is **30-35°C**.
- **Dhaincha** is an ideal green-manure crop for **rice** based cropping system.

- Incorporation of 10 tonnes/ha of green manure through *Sesbania* or *Crotalaria* supplements fertilizer N equivalent to **40-45 kg/ha**.
- The benefit of green manuring is felt only after continued application for **3-5 years**.
- **Green manuring** helps in reclamation of alkaline soils.
- ***Sesbania aculeata*** is most suitable for reclamation of **saline** and **alkali soils.**
- ***Delonix elata*** green leaf manure used for reclamation of **saline and sodic** soils.
- **Root-knot nematodes** can be controlled by **green manuring**.
- Botanical name of wild indigo is ***Tephrosia purpurea***.
- ***Tephrosia purpurea*** is a slow growing green manure crop.
- ***Sesbania rostrata*** is a **stem nodulating** green manure crop native of **West Africa**.
- ***Sesbania rostrata*** is a **short day plant**, length of vegetative period is short when sown in August or September.
- A mutant **TSR-1** developed by Bhabha Atomic Research Centre, Mumbai is **insensitive to photoperiod**, **tolerant to salinity** and **waterlogging.**
- **Sunhemp** accumulates higher biomass per ha (**30.6 tonnes/ha**).
- **Dhaincha** (***Sesbania aculeata***) accumulates **23.2 tonnes biomass/ha.**
- **Sunhemp fixes** higher nitrogen/ha (134 kg N/ha).
- Dhaincha fixes **133 kg N/ha**.
- Nitrogen content in Dhaincha is **3.50%**.
- Nitrogen content is highest in the green leaf manure ***Pongamia glabra*** **(3.31%)**.
- **Nitrogen fixation** by leguminous green manure crops can be **increased by** application of **phosphatic fertilizers**.
- Application to the field, green leaves and twigs of trees, shrubs and herbs collected from elsewhere is known as **green leaf manuring**.
- Forest tree leaves and plants growing in wastelands, field bunds are another source of green leaf manure.

- Important green leaf manure species are **neem**, **mahua, wild indigo, glyricidia, karanji (*Pongamia glabra*), Calotrops, avise (*Sesbania grandiflora*), subabul.**
- ***Gliricidia*** is used as a shade crop first and then incorporated as green manure.
- **Glyricidia** is more effective in sodic soil.
- **Nutrient** availability increases due to production of carbon dioxide and organic acids during decomposition.
- Incorporation of green leaf manures like sunhemp, *Sesbania rostrata*, *Calotropis* spp. *Tephrosia* spp. and *Glyricidia* spp. increases the **DTPA-Zn and Cu status** markedly.
- Most of the green manure crops are legumes which fix nitrogen and improve soil fertility.
- Most of the legumes derive **80-90%** of their nitrogen requirement from biologically fixed N.
- Water requirement of pulses varies from **250 to 300 mm**.
- Among pulse based cropping systems **rice-lathyrus** is the most extensive cropping system.
- Rice fallows are spread in **11.7 m ha** in India.

BIOFERTILIZERS

- **Microrganism – Function**

  Rhizobium spp. – Nodulation and nitrogen fixation

  Arbuscular Mycorrhizae – Nutrient mobilization

  Phanerochaete chrysosporium – Composting

  Azolla – Improve nitrogen availability in rice

  Bacillus megaterium – Silicate/Phosphate solubilization
- Biofertilizers can be applied as **seed coating**, **soil application** or **seedling dip**.
- Dry formulations of microbial inoculants can be in the form of dusts, wettable powders, granules, pellets, capsules and briquettes.
- Commonly used carriers for biofertilizers are **peat, lignite, soil, charcoal, vermiculite, talc, vermicompost, sawdust** and **pressmud**.

- ***Biofertilizer - specific crop***
  Azospirillum - Cereals, particularly grasses
  Blue green algae - Rice
  Frankia – Casuarina
  Azotobacter – cotton
- Frankia fixes **nitrogen**.
- *Rhizobium* establishes efficient symbiotic associations with pulses, leguminous oil-seeds and fodder crops.
- For seed treatment, *Rhizobium* inoculum @ **1.5kg/ha** is mixed in the jaggery solution and sprinkled over the seeds.

RHIZOBIUM SPECIES SUITABLE FOR DIFFERENT CROPS

Rhizobium sp.	Crops
R. leguminosarum	Peas (*Pisum*), lathyrus, Vicia, Lentil (*Lens*)
R. trifoli	Berseem (*Trifolium*)
R. phaseoli	Kidney bean (*Phaseolus*)
R. lupini	Lupinus
R. japonicum	Soybean (*Glycine*)
R. meliloti	Melilotus, Lucerne (*Medicago*), Fenugreek (*Trigonella*)
Cowpea miscellany	Cowpea, cluster bean, greengram, blackgram, redgram, groundnut, moth bean, dhaincha, sunhemp, *Glyricidia, Acacia, Prosophis, Dalbergia, Albizzia, Indigofera, Tephrosia, Atylosia, Stylo*
Separate group	Bengalgram (gram)

- Free living organisms that can fix atmospheric nitrogen are **blue green algae (BGA), *Azolla, Azotobacter* and *Rhizospirillum*.**
- BGA and *Azolla* can survive only in **lowland** conditions.
- Important species of BGA that fix atmospheric nitrogen are ***Anabaena* and *Nostoc*.**
- Amount of nitrogen fixed by BGA ranges from **15-45 kg N/ha**.
- BGA can grow at a temperature of **25 to 45°C**.
- Bright sunshine **increases** the growth rate of BGA while rains and cloudiness **slows** growth rate.

- BGA grows well in a pH range of **7 to 8** and in soils with high organic matter.
- BGA inoculum is applied after transplantation of rice crop in the main field.
- Amount of BGA inoculum required is **10 kg/ha**.
- Azolla is a **free-floating water fern** which forms symbiotic association with blue-green algae species ***Anabaena azollae*** present in the lobes of ***Azolla* leaves** and provides nitrogen to rice crop.
- ***Azolla pinnata*** is the most common species occurring in India.
- A thick mat of *Azolla* supplies **30-40 kg** N/ha.
- Unlike blue-green algae, azolla thrives well at **low** temperature.
- Normal growth of *Azolla* occurs in the temperature range of **20 to 30°C**.
- ***Azolla*** grows better under monsoon season with frequent rains and cloudiness.
- For *Azolla* suitable soil pH is **5.5-7.0**.
- Amount of *Azolla* inoculum required is **0.1 to 0.5** kg/m^2.
- As green manure crop, *Azolla* is allowed to grow on the flooded fields for 2 to 3 weeks before transplanting, later water is drained and *Azolla* is incorporated by ploughing in.
- Advantages of Azotobacter to crops are Biological nitrogen fixation, release of growth promoting substances, suppression of plant diseases.
- *Azotobacter chroococcum* is capable of fixing **20 to 30 kg N/ha**.
- Amount of *Azotobacter* inoculum required is **3-5 kg/ha**.
- *Azotobacter* can be used for **rice**, **cotton** and **sugarcane**.
- ***Acetobacter*** is commercially utilized for **Sugarcane**.
- *Azospirillum* inoculants are recommended in several crops such as **jowar, bajra, ragi** and **other millets**.
- Cell number or colony forming units at the time of manufacture should not be less than **10^8 and 10^7** per gram of carrier material, respectively for ***Rhizobium* and *Azotobacter***.
- ***Pseudomonas striata***, ***Aspergillus awamorii*** and ***Bacillus polymyxa*** are capable of solubilising phosphates.

- Liquid inoculants and biofilmed inoculants are **new generation** biofertilizers.
- Shelf life of liquid biofertilizers is **12-24** months.

CROP RESIDUES

- Gross quantity of crop residues annually available in India is **686 million tonnes**.
- **Crop – residue to economic yield ratio**

  Rice – 1.4

  Wheat – 1.3

  Maize – 2.0

  Barley – 1.5
- Out of the total residue produced in India, **cereal** crops contribute the highest amount followed by **sugarcane**.
- The silica content in rice straw is **12-16%** and wheat straw is **3-5%**.
- Wheat straw contains approximately **0.53% N**.
- C:N ratio of wheat straw is **more** than rice straw.
- The rice straw contains **50-100%** higher concentration of K than in wheat straw.
- Machines used for zero-till planting of crops under surface residue conditions is **turbo happy seeder, rotary disc drill and double disc drill.**
- Hydraulic conductivity and infiltration rate are **higher** in no-till with residue retention compared to conventional till with residue incorporation.
- **Gas – Qty released by burning 1 tonne of rice residue**

  CO_2 – 1515 kg

  CO – 92 kg

  NO_x – 3.83 kg

  CH_4- 2.7 kg

  Non-methane volatile organic compounds – 15.7 kg

  SO_2 – 0.4 kg

- **Nutrient - Content in 1 tonne rice straw**
  N – 5-8 kg
  P – 0.7 -1.2 kg
  K – 15-25 kg
  S - 0.5 -1 kg
  Ca – 3-4 kg
- Cellulose content in crop residues on dry weight basis is **15-60%.**
  Hemicellulose - **10-30%**
  Lignin - **5-30%**
  Protein - **2-15%**
- The potential of no-till can be fully realized only when it is practiced continuously and the soil surface is covered at least **30%** by crop residues or other organic materials.

INTEGRATED NUTRIENT MANAGEMENT

- The gap between fertilizer application to nutrient removal is estimated to be **8-10 million tonnes** of N + P_2O_5 + K_2O each year in the country.
- Legumes can fix **50-500** kg N/ha depending upon the crop and its growth period.
- Green manuring along with recommended level of fertilizers increases the total productivity of the system to the tune of **10-20%.**
- **French bean** has poor root nodulation, particularly when it is grown in **Indo-gangetic plains.**
- Loppings of perennial multi-purpose woody legumes, such as ***Gliricidia sepium, Cassia siamea*** and ***Leucaena leucocephala*** **(Subabool)** can be used for green leaf manuring.
- Green manures can add **60-120 kg N/ha** and in many situations can meet the entire N demand of a crop to which they are supplied.
- **Biogas slurry** is the residue left in biogas units after the fermentation and liberation of biogas.
- **Pressmud cake** is a waste product of sugar industry.
- About **52.8 million tonnes** rice residue is produced from about **10 million ha** under rice-wheat cropping system belt.

WATER AND NUTRIENT INTERACTIONS

- Nutrient availability is at a minimum as the soil water content approaches the **permanent wilting point**.
- Mobile nutrients like **calcium, magnesium, nitrate-N** and **sulphate** are transported to the root by **mass flow**.
- Excessive water use reduces N recovery by the means of nitrate – N **leaching**.
- Organic N - mineralization is **proportionately** related to increase in soil water content.
- Fe and Zn deficiencies are frequently associated with high soil moisture availability.
- Application of water and nutrients together is known as **fertigation**.
- Solubility of urea fertilizer is **1100 g/litre** at 20°C
- The lower the soil-moisture content, the **greater** the response to P.
- **Phosphatic** and **calcium** water-soluble fertilizers are compatible for mixing the solutions.
- Cultivation of undulating soil is possible with **fertigation**.
- **Deeper placement** of fertilizer in water limiting areas gives better response than surface application.
- For maximum use efficiency on sandy-loam soil, urea-N top dressing should be made **2-3 days** after irrigation.
- Plant requirements for P and K are mostly met by the process of **diffusion**.
- Application of K reduces water loss in plants through **stomatal movement and osmoregulation**.
- **Fertigation** improves water-use efficiency and Nutrient-use efficiency.
- Maximum water and nitrogen use efficiency in rice can be achieved by irrigation after **2-3 days** of disappearance of standing water.

Chapter 13

Growth and Development of Crops

- **Growth** is irreversible increase in size or weight.
- The main principle in agronomy is harvesting as much solar energy as possible and converting solar energy into chemical energy by photosynthesis.
- On the leaf surface, a thin layer of undisturbed air (boundary layer) offers resistance to the flow of CO_2 which is called **boundary layer resistance**.
- The resistance offered by stomata is called **stomatal resistance**.
- Resistance offered by mesophyll cells is called **mesophyll resistance**.
- In plants, the molecule absorbing radiant energy in the visible range is referred to as a **pigment**.
- Chlorophyll is **green**, carotenoids **red or yellow** and **phytochrome blue**.
- Plants also contain pigments such as **anthocyanins** and **flavones**.
- Only **chlorophylls** and **carotenoids** function in photosynthesis.
- Solar radiation contains small units called **photons**.
- By photolysis, water is broken down into **hydrogen** and **nascent oxygen**.
- Hydrogen ions released during break down of water are used for reducing NADP to NADPH which releases energy that is utilized for oxidative phosphorylation *i.e.*, conversion of ADP to ATP.
- Reduction of carbon dioxide is also called **dark reaction** as light is not necessary.
- Dark reaction does not mean that this reaction occurs only in dark.
- With the energy supplied by ATP (formed during light reactions), CO_2 combines with hydrogen (supplied by NADPH) and forms carbohydrates.

- Plants are classified into C_3, C_4 and CAM based on method of reduction of CO_2.

C_3 plants	**C_4 plants**	**CAM plants**
Initial product of carbon assimilation is 3-carbon compound	Primary product of carbon fixation is 4-carbon compound (Malic acid or aspartic acid)	• Stomata are open at night and CO_2 is fixed as malic acid and stored in vacuoles. • Stomata closed during day
Enzyme involved in primary carboxylation is RUBISCO (Ribulose-1,5-bisphosphate carboxylase)	Enzyme responsible for carboxylation is PEP (Phosphoenol pyruvic acid) carboxylase	CO_2 stored as malic acid, is broken down and released as CO_2
Photorespiration is high	• Photorespiration is negligible • Photosynthetic rate higher	-
Low water-use efficiency	High WUE	• High WUE • Lowest transpiration rate and use much less water
-	Able to utilize low concentrations of CO_2 and thrive under less CO_2 supply	-
Perform better under cool conditions with moderate insolation	Better adaptation to higher temperature and higher insolation conditions	-
Ex: rice, wheat, barley, oats, cotton, soybean, groundnut, sugarbeet, rye, tomato, potato, sweet potato	Ex: maize, sorghum, pearl millet, napier grass, sugarcane, amaranthus and other minor millets	Ex: Pineapple and sisal

- C_4 minor millets, even under good management do not out yield **C_3 rice**.

- Photosynthetic advantage of **C_4 plants** compared with C_3 plants at the level of carboxylation is **reduced** at the whole leaf level. It is due to combination of **stomatal and mesophyll resistance** at the leaf level and by mutual shading and periods of low light at plant community level. As a result, no consistent advantage of the C_4 pathway is evident in crop growth rates and crop yields of C_4 plants.
- In C_4 plants, as **PEP enzyme** has high affinity and activity with CO_2, for known size of stomatal aperture, more CO_2 is fixed for the same amount of water lost.
- C_4 plants use considerably **less** water per unit of additional dry weight than calvin cycle (C_3) plants.
- **Respiration** is a reverse process of photosynthesis.
- **Respiration** supplies the necessary energy for the execution of various biological and chemical reactions in plants.
- Growth respiration provides energy and products for the synthesis of structural and storage compounds.
- Growth respiration does not depend on temperature.
- **Maintenance** respiration provides energy for the entire plant for routine works such as maintenance of membranes, proteins, cellular organization and for ion uptake.
- **Growth** respiration is necessary for the normal growth.
- **Maintenance** respiration is considered as a wasteful process especially under higher temperature.
- Maintenance respiration depends on **temperature**.
- **Low light** and **high temperature** during grain filling period is considered as unfavorable for high yields.
- Respiratory mechanism common to all types of plants (C_3 and C_4) is called **dark reaction** since it occurs regardless of light.
- Photorespiration occurs only during **high light** and **oxygen availability**.
- Under high light intensity, high levels of energy and oxygen is available in the leaves.
- The enzyme in photo respiration is the same **ribulose 1,5-bisphosphate carboxylase** which fixes CO_2.
- As the enzyme RUBISCO also accepts oxygen, it is also called as **ribulose 1,5-bisphosphate oxygenase**.

- Photorespiration is high in **C_3 plants** which is considered as wasteful.
- Total amount of photosynthates produced due to the process of photosynthesis is called **gross photosynthesis**.
- **Net photosynthesis** is the amount of carbohydrates added in the plant by photosynthesis less the amount of carbohydrates spent in respiration.
- Amount of net photosynthesis depends on **light intensity** and **carbon dioxide concentration**.
- The light intensity at which photosynthesis and respiration are **equal** is called **light compensation point**.
- The light intensity at which there is no further increase in the rate of photosynthesis is called **light saturation point**.
- Light saturation is **high** in **C_4 plants** compared to C_3 plants.
- Concentration of carbon dioxide at which respiration and photosynthesis are equal is called **carbon dioxide compensation point**.
- Carbon dioxide compensation point is **lower** in **C_4 plants** than C_3 plants.
- Carbohydrates are usually translocated as **sucrose** and to some extent as **starch**.
- Dormancy may be due to
  1) Improper development of embryo
  2) High concentration of growth inhibiting substances
  3) Hard and impermeable seed coat
- **Positive** photoblastic seeds require **light** for inducing germination.
- **Negative** photoblastic seeds **do not germinate** when exposed to light.
- **Non-photoblastic** seeds germinate either in **light or dark**.
- Seeds of many cultivated crops are **non-photoblastic**.
- Flowering plants are classified into **monocotyledons** and **dicotyledons**.
- Cereals and millets belong to **monocotyledons**.
- When seed is sown in soil, it absorbs water **twice** its weight.

- **Embryo** secretes **gibberelin** which in turn induces the secretion of **hydrolytic enzymes** by **aleurone layer** in cereals.
- **Hydrolytic enzymes** break down complex food materials like starches and proteins into simple **sugars and aminoacids** respectively.
- Fats in the cotyledons of oil seeds and in the embryos of cereal seeds are split by **lipases** into **fatty acids and glycerol**.
- **Radical** is the first organ to emerge from the seed in all cases.
- Radical is followed by **plumule** of young shoot.
- In dicotyledonous plants such as groundnut **cotyledons** emerge from the soil and function as **first leaves**.
- In groundnut cotyledons are brought out of the soil by **curved elongation of hypocotyls**.
- Type of germination where cotyledons emerge out of the soil is called **epigeal germination**.
- In monocotyledons plants, cotyledons remain inside the soil. The plumule grows upward by the elongation of epicotyls. This type of germination is called **hypogeal germination** since the **cotyledon** is below or **inside the soil**.
- Dicotyledons also exhibit **hypogeal germination** when sown deep.
- The coleoptiles of grasses emerge from the soil as pale tube like structure that encloses the first true leaf.
- In monocotyledonous plants, **radical** elongates and constitutes **primary root**.
- **Primary root** usually grows **vertically** downwards while secondary roots that appear during the seedling stage grow **horizontally** for a few centimeters before turning downwards.
- High order laterals spread randomly and these roots are called **seminal roots**.
- At the end of seedling stage, fresh roots develop from lower nodes of stem called **nodal roots or adventitious roots**.
- **Seminal roots** penetrate downwards to the greatest depth.
- **Adventitious roots** constitute a major portion of total root mass and become important for the rest of the life of the plants, while the **seminal roots** decay gradually.

- When seedlings are transplanted, they establish by producing **nodal roots**.
- **Top leaves** contribute more to ear growth and almost **half** of the pre-anthesis weight of the ear is from the **flag leaf**.
- In wheat and barley, most of the contribution to grain is from **flag leaves**.
- Contribution of stored carbohydrates in stem to grain filling is **10 to 20%**.
- During moisture stress, when the normal photosynthesis is affected, stem contribution may exceed **20%** of final grain weight.
- Primordial differentiation stage is called as **panicle initiation stage** in cereals and millets, **squaring** in cotton, **flower bud initiation** in sunflower *etc.*
- With the start of **primordial differentiation** stage, plants enter reproductive phase.
- **Primordial differentiation** stage is more sensitive to moisture and solar radiation in cereals.
- Crop is said to be at 50% flowering when **50%** of plants put forth flowers.
- Opening of flowers and shedding of pollen is called **anthesis**.
- **Blooming** also indicates opening of flowers.
- Flowering stage is very sensitive to **moisture** stress.
- Total area of leaves per unit area of the land surface is **leaf area index (LAI)**.
- Optimum LAI for crops with horizontally oriented leaves is **3-4**.
- Optimum LAI for crops with upright leaves is **6-9**.
- The proportion of incident light that is intercepted by the crop canopy does not depend on LAI alone but also on the architecture of the plant community.
- **Extinction coefficient (K)** is a measure of the light intercepting efficiency of the leaf area.
- The maximum temperature above which no germination occurs is usually within the range of **35-45°C**.
- Most of the crop seeds germinate well within the moisture regime of field capacity to **50% available soil moisture**.

- Soil crust is the main hurdle for the emergence of crops like **foxtail millet, pearl millet** etc. as the seeds are **small.**
- **Oxygen content**, **light and dormancy** influence germination and emergence.
- Germination may be affected due to lack of **oxygen** by waterlogging if rains follow immediately after sowing.
- Seeds of **stylo and subabul** need treatment prior to soaking to break dormancy.
- Leaf expansion is normal if the relative water content (water content of leaves compared to water content at saturation) is **90-100%.**
- Leaf expansion stops when RWC is below **70-75%.**
- Relative water content of leaves is more in **young leaves** compared to old leaves.
- **Cell expansion** is more affected by **moisture stress** than **cell division.**

PLANT GROWTH SUBSTANCES

- Plant growth substances are biochemicals produced in plants (endogenous) or synthetic substances applied to plants externally (exogenous) which cause modifications in plant growth and development.
- There are **5** major groups of endogenous growth substances present in plants

  Ex: auxins, cytokinins, gibberellins, abscisic acid and ethylene
- Plant growth substances produced by the plant are called **phytohormones.**
- Plant growth substances are classified into
  1) Growth promoters : **auxins**, **cytokinins** and **gibberellins**
  2) Growth retardants : **abscisic acid**, **ethylene**
- Growth promoters exist in **multiple forms.**
- Growth retardants (abscisic acid and ethylene) exist in **single form.**

- **Important plant growth regulators and their use**

Common name	Trade name	Use
ABA	abscisin	Defoliant
Acifluorfen	Blazer	Growth retardant
Chlormequat (CCC)	Cycocel	Lodging preventor
Ethephon	Cepha	Sugarcane ripener
Glyphosate	Roundup	Sugarcane ripener
GA_3 (Gibberelic acid)	Berelex Pro-gibb	Grape enlarger
Kinetin	-	Dormancy breaker
IAA	Rhizopon-A	Plant cell enlarger
IBA	Seradix	Plant cell enlarger
Maleic hydrazide (MH)	Sproutstop	Growth retardant
NAA	Fruitone-N	Fruit thinner
TIBA	Regim-8	Growth retardant

- **Auxins** stimulate elongation of cells of stems and coleoptiles.
- Endogenous auxins are **Indoleacetic acid (IAA)** and **Phenolacetic acid**.
- Synthetic auxins are **Naphthalene acetic acid (NAA)**, **Indole-3-acetic acid**, **Indole-3-propionic acid** and **2,4-D**.
- **Auxins** promote cell enlargement resulting in elongation of coleoptiles, stem etc.
- Presence of auxins in apical bud suppresses the auxiliary buds and results in **apical dominance**.
- **Cell division** and **root formation** are important functions of auxins.
- Plant organ development in tissue culture affected by **balance of auxins to cytokinins**.
- Due to high concentration of auxins and cytokinins, cells grow amorphously without differentiation.
- High ratio of **auxin to cytokinin** - induction of **roots** in callus cells.
- High ratio of **cytokinin to auxin** - formation of **shoots**.
- Auxins are used to enhance fruit set.

- **Auxins** are used as herbicides at higher doses. Ex: **2,4-D and 2,4,5-T.**
- **NAA** induces flowering in **Pineapple**.
- **IBA** is used for inducing rooting of cuttings.
- Cytokinins stimulate **cell division**.
- Endogenous cytokinins are **Kinetin, Zeatin** and **Isopentenyladenosine**.
- Synthetic cytokinin is **6-Benzyladenine**.
- **Cytokinins** promote orderly development of embryos of seed.
- **Cytokinins** break dormancy of seeds and buds.
- **Cytokinins** delay senescence.
- **Gibberellin** is first isolated from the fungus ***Gibberella fuzikuroi***.
- Gibberellins increase **cell division** and **cell elongation**.
- Gibberellin commonly available is **GA_3 (gibberellic acid)**.
- Gibberellins promote **cell elongation** and **increase** in size of leaf, flower and fruit.
- Dormancy is broken and flowering is induced by **gibberellins**.
- **Abscisic acid** induces leaf and fruit abscission.
- **Abscisic acid** accumulation induces dormancy.
- Moisture stressed plants produce **abscisic acid** which facilitates stomatal closure and helps in maintaining cell turgidity.
- **Ethylene** stimulates the swelling or **isodiametric growth** of stems and roots.
- Regulation of **ethylene** can trigger **ripening** of fruits or delay in ripening process
- **Phenolics** inhibit cell division, cell enlargement and germination of seed.
- **Lucerne** leaves contain **triacontanol** which when applied as foliar spray improves the growth of crops.
- Examples of growth retardants are **cycocel (CCC), phosfon-D, maleic hydrazide (MH)**.
- **CCC and MH** retard stem elongation and the leaves of the treated plants become thick and dark green.
- **Maleic hydrazide** is used for **sucker control** in tobacco and as growth retardant.

- **Abscisic acid** is used as a cotton defoliant.
- **Cycocel** is used for reducing **excessive vegetative growth** in cotton.
- **Cycocel** is used as **dwarfing agent** in wheat.
- **NAA** increases **number of flowers.**
- **Gibberellins** are used for production of **seedless grapes.**
- **Gibberellins** are used for **increasing size** of fruits.
- **S-shaped or sigmoid curve** is typical of growth pattern of individual organs, of a whole plant and of population of plants.
- In **lag period** internal changes occur that are preparatory to growth. Increase in size or weight is **negligible.**
- In **log phase or grand period** of growth, growth is very fast. Logarithm of growth when plotted against time is a **straight line.**
- **Justus Von Liebig** proposed **law of minimum** in **1862.**
- **Blackman** in **1905** proposed **law of optima and limiting factors.**
- Mitcherlich's **law of diminishing returns** was proposed by **Mitcherlich** in **1909**. He developed an equation relating **growth** with **supply of plant nutrients.**

$$\frac{dy}{dx} = (A - y)C$$

where, dy/dx= growth rate

A = maximum possible yield with sufficient level of all growth factors

y = yield obtained at a given level of growth factor

x, C = proportionality constants

- **Wilcox** proposed **inverse yield-nitrogen law** in **1929.**
- According to inverse yield nitrogen law, yielding ability of any crop plant is **inversely** proportional to the mean nitrogen content in dry matter.
- **Macy-poverty adjustment** law was proposed by **Macy** in **1936.**
- **Watson** developed the concept of **leaf area Index (LAI).**
- Leaf area index = $\frac{\text{Leaf area}}{\text{Ground area}}$

- Absolute growth rate = $\frac{W_2 - W_1}{t_2 - t_1}$
  - ✓ W_1 and W_2 are dry weights of plants at times t_1 and t_2 respectively
  - ✓ AGR indicates at what rate the crop is growing, whether at faster rate or slower than normal
  - ✓ AGR is expressed as **g of dry matter produced per day**
- Crop growth rate is the rate of crop growth per unit area

$$CGR = \frac{1}{P} \times \frac{W_2 - W_1}{t_2 - t_1}$$

- CGR expressed as **g/m²/day.**
- **Relative growth rate** indicates rate of growth per unit dry matter.
- **Relative growth rate** expressed as grams of dry matter produced by a gram of existing dry matter in a day.

$$RGR = \frac{Log_e W_2 - log_e W_1}{t_2 - t_1}$$

- **Net assimilation rate** indirectly indicates the rate of **net photosynthesis.**
- **NAR** is expressed as g of dry matter produced per dm^2 of leaf area in a day.
- For calculating NAR, leaf area of **individual plants** has to be used but not leaf area index.

$$NAR = \frac{(W_2 - W_1)(log_e L_2 - log_e L_1)}{(t_2 - t_1)(L_2 - L_1)}$$

Here L_1 and W_1 are leaf area and dry weight of plants at time t_1, and L_2 and W_2 are leaf area and dry weight of plants at time t_2

- **Leaf area duration** of a crop is a measure of its ability to produce leaf area on unit area of land throughout its life.

$$LAD\ (days) = \frac{L_1 + L_2}{2} \times (t_2 - t_1) + ... + \frac{L_{n-1} + L_n}{2} \times (t_n - t_{n-1})$$

Where L_1, L_2 = leaf area at time t_1 and t_2

L_n = leaf area at time t_n

L_{n-1} = leaf area at time t_{n-1}

- Yield of dry matter is a function of **leaf area**, **net assimilation rate** and **duration of leaf area**.
- The total dry matter produced by a crop is known as **biological yield**.
- Fraction of the biological yield which is useful for man is known as **economic yield**.
- Biological yield × K = Economic yield
- K is a constant and called **harvest index** or **coefficient of effectiveness.**
- Harvest index = Economic yield/Biological yield
- In many cereals, most of the drymatter in the grain is produced by photosynthesis after the ears emerge.
- Most of the dry matter of the grain is produced by the part of the shoot above the flag leaf node.
- **Flag leaf** contributes nearly **40%** of the total dry matter in many cereals.
- In cereals, grain filling is largely dependent on **photosynthesis** and environmental conditions after **flowering**.
- In cereal, capacity for storage is determined by conditions **before flowering**.
- In plants where source and sink are developed simultaneously, like groundnut, redgram, cotton etc., the adjustment of two components may be more readily achieved.
- Economic yield is expressed as function of yield attributes

  $$Y = a \times b \times c \times d$$

  a = final plant population at harvest

  b = number of effective tillers (panicle or ear producing)

  c = number of filled grains/ear

  d = weight of individual grain
- Instead of individual grain weight, 100-grain weight (in case of bold grains) and 1000 grain weight (in case of small sized grains) are taken as yield attributes and this is also known as **test weight**.

Chapter 14

Dryland Agriculture

- Growing of crops entirely under rainfed conditions is known as **dryland agriculture**.
- Dryland agriculture grouped into 3 groups based on rainfall

Dry farming	Dryland farming	Rainfed farming
Cultivation of crops in areas where rainfall < 750mm/annum	Cultivation of crops in areas when rainfall > 750mm/annum	Cultivation of crops in areas where rainfall > 1150mm/annum
Prolonged dry spells during crop period are most common	Dry spells during crop period occur	-
Crop failures are more frequent	Crop failures are less frequent	Crop failures are rare
Dry farming regions equivalent to arid regions	Grouped under semiarid regions	Practiced in humid regions
Moisture conservation practices are important in this region	Adoption of soil and moisture conservation practices. Provision of drainage in black soils.	Drainage is the important problem

- **Pitcher farming** is a practice in dry farming where crop is irrigated through small holes made in the bottom of earthen pitcher. The practice is generally used for **wider spaced** plants.
- UNITED NATIONS ECONOMIC AND SOCIAL COMMISSION FOR ASIA AND PACIFIC distinguished dryland agriculture mainly into two categories

CONSTITUENT	DRYLAND FARMING	RAINFED FARMING
RAINFALL (MM)	< 800	>800
MOISTURE AVAILABILITY TO THE CROP	Shortage	Enough
GROWING SEASON (DAYS)	< 200	>200
GROWING REGIONS	Arid and semiarid as well as uplands of sub-humid and humid region	Humid and sub-humid region
CROPPING SYSTEM	Single crop or intercropping	Intercropping or double cropping
CONSTRAINTS	Wind and water erosion	Water erosion

- Cultivated land in India = **142** mha
- Dryland area = **34.5 mha** (24 %)
- Rainfed area (including flood prone area of 15 mha) = **65.5 mha** (45.5 %)
- Irrigated area = **43.8 mha** (30.5 %)
- Per cent area under rainfed and dryland = **69.5 %**
- Dryland contributes **42 %** of total food grains.
- All coarse grains, **75%** of pulses and oilseeds, **two thirds** of mustard, **most of soybean and groundnut** are grown under rainfed condition.
- **First famine commission** was appointed in **1880**.
- Important recommendation of the first famine commission was to provide facilities for **protective irrigation**.
- Systematic research work was started from **1923** with the start of research centre at **Manjre** near **Pune.**
- In **1933**, research stations established at **Bijapur** and **Sholapur**.
- In **1934** research stations established at **Hagari** and **Raichur**.
- In **1935** research station established at **Rohtak.**
- In **1944** Monograph on dry farming in India by Kanitkar.

- In **1953**, establishment of **Central Soil Conservation Board**.
- During **1954**, the Soil Conservation Training and Demonstration Centres were established by ICAR at **8** locations.
- During **1970**, ICAR started **AICRP on Dryland Agriculture** at **23** locations spread all over India.
- In **1972**, ICRISAT was established.
- In **1976**, establishment of **dryland Operational Research Projects (ORPs)**.
- In **1983**, **47 model watersheds** were developed.
- In **1985, Central Research Institute for Dryland Agriculture (CRIDA)** was established.
- Extended period of deficient rainfall compared to normal rainfall of the region is called **drought**.
- Drought can be classified based on **duration** and **nature of users**.
- **Meteorological drought** refers to substantial deficit of rainfall relative to average of the region.
- IMD defines **meteorological drought** as a situation when there is 25% decrease in the average rainfall for a given period in a region.
- **Atmospheric drought** is due to low air humidity, frequently accompanied by hot dry winds. It may occur even under conditions of adequate available soil moisture.
- Plants growing under favourable soil moisture regime are usually susceptible to **atmospheric drought**.
- **Agricultural drought** refers to extended dry period in which lack of rainfall results in **insufficient moisture in the root zone** of the soil causing adverse effects on crops.
- **Hydrological drought** is extended dry period leading to marked depletion of surface water and consequent drying up of reservoirs, lakes, streams, rivers, cessation of spring flows and fall in ground water levels.
- **Permanent drought** is the characteristic of the **desert climate** where sparse vegetation growing is adapted to drought and agriculture is possible only by irrigation during entire crop season.

- **Seasonal drought** is found in climates with well defined rainy and dry seasons. Most of the arid and semiarid zones fall in this category. Duration of the crop varieties and planting dates should be such that the growing season should fall within rainy season.
- **Contingent drought** involves an **abnormal failure** of rainfall. It may occur almost anywhere especially in most parts of humid or sub humid climates. It is usually brief, irregular and generally affects only a small area.
- **Invisible drought** can occur even when there are frequent rains in an area. When rainfall is inadequate to meet the evapotranspiration losses, the result is borderline water deficiency in soil resulting in less than optimum yield.
- **Invisible drought** occurs usually in **humid** regions.
- Dryspell is a rainless period more than **10 days** in light soil areas and **15 days** in heavy soil areas.
- **Drought** is prolonged dryspell resulting in wilting or drying of crops.
- Severe form of drought is called **famine**.
- **Desertification** process mainly occurs due to recurrent droughts, over grazing, reduction in vegetation, soil degradation and reduction in water resources.
- Though there is sufficient amount of soil moisture, water deficits develop due to higher transpiration than absorption especially on hot mid days. This temporary wilting is known as **incipient wilting or mid day depression.**
- Stomatal closure occurs when leaf water potential approaches about -**1.0 to -1.2 MPa** or **-10 bars to -12 bars**.
- If soil moisture depleted to a level of **-6 MPa (-60 bars)**, plants die permanently and this is known as **ultimate wilting point**.
- Moisture stress reduces photosynthetic rate due to reduction in CO_2 entry, decrease in mesophyll conductance, due to stomatal resistance.
- Reduction in photosynthesis due to moisture stress is mainly by the **reduction in leaf area** than by photosynthetic rate.
- Decreasing the tissue water potential by only – 0.1 MPa (–1 bars) or less result in a perceptible decrease in cellular growth while photosynthetic rate is affected only at **–1.6 MPa (–16 bars)**.

- Translocation of assimilates is affected by water stress, resulting in assimilate saturation, there by leading to reduction in photosynthesis.
- Drought stress induces **oxidative** damage due to release of **free radicals**.
- Activity of **superoxide dismutase** and **catalase** increases in response to moisture stress.
- Respiration **increases** with mild stress.
- Respiration **decreases** under severe water deficit.
- Stomata per unit leaf area tend to **increase** under moisture stress.
- Severe water deficits cause **decrease** in enzymatic activity. **Peroxidase** activity decreases.
- Enzymes involved in hydrolysis **increase** resulting in breakdown of starch and protein.
- Accumulation of **sugars** and **amino acids** takes place under moisture stress.
- **Proline**, an aminoacid accumulates under moisture stress.
- Under moisture stress activity of growth promoting hormones like cytokinin, gibberellic acid and indoleacetic acid **decreases**.
- Growth regulating hormones like abscisic acid, ethylene, betain etc. **increases** under moisture stress.
- Translocation of growth promoting hormones is also reduced by moisture stress.
- Abscisic acid content is **inversely** related to leaf water potential.
- **Abscisic acid** acts as water deficit sensor to minimize the loss of tissue water potential.
- **Abscisic acid** controls stomata and thus reduces water loss when there is moisture stress.
- **Ethylene** production due to moisture stress is the cause for **leaf and fruit drop**.
- **Betain** produced by moisture stressed plants is an indicator of moisture stress.
- Moisture stress affects **nitrogen fixation**, **uptake and assimilation**.

- Moisture stress **delays** maturity.
- If stress occurs **before flowering**, duration of the crop **increases**.
- If stress occurs **after flowering**, duration of the crop **decreases**.
- During ripening, which involves dehydration and certain biochemical processes, moisture regime has **very little effect** on yield components.
- In cereals, moisture stress at **panicle initiation** is critical.
- Pod abortion takes place due to drought in several legumes including in soybean.
- Drought **decreases** leaf sucrose and starch concentrations.
- Drought **increases** hexose (glucose + fructose) concentrations.
- When the yield is fibre or chemicals where economic product is a small fraction of total dry matter, moderate stress on growth does not have adverse effect on yields.
- Ability of crop to grow satisfactorily under water stress is called **drought adaptation**.
- **Evading** the period of drought is the simplest means of adaptation of plants to dry conditions.
- Many desert plants, the so called **ephemerals**, germinate at the beginning of the rainy season and have an extremely short life period (**5 to 6 weeks**) confined to the rainy season.
- **Ephemerals** have no mechanism for overcoming moisture stress, therefore not drought resistant.
- Certain varieties of pearl millet mature within **60 days** after sowing.
- Short duration pulses like **cowpea, greengram, blackgram** included under ephemerals.
- The disadvantage of breeding early varieties is that yield is **reduced** with reduction in duration.
- Stress avoidance is the ability to maintain water balance, and turgidity even when exposed to drought conditions.
- Favourable water balance under drought conditions achieved by
  1. Conserving water by reducing transpiration
  2. Accelerating water uptake

- Photosynthetic efficiency is higher in **C_4 plants** than C_3 plants.
- In C_4 plants, the carboxylating enzyme **PEP carboxylase** has very high affinity for **CO_2**.
- C_4 plants are said to be drought resistant as they are able to grow better even under moisture stress.
- **CAM** plants are highly drought resistant.
- CAM plants open stomata only during **night** when they take CO_2 into the leaves and store it as **organic acid**.
- Examples of CAM plants are **Pineapple and Agave**.
- **Soybean**, **sorghum** etc., reduce water loss by depositing **lipids** on leaves and plant surface.
- In **grasses**, leaves roll or curl due to moisture stress and reduce the area exposed to solar radiation resulting in low transpiration.
- **Leguminous** plants show **parahelionastic** movements *i.e.*, the leaves are oriented parallel to sun rays thus avoiding the load of solar radiation.
- Moisture stressed **groundnut** plants reduce radiation load during midday by about 60 to 70% due to **folding of leaves**.
- Pubescence (hairyness) **increases** leaf reflectance and **reduces** solar radiation incidence.
- Awned varieties give **more** yield under drought conditions compared to awnless varieties.
- Awns contribute **12%** of photosynthates to grain.
- Compared to transpiring area of awns, its contribution of photosynthates to grain is more.
- Water uptake is improved by well developed deep root system.
- Drought **increases** root growth and **root-shoot ratio** which is an important mechanism of drought resistance.
- By improving **water uptake**, **high water potential** is maintained in leaves and the rate of photosynthesis is not reduced.
- Lowering of resistance to water can be achieved by increasing either **diameter of xylem vessels** or their **number**.
- **Abscisic acid** produced in leaves at lower turgor reduces seed set through its effect on pollen viability.

- By **osmotic adjustment**, production of abscisic acid is reduced.
- At **low osmotic potential**, photosynthetic activity and rate of hypocotyl extension are **reduced** due to inhibition of enzymatic activity.
- **Osmotic adjustment** allows turgor to be maintained as the leaf water potential and water content decreases.
- **Turgor pressure** is the pressure exerted on the cell wall by the cell contents inside it when the cell contents are **fully turgid**.
- In **drought tolerance**, water potential of plant is reduced and its adverse effects are felt.
- **Drought tolerance** can be defined as tolerance of the plants to a level of stress at which **50 % of cells die**.
- Simplest way of mitigating stress is by resisting dehydration and by maintenance of **higher osmotic pressure** by accumulating higher amounts of solutes.
- Leaves with thick cuticle resist cell collapse.
- **Plastic strain** indicates irrevocable loss of plant tissues due to moisture stress.
- Crops with **C_4** and **CAM** type of photosynthesis are preferred in **dry regions**.
- Under normal conditions, contribution of preanthesis assimilates to grain is **less than 20%** in most plants except in rice where it ranges from **20 to 40%**.
- Under moisture stress conditions preanthesis assimilates contribution may be up to **50 to 75%**.
- Collecting and storing rain water for subsequent use is known as **water harvesting**.
- Water harvesting is a method to induce, collect, store and conserve local surface runoff for agriculture in arid and semiarid regions.
- **Catchment area** is the part of the land that contributes the rain water.
- **Command area** is where water is used.
- In **arid** regions, collecting area or catchment area is substantially in **higher proportion** compared to command area.

- In **arid lands**, runoff is induced in **catchment area**.
- In **semi arid regions**, runoff is not induced in catchment area, only excess rainfall is collected and stored.
- Treating soils with chemicals like sodium salts of **silicon, latexes, asphalt** and **wax** fill soil pores or make soil repellant to water.

WATER HARVESTING METHODS IN ARID REGION

- In arid regions water is harvested by different methods like **runoff farming**, **water spreading**, **microcatchments**, **inter-row water harvesting systems** and **traditional water harvesting systems** like **tanka**, **nadi**, **khadin**.
- In **water spreading method** flood waters are deliberately diverted from their natural courses and spread over adjacent plains.
- In **microcatchment** method, rain water catchment basin is built around the plant.
- In **inter-row water harvesting systems,** water collected from ridge is stored in furrow and the crop is benefitted by high moisture.
- **Ridge and furrow system** is better for getting higher yield of **pearl millet** than flat bed method.
- Ridge provides partial shading of the furrow for 6 to 7 hours a day and reduces evaporation.
- **Tanka**, **nadi**, **khadin** are the important traditional water harvesting systems of **Rajasthan**.
- **Tanka** is an underground tank or cistern constructed for collection and storage of runoff water from natural catchment or artificially prepared catchment or from a roof top.
- Nadi or village pond is constructed for storing water from natural catchments.
- **Khadin** is unique land use system wherein runoff water from rocky catchments are collected in valley plains during rainy season.
- In **Khadin** method crops are grown in the winter season after water is receded in shallow pond on the residual moisture.

WATER HARVESTING METHODS IN SEMIARID REGIONS

- In **semiarid regions** water harvesting techniques include **dug wells**, **tanks, percolation tanks, farm ponds, inter-row water harvesting, broad bed and furrows.**
- Quality of water is generally **poor** in dug wells due to dissolved salts.
- To avoid the breaching of tank bund, spillways are provided at one or both the ends of the tank bund to dispose of excess water.
- **Sluice** is provided in the central area of the tank bund to allow controlled flow of water into the command area.
- Unlike wells, quality of water is good in **tanks**.
- Flowing rivulets are obstructed and water is ponded in percolation tanks, which percolates into the soil and raises the water table of the region.
- Problem associated with farm ponds in red soils is **high seepage loss**.
- Seepage loss controlled by the use of bentonite, **soil dispersants** and **soil-cement mixture**.
- In alfisols mixture of red soil and black soil in the ratio of **1:2** is used for lining farmponds to reduce seepage losses.
- In high rainfall areas, there is possibility for occasional waterlogging and yield of **maize** is affected.
- In inter-row water harvesting maize is grown on **beds** and rice in **furrows** helps in increasing the yields of both the crops. Excess water collected on beds is stored in furrows which is beneficial for rice.

EVAPOTRANSPIRATION

- Evapotranspiration losses can be reduced by mulches, antitranspirants, wind breaks and weed control.
- About **60 to 75 %** of the rainfall is lost through evaporation.
- **Mulch** is any material applied on the soil surface to check evaporation and improve soil water.
- Application of mulches results in soil conservation, moderation of temperature, reduction in soil salinity, weed control and improvement of soil structure.

- If the surface of the soil is loosened, it acts as mulch for reducing evaporation. This loose surface soil is called **soil mulch or dust mulch**.
- Soil mulch helps in closing deep cracks in **vertisols**.
- Crop residues like wheat straw or cotton stalks etc. are left on the soil surface as a **stubble mulch**.
- If straw is used as mulch, it is called **straw mulch**.
- In plastic mulching plastic materials like **polyethylene**, **polyvinyl chloride** used as mulching materials.
- **Subsoiling** is the most effective method of breaking hard pans to improve root penetration, aeration and water percolation.
- Effects of subsoiling are not long lasting.
- Slots left by the subsoiler are closed and sealed off within a few months.
- In order to prolong the beneficial effect of subsoiling **vertical mulching** is adopted.
- The objective of vertical mulching is to fill slots with organic matter and keeping them open and functional for a longer period.
- In black soils infiltration of water is **slow** and rainfall is lost as runoff.
- To improve infiltration and storage of rain water in black soils, **vertical mulches** are formed.
- In vertical mulching narrow trenches are dug across the slope at intervals and placing the straw or crop residues in these trenches.
- Nearly **99% of water** absorbed by the plants is lost in **transpiration**.
- **Antitranspirant** is any material applied to transpiring plant surfaces for reducing water loss from the plant.
- **Fungicide** like **phenyl mercuric acetate (PMA)** and **herbicides** like **Atrazine** in **low concentrations** function as **stomatal closing** antitranspirant.
- Stomatal closing antitranspirants reduce **photosynthesis**.
- **Mobileaf**, **hexadeconol**, **silicone** are **film forming** type of antitranspirants. They also reduce photosynthesis.

- **5% kaolin spray**, **diatomaceous earth product (celite)** are **reflectant** type of antitranspirants. These are **white materials**.
- **Cycocel** is a growth retardant. It **reduces shoot growth** and **increase root growth**. It also induces stomatal closure.
- **Wind breaks** are any structures that obstruct wind flow and reduce wind speed.
- **Shelterbelts** are rows of trees planted for protection of crops against wind.
- The direction from which wind is blowing is called **windward side**.
- The direction to which wind is blowing is called **leeward side**.
- Shelterbelts give protection from desiccating winds to the extent of **5 to 10 times** their height on **windward side** and up to **30 times** on **leeward side**.
- **Contingency cropping** is growing of a suitable crop in place of normally sown highly profitable crop of the region due to aberrant weather conditions.
- Generally short duration pulses like green gram, blackgram and cowpea may suit the situation.
- However if the monsoon turns to be extraordinarily good, opportunity is lost if only short duration crops are sown.
- Farmers with economic strength and motivation for high profits with some amount of risk can go for crops of **long duration**.
- Long duration crops with flexibility or elasticity in yield are more suitable. **Pearl millet and sorghum** can be ratooned if monsoon extends.
- **Sunflower** can be introduced for higher profits with certain amount of risk.
- Crops like sorghum, pearl millet can be grown for grain if monsoon extends and if not, fodder can be obtained.
- Groundnut is sown up to **July** in the rainfed areas of Andhra Pradesh. If the monsoon is delayed, **sunflower, pearl millet, setaria** etc. are taken up.
- In case of contingency crops sown in the month of September, spacing of the crops has to be **reduced**.
- Sunflower, sorghum and pearl millet have to be sown with **30 cm** inter row spacing instead of normally adopted **45 cm**.

- In general a **single crop** is being taken in dry farming areas where the annual rainfall is **below 500 mm**.
- **Rainy season** crop is taken in light soils like **alfisols, inceptisols and oxisols**.
- Crops are being grown on residual moisture in **vertisols** in the post **rainy season** or winter season.
- In areas where annual rainfall is in the range of **600-850 mm**, **intercropping** is being recommended and practiced.
- **Double cropping** is feasible in areas receiving rainfall **more than 850 mm** and soil moisture storage capacity of 200 mm/m depth or 20 cm/m depth.
- Water use efficiency is more in CAM plants about **20 g** dry matter for kilogram of water for pineapple compared to **3 to 5 g** for C_4 plants and **2 to 3 g** for C_3 plants.
- Yield of maize can be improved by selecting genotypes for **shorter interval between tasselling to silking**.
- Popular hybrids of pearl millet are **ICMH-451, HHB-67 and RHRBH-8609**.
- Among composites of bajra, **ICTP-8204** is very popular.
- Special characters of sunflower are **photoperiod insensitivity** and faster recovery from drought.
- Sunflower hybrids are performing better than varieties due to higher degree of **self fertility** and **uniform seed development**.
- Traditional varieties of castor are **tall** and **long** duration. **Kranthi and Haritha** among the varieties and **GCH-3 and GCH-4** among hybrids are medium duration and high yielding.

DOMINANT INTERCROPPING SYSTEMS IN DIFFERENT REGIONS

Location	Soil	Rainfall (mm)	Intercropping	Row ratio
Anantapur	Alfisols	550	Groundnut + pigeonpea	11:1
Akola	Vertisols	825	Sorghum + pigeonpea	2:1
Rajkot	Vertisols	590	Groundnut + castor	4:1
Sholapur	Vertisols	560	Chickpea + safflower	3:1
Bangalore	Alfisols	890	Finger millet + pigeonpea	8:1

IMPORTANT DOUBLE CROPPING SYSTEMS OF DIFFERENT LOCATIONS

Location	Rainfall (mm)	Soils	Double cropping
Ranchi	1370	Oxisols	Rice-linseed or chickpea
Indore	960	Vertisols	Soybean-Wheat
Pune	1050	Vertisols	Rice-Chickpea
Bangalore	890	Alfisols	Cowpea-finger millet

- **Watershed** is defined as any surface area from which rainfall is collected and drains through a common point.
- Watershed is synonymous with a **drainage basin** or **catchment area**.
- **Watershed** is a biological, physical, economic and social system.
- **Watershed management** is the integration of technologies within the natural boundaries of a drainage area for optimum development of land, water and plant resources to meet the basic needs of the people and animals in a sustained manner.
- **Watershed management** is the planned use of watershed lands in accordance with predetermined objectives, such as the control of erosion, stream flow, sedimentation and improvement of vegetative cover and other related resources.
- **Classification of watersheds**

  River basin: > 1000 ha

  Macro watershed: 400-1000 ha

  Sub watershed: 200-400 ha

  Mini watershed: 40-200 ha

  Small watershed: 10-40 ha

  Micro watershed: 0-10 ha

Chapter 15

Soil Conservation

- Agents causing erosion are **wind** and **water**.
- Sheet erosion is **uniform removal** of top soil in thin layer from the field.
- **Sheet erosion** is least conspicuous and is the **first stage** of erosion.
- In **rill erosion** due to runoff, channelization begins and erosion is no longer uniform.
- In **rill erosion** incisions are formed on the ground and erosion is more apparent than sheet erosion.
- **Rill erosion** is the **second stage** of erosion.
- Gullies are formed when channelized runoff from vast sloping land is sufficient in volume and velocity to cut deep and wide channels.
- **Gullies** are the most spectacular symptoms of erosion.
- **Gullies** if unchecked cultivation becomes difficult.
- **Ravines** are the manifestation of a prolonged process of gully erosion.
- Ravines are typically found in the large expanses of **deep alluvial soils**.
- Ravines are deep and wide gullies and their formation indicates very **advanced stage** of gully erosion.
- Sliding down of large chunk of soil due to steep slopes is called **landslides**.
- Landslides occur in mountain slopes when the slope exceeds **20 per cent and width 6 m**.
- Along with runoff, soil is carried away as fine particles of less than 0.5 mm in diameter are suspended in water.
- **Rill erosion** starts only when the amount of runoff exceeds **0.3 to 0.7 mm/s**.
- Majority of rain drops are between **1 and 4 mm** in diameter though the size may vary from tiny droplets to a maximum diameter of 7 mm.

- The rainfall intensity of more than **5 cm/h** is considered as **severe**.
- For a wide range of soils and crop conditions, erosion (E) is related to intensity of rainfall (I) as power equation.

  $E = CI^b$

  b = slightly **above 2** for soils of **low clay content**

  b = **1** for soils with **50% clay**
- For low clay soils like silts, silt loams and sandy loams, above equation is written as

  $E = CI^2$

  C = relative inter rill erodibility of different soils
- **Erosivity** is the capacity of agents causing erosion.
- **Erodibility** is the susceptibility of soil to erosion.
- Universal soil loss equation was developed by **Wischmeir and Smith**.
- Soil loss equation due to water erosion

  A = RKLSCP

  A = Predicted soil loss (t/ac/year)

  R = Rainfall and runoff factor

  K = Soil erodibility

  L = Slope length

  S = Slope gradient or steepness

  C = Soil cover and management

  P = Erosion control practice
- **Soil erodibility factor (K)** gives an indication of the soil loss from a unit plot of **22 m long** with a **9 per cent slope** under continuous fallow.
- K value varies from **0 to 0.6**.
- K value is **low** for soils into which water readily **infiltrates**.
- Soils with **intermediate infiltration capacity** and moderate soil structural stability have a K factor of **0.2 to 0.3**.
- More easily eroded soils with **low infiltration capacities** have a K value of **0.3 or higher**.
- **Topographic factor (L.S)** reflects influence of length and steepness of slope.

- **Topographic factor** is the ratio of soil loss from the field in question to that of a unit plot with **9% slope, 22 m long** and **continuously fallowed.**
- **Soil cover and management factor (C)** indicates influence of cropping systems and management on soil loss.
- **Forests and grass** are the best natural soil protective agencies known and are about **equal in their effectiveness.**
- Forage crops, both legumes and grasses are next in effectiveness because of their relatively dense cover.
- C is the ratio of soil loss under the conditions found in the field in question to that which would occur under clean tilled continuous fallow conditions.

  C =1 for **bare soil** before crop canopy develops

  C < 0.1 when **large amounts of crop residues** are on the land or in areas of dense forests
- **Support Practice factor (P)** reflects the benefits of contouring, strip cropping and other supporting factors.
- **Support practice factor (P)** is the ratio of soil loss with a given support practice to the corresponding loss when crop culture is along the slope.
- Annual soil loss in India is **16.35 t/ha.**
- Permissible limit of soil loss is **11 t/ha.**
- **29%** of the total eroded soil is lost permanently to the sea and **10%** is deposited in reservoirs.
- About **175 mha** constituting **53.3%** of India's geographical area of 328 mha is subject to some kind of degradation.
- Active soil erosion by water and wind is prevalent over **140 mha** resulting in the loss of **6000 mt** of fertile soil containing **5.53 mt of NPK.**
- Based on the capability or limitations, the lands are grouped into **eight classes** by the **U.S. SOIL CONSERVATION SERVICE.**
- **First four classes** are used for **agriculture or cultivation of crops.**
- Classes from **five to eight** are not capable of supporting cultivation of crops.

- Classes from five to eight are used for **growing grasses, forestry and supporting wild life**.

CLASS I	CLASS II	CLASS III	CLASS IV
Ex: Alluvial soils of Indo-gangetic plains	• Deep red soils • Black soils	• Shallow red soils • Slightly saline black soils	• Shallow soils • Saline soils • Alkaline soils
No limitations, need only ordinary management practices to maintain their productivity	Some limitation, require moderate conservation practices	Severe limitations, require special conservation practices or both	Very careful management is required
Well suited to growing of crops intensively	reduce choice of crops	reduce the choice of crops	Very severe limitations on choice of crops
1) Deep well drained level lands with high water holding capacity 2) Naturally fertile or have characteristics which encourage good response of crops to fertilizers	Limited by one or more factors such as 1) Gentle slope (1-3%) 2) Moderate erosion hazard (sheet and rill) 3) Inadequate soil depth 4) Less than ideal structure and workability 5) Slight to moderate alkali or saline conditions 6) Somewhat restricted drainage	Limitations include 1) Moderately steep slope 2) High erosion hazard 3) Very slow water permeability 4) Shallow depth and restricted root zone 5) Low water holding capacity 6) Low fertility 7) Moderate alkali and salinity 8) Unstable soil structure	Limitations include 1) Steep slopes 2) Severe erosion susceptibility 3) Severe past erosion 4) Shallow soils 5) Low water holding capacity 6) Poor drainage 7) Severe alkalinity and salinity
Soils of arid and semiarid regions with all above characters grouped under Class I provided they are irrigated by permanent irrigation system	-	-	-

Ordinary management practices include 1) Use of fertilizers 2) Use of manure 3) Crop rotation	Management practices (in addition to ordinary practices) include 1) Strip cropping 2) Contour tillage 3) Rotation involving grasses and legumes 4) Grassed water ways	Management practices (in addition to ordinary practices) include 1) Strip cropping 2) Contour tillage 3) Rotation involving higher proportion of grasses and legumes 4) Grassed water ways 5) Drainage may be needed	Soil conservation practices have to be applied more frequently than on soils of Class III

CLASS V	CLASS VI	CLASS VII	CLASS VIII
Ex: Arid soils Rocky soils Uneven or rolling soils	-	-	Ex: Sandy beaches River wash
Limitations include 1) Interference from stream flow 2) Short growing season 3) Stony or rocky soils 4) Ponded areas 5) Drainage not possible	Have extreme limitations	• Very severe limitations • Improvement of pastures is not possible due to physical limitations	Not useful for any kind of crop production
-	Restrict their use mainly for 1) pasture or range 2) woodland or wildlife	Restrict their use to 1) Grazing 2) Woodland or wildlife	Use is restricted to 1) Recreation 2) Wild life 3) Aesthetic purpose

- Measures to prevent erosion grouped as **agronomic, mechanical, forestry and agrostological measures**.
- When these are used in combination, erosion can be reduced even if the slope is more than **2 per cent**.
- Soil erosion can be controlled by **agronomic methods** when the slope is gentle *i.e.*, **less than 2 %**.
- Agronomic measures include **contour cultivation, tillage, mulching, strip cropping** and other improved dryland practices.
- **Guatemala grass (*Tripsacum laxum*)** can be used for **mulching**.
- **Strip-cropping** is a system of crop production in which long and narrow strips of **erosion resisting crops (close growing crops)** are alternated with strips of **erosion permitting crops (erect growing crops)**.
- Erosion resistant crops are **groundnut, moth bean, horse gram (pulses).**
- Erosion permitting crops are **sorghum, maize and millet**.
- Aggregate stability can be increased by spraying chemicals like **polyvinyl alcohol** at **480 kg/ha**.
- Soils treated with **bitumen** increase water stable aggregates and infiltration capacity of the soil.
- **Dead furrows** (with closed ends) formed at **3.6 m interval** after emergence of the crop sown across slope, reduce the length of the run of rain water, hold water and increase opportune time for infiltration.
- Mechanical measures to control soil erosion include **contour bunding**, **graded bunding**, **bench terracing**, **gully control** etc.
- Contour bunding = upto 6% slope

  Graded bunds = 6 - 10% slope

  Graded trenches = 10 - 16% slope

  Bench terracing = 16 - 33% slope
- $VI = \frac{S}{2} + 3$

  S = percent slope

  VI = vertical interval between bunds
- Height of contour bund depends on the **spacing between bunds, soil conditions** and **maximum intensity of rainfall**.

- $D = FR/6$

  D = Depth of water to be impounded in feet

  Or

  Theoretical height of the bund to be put up

  R = Total runoff in inches

  F = vertical fall between bunds in feet
- Contour bunds are usually laid in areas with less than **1500 mm rainfall** and up to **6 per cent** slope of land.
- **Graded bunding** is recommended in situations where the rain water is **not readily absorbed** due to **high rainfall** or **low intake** of the soil.
- In **graded bunds** soil from the excavation of the channel is formed into a bund on the downstream to guide the water into a **grassed waterway**.
- In deep black soils with high clay content develop deep cracks in summer and bunds in these soils breach extensively during rainy season, especially where rains are of high intensity.
- In deep black soils **broad based terraces** are constructed.
- A terrace is a combination of **ridge and channel** built across the slope on a controlled grade.
- In broad base terrace excess rain water is led at non-erosive velocity into grassed water ways.
- On steeply sloping and undulated land, intensive farming is possible only with **bench terracing**.
- **Bench terracing** consists of principally transforming relatively steep land into a series of level strips or platforms across the slope of the land.
- **Bench terracing** reduces the **slope length** and consequently erosion.

Type of terraces for different soil and rainfall conditions

Type	Suitability
Level and table top	Area receiving medium rainfall (750 mm) of even distribution with highly permeable deep soils
Sloping outwards	Low rainfall (< 750 mm) area with permeable soil of medium depth
Sloping inwards	Heavy rainfall areas (> 750mm) with soil of poor infiltration rate

- **Zing terracing** is adopted in lands with **3 – 10% slope**.
- Zing terraces are constructed in **medium to deep soils** in **moderate to high rainfall areas**.
- In zing terracing length of the field is divided into donor area and receiving area in the ratio of **2:1 to 5:1**, but **usually 2:1.**
- Vegetative barrier = **Khus khus grass (*Vetivaria zeylanica*)**.
- **Check dams** are constructed across gullies to reduce the velocity of runoff, heal the gully, store water for use by livestock and recharge groundwater in wells lower down.
- Grasses are used for stabilizing the surfaces of waterways, contour bunds and front faces of bench-terraces.
- ***Cenchrus ciliaris* + *Clitoria ternate*** is the best mixture for eroded soils of UP.
- ***Cenchrus ciliaris* + *Stylosanthes hamata*** combination is the best for Andhra Pradesh.
- Growing a mixture of grasses instead of any single grass proved to be better to stabilize newly formed bunds or terraces.
- Wind erosion is a natural phenomenon in **arid** and **semi-arid zones**.
- Minimum wind velocity necessary for initiating the movement of most erodible soil particles is about **16 km hr^{-1}** at a height of 30.5 cm.
- Movement of soil particles through wind erosion takes place in **three** stages *i.e.,* **saltation, surface creep and suspension**.
- **Saltation** is the **first stage** of movement of soil particles in **series of jumps**.
- Soil particles moved by saltation are between **0.1 to 0.5 mm** in diameter (fine sand).
- In **saltation** soil particles jump up vertically into air and rise to a height of **30 to 60 cm**.
- **50 to 75%** of the weight of soil lost by wind erosion is carried in **saltation.**
- Rolling of coarse grains, larger than **0.5 to 3 mm** in diameter and too heavy to be lifted, by wind along the surface of the ground is called **surface creep**.

- **5 to 25 %** weight of the soil lost by wind erosion is carried in **surface creep**.
- Floating of fine dust particles smaller than **0.1 mm** diameter through the air is known as suspension.
- **3 to 4 %** of the weight of soil lost by wind erosion is carried in suspension.
- Equation to predict soil loss due to wind erosion

  E = I.R.K.F.C.W.D.B

  E = Soil loss by wind erosion

  I = Soil cloddiness factor

  R = Surface cover factor

  K = Surface roughness factor

  C = Local wind factor

  W = Field width factor

  D = Wind direction factor

  B = Wind barrier factor
- Trees selected for agroforestry should have quick growth and **less crown**.
- **Casuarina**, **cashew** and **coconut** are useful for coastal sands and **date palms** are suitable for deserts.
- Among the pasture grasses ***Cenchrus ciliaris*** is drought resistant and persistent grass.
- Among the fodder trees, **subabul** is best suited because of its fast growth, adaptability and multiplicity of uses.
- For establishment of pastures in wastelands, it is better to grow **leguminous** plants initially.
- During subsequent years *i.e.,* after improvement of soil fertility, grasses can be included to increase fodder production.

Chapter 16

Water Management

- Water is the most abundant compound on Earth's surface, covering **70 per cent** of the planet.
- Water present in sea, lakes, rivers, groundwater and stream base flow is called **blue water**.
- **Blue water** is extensively used in agriculture.
- **Green water** denotes soil moisture and water present in plants and used in photosynthesis.
- **Grey water** is waste water from bathrooms, kitchens and wash basins.
- **Grey water** is used in crop production, particularly in kitchen gardens and lawns.
- **Black water** is the water coming out as **domestic sewage or industrial waste**.
- **Black water** can be used in crop production after proper treatment.
- The water consumed in the production process of an agricultural or industrial product has been called the '**virtual water**' contained in the product.
- To produce one kilogram of wheat we need about **1,000 litres** of water, *i.e.*, the virtual water of this kilogram of wheat is **1000 litres**.
- **400 to 500** litres of water is necessary for the production of a kilo of plant dry matter.
- **Water footprint** is an indicator of freshwater use that looks at both direct and indirect water use of a consumer or producer.
- **Root proliferation** is reduced due to high **mechanical resistance** of dry soil.
- **Irrigation** is the artificial application of water to soil to supplement rainfall for crop production.
- About **97** % of water is in the oceans and not useful for irrigation.
- Of the total quantity of water, only **2.60** % is fresh water.

- Of the total fresh water, **77.23** % is in polar icecaps, ice-bergs and glaciers.
- Average rainfall of India is **1194** mm.
- Total quantity of rainfall received on a geographical area of 328 m ha in India is **400 m ha m** (including snow fall).
- Out of the 400 m ha m of rainfall, **75 %** of it is received during **South-west monsoon period (June to September**) and the rest in the remaining 8 months.
- **215** m ha m soaks into the soil.
- **70** m ha m is lost as evapotranspiration
- Water moves from **higher** potential to **lower** potential.

Saturated flow	Unsaturated flow	Vapour movement
Saturated flow of water occurs when all pores are filled with water	Unsaturated flow occurs in micropores. Macropores are empty	Occurs when soil becomes dry, micropores are also emptied and water is present in the form of water vapour
Flow of water is due to a gradient in metric potential from one region to another	-	Water vapour moves from high vapour pressure area to low vapour pressure area
Direction of flow is from higher potential to lower potential	Direction of flow is from higher to lower potential	Water vapour moves from higher temperature region to cooler region
Major force in driving water is gravity and major direction is downward movement	Major driving force is metric potential. Major direction of flow is lateral	Major driving force is vapour pressure gradient. Direction of flow is in all directions
Rate of movement depends on hydraulic conductivity which is a measure of ease with which water moves in the soil	Unsaturated flow is important from crop production point of view	Amount of water supplied through vapour movement to plants is very small but is important for survival of plants under severe drought conditions
Hydraulic conductivity can be expressed as V = Kf V = Volume of water moved/unit time f = Water moving force **K = Hydraulic conductivity**		

Hydraulic conductivity of a saturated soil is constant and depends on size and configuration of soil pores		
Flow rate in soil pores is proportional to the **fourth power of radius**		
In saturated condition, sandy soils have higher conductivity due to the presence of higher macropore space compared to clay soils	Hydraulic conductivity is higher in heavy soils under low water potential compared to sandy soils	-

- **Darcy's** law states that the velocity of a fluid in permeable media is directly proportional to the **hydraulic gradient**.
- In this law, **hydraulic conductivity (K)** is taken as **proportionality constant**.
- **Darcy** stated that the rate of flow increases with an **increased** depth of water above the bottom of the soil, and **decreases** with an increased depth of soil, through which water flows.
- **Poisseuille's law** expresses the flow of water in a **narrow tube**. According to it rate of flow of water in **sandy soil** is more than that of loam and least in the clay. Sandy > loam > clay
- **Passive absorption** takes place when water is drawn into the roots by **negative pressures** in the conducting tissue created by **transpiration**.
- When there is a little transpiration, the roots of many plants absorb water by spending energy which is called **active absorption**.
- Under normal conditions of transpiration, the contribution of active absorption to the water supply of plants is negligible and it is usually **less than 10%** of the total absorption.
- **Evaporation** from the surface of the soil or free water surface or vegetative cover is a **diffusive** process by which water in the form of vapour is transferred to the atmosphere.
- **Transpiration** is the process by which water vapour leaves the living plant body and enters the atmosphere.
- Transpiration is basically an **evaporative** process.

- Amount of water on dry weight basis is obtained by

  Amount of water on weight basis (P_w) =

$$\frac{\text{Weight of water (g)}}{\text{Weight of oven - dry soil (g)}} \times 100$$

- Amount of water on soil volume basis is obtained by

  Amount of water on volume basis (P_v) =

$$\frac{\text{Weight of water (g)}}{\text{Weight of dry soil (g)}} \times 100 \times \text{B.D}$$

B.D = Bulk Density

Amount of water (depth basis) = P_w × B.D × Depth of soil

$$(\text{Since } P_v = P_w \times \text{B.D}) \because = \frac{P_v \times D}{100}$$

D = depth of soil in cm

- Amount of water present in the soil does not correctly indicate its availability unless **soil type** is mentioned.
- At **12 per cent soil moisture**, crops in **alfisols** grow normally while those in **vertisols** show wilting symptoms due to variation in **energy status** of water in different soils.
- Energy status of water in soil indicates the **tenacity with which water** is held in the soil and the **ease with which it is available**.
- Shape of water molecule is a **sphere** and the position of two hydrogen ions is at the corners of a **tetrahedron** that exists within a **sphere**.
- One end of water molecule has positive charge and another end has negative charge making it a **dipole**.
- Hydrogen in the water serves as a connecting link from one molecule to the other end and it is known as **hydrogen bonding**.
- Water sticks to itself with great energy and this property is called **cohesion**.
- Water attaches itself to surfaces of many substances and this property is known as **adhesion**.
- By **adhesion**, water is held tightly at the soil-water interface.
- Water contents under certain standard conditions are referred to as **soil moisture constants**.

- The water content of soil at which all the soil pores are filled with water is referred to as **saturation or maximum water holding capacity**.
- Energy status of water at saturation is **zero**.
- Water content of a soil at saturation is approximately **double** that of field capacity.
- Soil moisture held by the soil against gravitational force is called **field capacity**.
- Energy status of water at field capacity is **-0.1 to -0.33** bars.
- **Field capacity** is considered as the **upper limit** of water availability to plants.
- As the **thickness** of water around soil particles **decreases**, more and more energy is required to remove the water.
- When the energy status of soil moisture reaches **-15 bars**, plants cannot absorb sufficient moisture and show wilting symptoms even under high humidity conditions. This is called **permanent wilting point**.
- **Permanent wilting point (PWP)** was proposed by **Briggs and Shantz** in 1912. They utilized dwarf **sunflower** as indicator plant.
- At **PWP** plants wilt but do not die and are able to absorb small quantity of water just sufficient for their survival and plants recover if water is supplied.
- Soil moisture at **-60 bars** is not available to plants and they die due to lack of water. Soil moisture content at which plants die is known as **ultimate wilting point**.
- **Hygroscopic coefficient** of water is defined as the amount of water that soil contains when brought to equilibrium with air at **one standard atmosphere** at **98% relative humidity** at the room temperature.
- **Moisture equivalent** is the amount of water retained by a sample of initially saturated soil material after being subjected to a centrifugal force of 1000 times that of gravity for a definite period of time, usually half an hour.
- **In medium textured soils**, the values of field capacity and moisture equivalent are nearly **equal**.
- **In sandy soil FC>ME**

  In very clayey soil FC<ME

- **Sandy soil** has the **lowest** amount of available water (8 cm/m depth) while **clay soil** has the **highest** amount (23 cm/m depth).
- Amount of water present in the soil between field capacity and permanent wilting point is called as **available water**.
- **Veihmeyer and Hendrickson** (1927, 1949, 1950) proposed that water is available to plants with **equal ease** throughout the available range.
- **Richards and Wadleigh** (1952) proposed that soil water availability to plants actually **decreases** with decreasing soil moisture.
- Recent evidence indicates that yield of several crops do not reduce if the soil moisture is depleted up to **25 %** of available moisture, but further decrease in soil moisture decreases the yield.
- The main defect of the above three theories is that they relate plant growth with soil moisture only without considering **climate**.
- When a water molecule is kept in a hypothetical situation, wherein it is not subjected to the influence of any force, its potential to move in any direction is **zero**.
- When the water molecule is attached to any substance, its ability or potential to move is **reduced**.
- Water potential of soil is always **less than zero** and is expressed in **negative values**.
- The total potential of soil water is the amount of work that must be done per unit quantity of pure water in order to transport reversibly and isothermally an infinitesimal quantity from a pool of pure water at a specified elevation at atmospheric pressure.
- The total potential of soil water is the sum of **matric, osmotic and gravitational** potentials.
- **Matric potential** is the portion of the total water potential that is attributable to the solid matrix of the soil or plant.
- **Matric potential** is the negative potential which results from the **capillary and adsorptive forces** emanating from the **soil matrix**.
- At saturated condition in soil matric potential is zero
- **Osmotic potential** is the portion of water potential that results from the solutes present in the soil.
- **Gravitational potential** is the potential attributable to gravitational force.
- **Pressure potential** at a point is a direct result of the overlying water.

- Pressure potential is always **positive**.
- **P^F** means potenz meaning power at 10.
- **P^F** value was first time introduced and defined by **Schofield (1935).**
- **P^F** is the scale through which we measure the force with which water is retained in capillary or soil.
- **P^F** is defined as the logarithm to the base 10 of the height of water column expressed in centimeter of water.
- P^F at field capacity is **2.5**.
- P^F at permanent wilting point is **4.2.**
- In **direct methods** soil moisture is estimated **thermo-gravimetrically** either by **oven-drying** or by **volumetric method.**
- Soil moisture is estimated **indirectly** by **tensiometer**, **gypsum block**, **neutron probe**, **pressure plate and pressure membrane apparatus**.
- Tensiometers are also called **irrometers** since they are used in irrigation scheduling.
- Length of tensiometer tube varies from **30 cm to 100 cm**.
- Tensiometers are sensitive up to **0.85 – 0.9** bars of soil moisture.
- Tensiometers are suitable for **sandy soils** as most of the available water in the sandy soil is within **one bar potential**.
- **Irrometers** do not give any information on the amount of irrigation water to be applied at each irrigation.
- Gypsum blocks are not suitable for **saline soils** as salts in the soil **increases** conductivity.
- In gypsum block the resistance reading is about **400-600** ohms at field capacity and **50,000 – 75,000** ohms at wilting point.
- Soil moisture can be estimated quickly and continuously with **neutron moisture meter** without disturbing the soil.
- By **neutron moisture meter** soil moisture can be estimated from large volume of soil.
- **Neutron moisture meter** consists of a **probe** and a **scalar or rate meter**.
- **Probe** contains **fast neutron source** which may be a mixture of **radium and beryllium** or **americium and beryllium.**

- Probe consists of a tube filled with lithium enriched with **boron trifuoride gas (BF_3)** as a **detector.**
- Drawbacks of neutron moisture meter are that it is **expensive** and moisture content from **shallow top layers** cannot be estimated.
- Fast neutrons are also slowed down by other sources of hydrogen (present in organic matter), **chlorine, boron and iron** overestimating the soil moisture content.
- **Pressure membrane** and **pressure plate apparatus** are generally used to estimate **field capacity**, **permanent wilting point** and **moisture content** at different pressures up to 2 atmospheres. (Richards).
- **Time domain reflectometry (TDR)** is a relatively new highly accurate and automatable method for measurement of soil water content and electrical conductivity.
- Water content is inferred from the **dielectric permittivity** or **dielectric constant** of the medium, whereas electrical conductivity is inferred from TDR signal attenuation.
- The first application of TDR to soil water measurements was reported by **Topp *et al.* (1980)**.
- The main advantages of TDR over other soil water content measurement methods are
  1) Superior accuracy to within 1 or 2% volumetric water content.
  2) Calibration requirements are minimal – in many cases soil-specific calibration is not needed.
  3) Lack of radiation hazard associated with neutron probe or gamma – attenuation techniques.
  4) TDR has excellent spatial and temporal resolution.
  5) Measurements are simple to obtain, and the method is capable of providing continuous measurements through automation and multiplexing.
- The energy status of water and amount of water in the soil are related with the **soil moisture characteristic curve**.
- As the energy status of water decreases (moving towards more negative values) soil water content also **decreases**.
- As soil moisture content decreases, **more** energy has to be applied to extract moisture from the soil.

- The relation between **suction** (externally applied force) and **water content** of the soil are represented graphically by a curve which is known as **soil moisture characteristic curve**.
- The shape of the clay soil curve is almost a **straight line with bends** on ends while it is **L shaped** in case of sandy soil.
- The moisture content at a given suction is greater in **desorption** than in **sorption** and this phenomenon is known as **hysteresis**.
- Generally, **desorption** curve of soil moisture is determined in laboratory.
- Water is needed mainly to meet the demands of evaporation (E), transpiration (T) and metabolic needs of the plants, all together known as **consumptive use (CU)**.
- Since water used in the metabolic activities of the plant is negligible, being only less than **1** % of the quantity of water passing through the plant, ET is practically considered as equal to **consumptive use (CU)**.
- Water requirement = CU + application losses + water needed for special operations.
- Water requirement = Irrigation requirement + effective rainfall + soil profile contribution.

  $$WR = IR + ER + S$$
- Evapotranspiration and crop growth are **directly** related in several crops.
- Relationship between dry matter of crop and ET is **linear**.
- Relationship between ET and crop yield is **linear** incase of **Cereals**.
- Relationship between ET and crop yield is **quadratic** incase of **Pulses**.
- **Reference evapotranspiration** can be defined as the rate of evapotranspiration of an extended surface of an **8 to 15 cm tall** green grass cover, actively growing completely shading the ground and **not short of water**. Ex: Alfalfa grass.
- **Modified Blaney-Criddle** method is simple, easy to calculate and require only **temperature** data of the region.
- **Modified Penman** method is complicated, more reliable with a possible error of **10** per cent only.

- Possible error for pan evaporation is 15%
  Radiation method = 20%
  Modified Blaney – Criddle method = 25%
- **Modified Blaney-Criddle Method:**
  $ET_o = C [P (0.46 T + 8)]$
- **Radiation method:**
  $ET_o = C (W.Rs)$
  $R_s = (0.25 + 0.50 n/N) R_a$
- **Pan evaporation method:**
  $ET_o = K_p.E_{pan}$
- **Pan evaporation** method is simple, fairly reliable and inexpensive and can be adopted under **Indian conditions.**
- Modified Penman method
  $ET_o = c [W.R_n + (1 - W). f(U) (e_a - e_d)]$
- **Crop coefficient** is the ratio between evapotranspiration of crop (ET_c) and potential evapotranspiration (ET_o).
- Crop coefficient depends on **soil cover, soil moisture** and **crop height**.
  $ET (crop) = Kc \times ET_o$
- ET (crop) is also known as **maximum evapotranspiration** (ET_{max}).
- Crop coefficients vary with **relative humidity** and **wind velocity**.
- For most of the crops, Kc value increases from a low value at the time of crop emergence to a **maximum value** during the period when the crop reaches **flowering**, and **declines** as the crop approaches **maturity**.
- Actual evapotranspiration depends on both **climate** and **soil moisture**.
- Maximum evapotranspiration depends on **climate** only as full soil moisture supply is assumed.
- Actual evapotranspiration **equals** maximum evapotranspiration when available water to the crop is **adequate**.
- Actual evapotranspiration is measured from field experiments by estimating soil moisture loss during crop growth period.
- Actual evapotranspiration (ETa) is measured accurately with **Lysimeters**.

- A **lysimeter** is a container of soil that facilitates the measurements of gains and losses of soil water by weight during crop growth.
- **Lysimeters** are large in order to avoid edge or border effect and are to be located in the middle of the crop field.
- In **non-weighing** lysimeters changes in water balance are measured volumetrically **weekly or biweekly**.
- **Weighing** lysimeters provide precise information on soil moisture changes on **daily or even hourly basis**, but are **expensive**.
- **Effective rainfall** is a part of rainfall available for the **consumptive** use of the crop.
- **Available soil moisture** in the root zone is a good criterion for scheduling irrigation.
- For crops like **maize**, **wheat** etc. scheduling irrigation at **25 per cent** depletion of available soil moisture (DASM) is adequate.
- For drought resistant crops like **sorghum, pearl millet, finger millet, cotton** etc. it is sufficient to irrigate at **50 %** depletion of available soil moisture
- Soil moisture depletion approach is reliable, but cannot be recommended to farmers because the means to measure soil water content or soil moisture tension are not easily available.
- Soil moisture content is approximately estimated by **feel and appearance method** and irrigation is scheduled accordingly.
- **Deficit irrigation** is applying water less than the requirement.
- Climatological approach of irrigation scheduling includes
  1) IW/CPE method
  2) Can Evaporimeter method
- In IW/CPE approach, a known amount of irrigation water (IW) is applied when cumulative pan evaporation (CPE) reaches a predetermined level.
- Combination approach was given by **Doorenbos and Kassam (1979)**.
- Doorenbos and Kassam (1979) combined soil moisture depletion approach and climatological approach.

CRITICAL STAGE APPROACH FOR SCHEDULING IRRIGATION

- In each crop, there are some growth stages at which moisture stress leads to irrevocable yield loss, these stages are known as **critical period or moisture sensitive period**.
- In cereals, **panicle initiation** and **flowering stages** are moisture sensitive stages.
- In pulses, **flowering** and **pod development** stages are most important moisture sensitive stages.

CROP	MOISTURE SENSITIVE PERIOD
Rice	Panicle initiation, flowering
Wheat	Crown-root initiation, jointing, milking
Sorghum	Seedling, flowering
Maize	Silking, tasseling
Pearl millet	Flowering, panicle initiation
Finger millet	Panicle initiation, flowering
Groundnut	Rapid flowering, pegging, early pod formation
Sugarcane	Formative stage
Sesame	Blooming stage
Sunflower	Two weeks before flowering to two weeks after flowering
Safflower	From rosette to flowering
Soybean	Flowering and seed formation
Cotton	Flowering and boll development
Tobacco	Transplanting to full bloom
Potato	Tuber initiation to tuber maturity

- Canopy temperature is measured with **infrared thermometer**.
- When transpiration is normal, due its cooling effect, canopy temperature is less than air temperature.
- The **negative** values of $T_c - T_a$ indicate that plants have **sufficient amount of water**.
- When $T_c - T_a$ values are **zero or positive**, which indicates **stress**, irrigation is scheduled.

  Stress-degree days (SDD) = $\Sigma (T_c - T_a)$
- 1 ha mm = 10,000 litres

  1 ha cm = 1,00,000 litres

  1 m^3 = 1000 litres

- Pipeflow is measured by **pipe orifices**, **water meters** and **co-ordinate methods**.
- **Venturimeter** is used for measuring the flow of water in pipes under pressure.
- Channel flow is measured by **Parshall flumes** and **'V' notches**.
- **Coordinate methods** are **less accurate** due to the difficulty in measuring the coordinate of jet from the pipe.
- **90° 'V' notch weir** is an excellent device for measuring **small flows**.
- 90° 'V' notch weir has to be installed in such a way that each side will make an angle of **45°**.
- Discharge of 90° 'V' notch weir is computed by the formula

  $Q = 0.0138\ H^{2.5}$

  Q = Discharge (l/s)

  H = Head of the crest (cm)
- Parshall flume is placed in an open channel with **wide** mouth towards the **down** stream.

METHODS OF IRRIGATION

- **Sprinkler irrigation** is adopted where land leveling is uneconomical or impractical.
- **Drip irrigation** is used where water is **scarce**.
- **Flood method** of irrigation is exclusive for **lowland rice**.
- Labour requirement for irrigation is minimum in **flooding**.
- **Check basin** method of irrigation is the **most common method** among surface methods of irrigation.
- Check basin method is suitable for close growing crops like **groundnut, wheat, finger millet, pearl millet, paragrass** etc.
- In check basin method water can be applied uniformly.
- In **check basin** method **more land is wasted** under channels and bunds and intercultivation is difficult.
- **Basin method** is suitable for **fruit crops**.
- In **border strip** method of irrigation, field is laid out into **long, narrow strips**, bordering with small bunds.

- Length of border strips ranges from **30 to 300m** and width from **3 to 15m**.
- **Border strip** method is suitable for **close growing crops** and **medium to heavy** textured soils, but not suitable for **sandy soils**.
- Size of border strips depends on **stream size** and **soil texture**.
- For larger size streams and heavy soils, **longer strips** are made.
- **Furrow** method of irrigation is adopted to crops grown with ridges and furrows.
- **Furrow irrigation** is suitable for crops like sorghum, maize, cotton, tobacco, brinjal, tomato, potato, Napier grass, sugarcane etc.
- Length of furrow ranges from **30 to 300m**.
- Close growing crops like wheat, setaria, groundnut etc. are occasionally given supplemental irrigation though they are originally planned as rainfed crops.
- Intercultivation is done so as to make shallow furrows. Applying irrigation through these shallow furrows is called **corrugation irrigation**.
- Water in the furrows contacts only **one-half to one-fourth** of the land surface, thereby reducing evaporation losses.
- Crust problem is avoided in **furrow irrigation**.
- **Surge irrigation** is defined as the **intermittent** application of water to the field surface under gravity flow which results in a series of 'on' and 'off' modes of constant or variable time spans.
- In **surge irrigation** large intermittent flows rather than a continuous one are used with two sets of furrows and gated pipes laid in the **'Tee" configuration**.
- **Cablegation** is an **automated method** of surface irrigation.
- **Cablegation** is a form of **gated pipe system**.
- Subsurface irrigation through trenches causes deep percolation losses.
- **Subsurface irrigation** method is suitable where water table is **shallow**.
- **Subsurface irrigation** is practiced in a few places in Kerala for coconut gardens and in Kashmir for vegetables.

- **Rotational** irrigation is a system of rotational supply of irrigation water to ensure equitable supply to all the farmers in the realized area of an irrigation system, irrespective of the location of the field.
- **Rotational irrigation** is also known as warabandi irrigation.
- **Flood recession farming** is the practice of growing crops on land that is flooded annually and crops are grown during the recession period. By way of sediment deposits soil fertility is improved.
- **Deficit irrigation** is an irrigation water management alternative where the soil in the plant root zone is not refilled to field capacity in all or part of the field.
- In sprinkler irrigation height of riser pipes depends on the **height of the crop**. It should be **equal** to maximum height of the crop.
- To achieve uniform sprinkling of water, it is necessary to **overlap** the area of influence of each of the sprinklers.
- Conveyance losses with surface irrigation ranges from **15 to 20%** in well irrigated areas and **30-50%** in canal and tank irrigated areas.
- In sprinkler irrigation saving of water ranges from **25 to 50%** for different crops.
- It is difficult to irrigate sandy soils with surface irrigation and it is easy with **sprinkler irrigation**.
- **Sprinkler irrigation** does not work well under **high wind velocity**.
- **Sprinkler irrigation** is not suitable for areas with **hot dry winds**.
- Power requirements are usually high since sprinklers operate at a **pressure**.
- **Christiansen** developed **uniformity coefficient** to measure the uniformity of sprinkler systems, and it is most often applied in sprinkler irrigation situation. It is seldom used in other types of irrigation.
- **Uniformity coefficient** is defined as the ratio of the difference between the average infiltrated amount and the average deviation from the infiltrated amount, to the average infiltrated amount.
- Values of Uniformity coefficient varies from **0.6 to 0.9**.
- **Drip irrigation** is defined as the precise, slow application of water in the form of discrete or continuous or tiny streams or miniature sprays through mechanical devices called emitters or applicators located at selected points along water delivery lines.

- The terms **trickle or drip irrigation** are used synonymously.
- In **1964 Symcha Blass**, an **Israeli engineer** developed the **first patented** drip irrigation system.
- **Screen (mesh) filter** is primarily useful for removing suspended organic particles in water containing sufficient amounts of organic matter.
- Screen filters of 100-200 mesh remove particles of size range > 100-150 μm.
- **Sand filter** is most effective in the removal of **inorganic and organic particles** from water.
- Sand filters remove suspended particles of size range > 20 μm to 100 μm.
- **Sand filter** is provided with a back flushing arrangement.
- **Point source** drippers or emitters discharge water from individual or multiple outlets that are spaced at least 1m apart.
- Point source systems are used for **widely spaced** crops.
- **Line source** emitters or drippers have perforations, holes or porous walls in the irrigation tubing that discharge water at close spacing or even continuously along a lateral line.
- Line source emitters or drippers are used for **close growing** crops.
- Water discharge rate per dripper is normally between **1 to 4 l/h** though the discharge rate of emitters is up to **15 to 20 l/h**.
- Rate of application of water through dripper has to be **less** than the infiltration rate of the soil.
- Number of emitters per unit area depends on **plant spacing**, **soil characteristics**, **root development** and **discharge of emitter**.

$$\text{Number of emitters/plant} = \frac{\text{Rate of delivery needed}}{\text{Average discharge of an emitter}}$$

- Formula for calculating horse power of the pumpset required in drip system is

$$\text{Horsepower of pumpset} = \frac{Q \times H}{75 \times E}$$

Where Q = Discharge (l/s)

H = Head (m)

E = Pumping efficiency (0.6)

- Chlorine in the form of bleaching powder is used to control **algae** and **bacterial slimes**.
- **HCl (36%)** of 0.5-2.0% concentration removes precipitates in drip system.
- **Sulphuric** and **hydrochloric** acids can be used to remove chemical precipitates.
- Acid treatment is given when Ca and Mg in irrigation water exceeds **50 ppm** of each.
- **Sodium hypochlorite** at **500 ppm** helps to remove clogging of drippers.
- In drip irrigation saving in irrigation water compared to conventional method of irrigation was **40-70%**.
- Disadvantages of drip irrigation
  1) High initial cost
  2) High energy consumption to pump water with pressure for distribution
  3) Restricted area of root growth
  4) Requirement of higher level of design, management and maintenance
  5) Clogging of emitters
- In **sugarcane** an efficient irrigation system known as **Typhoon system** has been developed.
- **Bubbler irrigation** is designed to **reduce energy** requirements through inexpensive, thin walled, corrugated plastic pipe with a diameter that even the low pressure head from a surface ditch might suffice.
- **Siphon tubes** are curved pipes which are used to take water from supply channel into the field.

IRRIGATION EFFICIENCY

- Irrigation efficiency at the field level can be increased by selecting suitable method of irrigation, adequate land preparation and engaging an efficient irrigator.
- At project level, irrigation efficiency can be increased by proper conveyance and distribution system.

- **Irrigation efficiency** is the ratio usually expressed as per cent of the volume of irrigation water transpired by plants, plus that evaporated from the soil, plus that necessary to regulate the salt concentration in the soil solution and that used by the plant in building plant tissue to the total volume of water diverted, stored or pumped for irrigation.

$$E_i = \frac{W_t + W_s - R_e}{W_i} \times 100$$

E_i = Irrigation efficiency

W_t = Volume of irrigation water per unit area of land transpired by plants, evaporated from the soil during the crop period (including field preparation and nursery)

W_s = Volume of irrigation water per unit area of land to regulate the salt content of soil solution

R_e = Effective rainfall

W_i = Volume of water per unit area of land that is stored in a reservoir or diverted for irrigation

- Efficiency of irrigation projects in India is as low as **20 to 40** per cent.
- Major project can irrigate **more than 10,000 ha.**
- Medium project can irrigate an area between **2,000 to 10,000 ha.**
- Minor irrigation project is an irrigation project with a capacity to irrigate **less than 2,000 ha.**
- **Conveyance efficiency** indicates the efficiency with which water is conveyed from source of supply to the field. Conveyance efficiency estimates conveyance losses.

$$E_c = \frac{W_f}{W_s} \times 100$$

E_c = Water conveyance efficiency (per cent)

W_f = Water delivered at the field

W_s = Water delivered at the source

- **Water application efficiency** is the measure of efficiency with which water delivered to the field is stored in the root zone.

$$\text{Water application efficiency} = \frac{\text{Water stored in the root zone}}{\text{Water needed in the root zone}} \times 100$$

- **Water storage efficiency** is expressed as the percentage of water delivered to the field prior to irrigation to that stored in the root zone during irrigation.

$$\text{Water storage efficiency} = \frac{\text{Water stored in the root zone}}{\text{Water needed in the root zone}} \times 100$$

- **Water distribution efficiency** is defined as the percentage of difference from the unity of the ratio between the average numerical deviation from the average depth stored during the irrigation.

$$\text{Water distribution efficiency} = \left[1 - \frac{\bar{y}}{\bar{d}}\right] \times 100$$

Where,

$\bar{d}$ = Average depth of penetration along the run during irrigation

$\bar{y}$ =Average numerical deviation from d

- **Water productivity (WP)** is used to define the relationship between crop produced and the amount of water involved in crop production, expressed as crop production per unit volume of water.

WP = Grain or seed yield/water applied to the field

- **Water use efficiency** is defined as the yield of marketable crop produced per unit of water used in evapotranspiration.

WUE = Y/ET

Where, WUE = water-use efficiency (kg/ha mm of water)

Y = Marketable yield (kg/ha)

ET = Evapotranspiration (mm)

- Yield is more influenced by **crop management** practices.
- ET is mainly dependent on **climate and soil moisture**.
- Fertilizers and other cultural practices usually increase WUE, because they relatively increase crop yield more than crop water use.
- Water-use efficiency is **highest in finger millet** (13.4 kg/ha mm) followed by wheat (12.6 kg/ha-mm), groundnut (9.2 kg/ha-mm), sorghum (9.0 kg/ha-mm), Maize = pearl millet (8.0 kg/ha-mm) and **lowest in rice** (3.0 kg/ha-mm).
- Factors affecting water use efficiency are

1) Nature of the plant

2) Climatic conditions
3) Soil moisture content
4) Fertilizers
5) Plant population

- Under adequate irrigation, application of fertilizers increases yields considerably, with small increase in ET and improves WUE.
- Highest yield and WUE is possible only through optimum levels of soil moisture regime, plant population and fertilization.
- **Irrigation period** is the number of days that can be allowed for applying one irrigation to a given area during the peak consumption use period of the crop that is irrigated.

  Irrigation period = Net irrigation requirement/peak use rate
- **Duty of water** is the quantity of water required for irrigation to bring a crop to maturity.
- **Base period** is the period of irrigation which crop requires for full maturity.
- **Delta** is the total depth of water required by a crop during the entire period the crop is in the field.
- **Duty** is the area irrigated by one cusec discharge of water during the crop period. It is equal to twice the base divided by delta.
- **Duty** of water is the total volume of irrigation water required for a particular type of crop to mature. It includes consumptive use, evaporation and seepage from ditches and canals, and the water eventually returned to streams by percolation and surface runoff.

  Duty of water = 8.64 × Base period (B)/Delta (D)
- The main soluble constituents of irrigation water are **calcium, magnesium, sodium as cations and chloride, sulphate, bicarbonate** as anions.
- Other ions present in minute quantities in irrigation water are **boron**, **selenium**, **molybdenum** and **fluorine** which are harmful to animals fed on plants grown on excess concentration of these ions.
- Quality of irrigation water is judged by three parameters

  1) Total salt concentration
  2) Sodium adsorption ratio
  3) Bicarbonate and boron content

- Salt content of irrigation water is measured as **electrical conductivity** (EC).
- Water containing total dissolved salts to the extent of more than **1.5 dS/m** has been classified as **saline**.
- Saline waters are those which have **sodium chloride** as the predominant salt.
- **Brackish water** contains more of salts other than sodium chloride.
- **Brackish water** is one that is contaminated with **acids, bases, salts** or **organic matter**, whereas saline water contains mainly dissolved salts.
- In addition to **EC**, to determine the quality of irrigation water, **sodium adsorption ratio (SAR)**, **residual sodium carbonate (RSC)** and **boron content** are also used to find suitability of irrigation water.
- Classification of irrigation water based on total salt content

Class	EC (dS/m)	Quality characterisation	Soils for which suitable
C_1	< 1.5	Normal waters	All soils
C_2	1.5-3	Low salinity waters	Light and medium textured soils
C_3	3-5	Medium salinity waters	Light and medium textured soils for semi-tolerant crops
C_4	5-10	Saline waters	Light and medium textured soils for tolerant crops
C_5	> 10	High salinity waters	Not suitable

- **Residual Sodium Carbonate (RSC)** is an indicator of the tendency to precipitate Ca as $CaCO_3$ in irrigation water.

$$\text{RSC (me/l)} = (CO_3^{2-} + HCO_3^{-}) - (Ca^{2+} + Mg^{2+})$$

- Irrigation water is considered safe if its **RSC is < 1.25** and unsafe at **RSC > 2.5**.
- Irrigation water which contains more than **3 ppm boron** is harmful to crops, especially on **light soils**.

- Classification of irrigation water based on boron content

Class	Boron (ppm)	Quality characterisation	Soils for which suitable
B_1	< 3	Normal waters	All soils
B_2	3-4	Low boron waters	Clayey soils and medium textured soils
B_3	4-5	Medium boron waters	Heavy textured soils
B_4	5-10	Boron waters	Heavy textured soils
B_5	> 10	High boron waters	Not suitable

- Water quality of most of the Indian rivers is good with EC values < 0.7 dS/m except in Krishna (1.4), Hagari (1.6) and Tungabhadra (1.7) rivers.
- Water quality in tanks and lakes is **good**.
- Quality of ground water is influenced by **soil characteristics, water table** and **rainfall** of the region.
- Water quality in semi arid and arid regions is generally **poor with high salt content**.
- Crop growth in soils irrigated with poor quality water **decreases** due to increased **osmotic stress** and **poor physical condition** of highly dispersed **sodic soils**.
- **Salinity** delays flowering and reduces flower number.
- Irrigation with saline water from **fruiting to maturity** has less influence on yield'.
- Sodium and chloride of irrigation water is retained in stems in **melons**.
- Reclamation of **alkali soil** is more difficult than saline soil because alkali soils have **very low permeability**.
- **Permeameter** is a device for measuring the **permeability** of soils or other materials.
- Exchangeable sodium has to be replaced by **calcium** and the replaced sodium has to be leached down to lower layers.
- Replacement of excessive exchangeable sodium can be done by any soluble source of calcium and magnesium salts such as **calcium chloride, magnesium chloride or gypsum**.
- Calcium and magnesium chlorides are too expensive.

- However, **gypsum** by virtue of its **low solubility and cost** is quite suitable.
- In calcareous alkali soils, some acid forming reagents can also bring about reclamation by solubilising calcium carbonate thus creating acidity.
- Acidifying materials are
  1) Sulphur
  2) Sulphuric acid
  3) Iron sulphate
  4) Aluminium sulphate
  5) Lime sulphur
- In the above materials, sulphur acts slowly because it has to be oxidized by microbial activity before it could act as an ameliorating agent.
- The quantity of amendment necessary for reclamation of any area depends on the quantity of **exchangeable sodium** present on the clay surface.
- To replace each milliequivalent of sodium by calcium in an area of 1 hectare for a soil depth of 30 cm requires **4.1** tonnes of gypsum.
- **Barley, sugarbeet, mustard, cotton, turnips, beetroot, datepalm, coconut** etc. are salt tolerant crops.
- **Sorghum, pearl millet, finger millet, rice, castor** etc. are semi tolerant to salinity.
- Application of **FYM or incorporation of green manure** crops helps in reducing the adverse effects of irrigation with **poor quality** water.
- Under **salinity** conditions, planting seeds on the **side of the ridge** helps in **better germination** than those planted on the top of the ridge.
- Heavy water (D_2O) is the water in which hydrogen has been replaced by **deuterium** (hydrogen isotope of mass 2).

DRAINAGE

- **Pearl millet** is susceptible to water logging during **seedling stage** while it can tolerate at later stages.

- Yield of cereals is depressed if the soil is waterlogged during **panicle development**.
- Pulses are susceptible to water logging at **initial period of reproductive stage**.
- **Temperature** is the important climatic factor influencing the extent of damage due to excess moisture.
- Injury due to water logging is severe under **warm** weather conditions.
- Flooding is more harmful on **sunny days** than on cloudy days.
- **Flopping or wilting** of tobacco takes place only when sunshine occurs after prolonged dry spell.
- Under water logged conditions proportion of **aerenchymatous** tissue in the root system **increases**.
- Ethanol production **increases** and activity of **alcohol dehydrogenase** increases in roots of waterlogged plants.
- Under waterlogged conditions permeability of roots **decreases** due to shortage of oxygen resulting in decreased water uptake and wilting symptoms appear even though soil contains excess water.
- **Permeability** of roots for nutrients also **reduced** under waterlogged conditions.
- Adverse effects of waterlogging can be reduced to some extent by supplying **nitrogenous** fertilizers.
- Waterlogging can be avoided by providing **drainage**.
- **Agricultural drainage** is the provision of a suitable system for the removal of excessive irrigation or rain water from the land surface so as to provide suitable soil conditions for better plant growth.
- Rate of drainage is amount (expressed in depth) of water drained off from a given area in **24 hours**.
- Rate of drainage also called as **drainage coefficient** or **drainage design rate**.
- Rate of drainage expressed in terms of **flow rate per unit area (m^3/ha/day)**.
- **Runoff coefficient** is the amount of runoff expressed as a percentage of the total rainfall in a given area.
- Drainage improves soil aeration and **increases** soil temperature.

- **Surface drainage** is the **simplest** and **most common method** in India.
- Provision of **surface** drainage is cheap.
- Disadvantages of surface drainage
  1) Land is wasted for open drains
  2) Drains cause obstruction to field preparation and intercultivation
  3) Drains get silted and periodical desilting is necessary
  4) Weed growth in the drains is heavy
  5) Open drains are damaged by rodents and farm animals
- **Subsurface** drainage requires less maintenance, high initial investment.
- Failure of the **sub surface** drainage system is difficult to detect.
- **Subsurface** drainage system is ineffective in soils with **low permeability**.
- **Open trenches**, **tile drains**, **mole drains**, **perforated drains** are used in **subsurface drainage**

Chapter 17

Weed Management

- ***Phalaris minor*** developed resistance to **isoproturon** due to its longer usage.
- **Orobanche** is a complete root parasite on **tobacco** and **tomato**.
- **Striga** is a partial root parasite.
- **Onion** is a poor competitor with weeds because of shallow roots, slender leaves, sparse leaves and slow growth.
- **15-45 Days after transplanting (DAT)** is the critical period of crop weed competition in **onion**.
- For the control of weeds
  a) Recommended herbicide should be used
  b) Recommended dosage should be used
  If increased dosage is used herbicide will lose selectivity
  c) Herbicide should be applied at correct time
- Of the more than **3 lakh species** known in this world **3000 species** are of economic value for us and are cultivated ones.
- **Weed** is a plant growing where it is not desired.
- **Jethro Tull** a great **British** farmer was the first person to refer the word weed and its definition in his famous writing "**Horse Hoeing Husbandry**".
- **Bermuda grass, *Cenchrus ciliaris, Eleusine indica, Panicum maximum*** (**Guinea grass**) when grown in crops considered as weeds otherwise forages.
- Plants may become weeds only in a particular situation and time so long as any plant growing on time without interfering with man's interest.
- While all weeds are unwanted plants, all unwanted plants may not be the weeds.
- **Weed Science Society of America** defined weed as a plant growing where it is not desired.

- **European Weed Research Society** defined weed as any plant or vegetation excluding fungi interfering with the objectives or the requirements of the people.
- **W.S. Blatchley** defined weed as a plant out of place or growing where it is not desired
- **W.W. Robbins** *et al.*, defined weeds as obnoxious (unpleasant) plants.
- **J.L. Harper** defined weeds as higher plants which are a **nuisance**.
- **G.C. Klingman** defined weed as a plant growing where it is not desired or a plant out of place.
- Weed control as a science was initiated in **1942**.
- 2,4-D was first used in a large scale in **1947**.
- The development of **2,4-D** in **1946** and later triazines, ureas which shows tremendous potential for plantation crops was beginning of herbicide usage in India.
- Weeds account for **45%** loss of agriculture produce

  Insects – 30%

  Diseases – 20%

  Others (rodents) – 5%
- Weeds compete with crop plants for **moisture**, **nutrients**, **space** and **sunlight** and reduce the crop yields.
- The reduction in crop yields depends on **crop-weed competition**.
- Crop-weed competition depends on **types of weed flora associated with crop, weed density, duration of infestation, and competitive nature of crop plants**.
- **Crop – reduction in yield due to weeds**

  Wheat = 15-30%

  Rice = 30-35%

  Maize, sorghum, pulses, oilseeds = 18-85%

  Bengalgram = 30%

  Redgram = 34%

  Onion = 90.7%

  Potato = 28%
- **Redgram** is **very deep rooted** so sustain from weed competition by obtaining nutrients from deeper layers.

- Weed infestation in sugarcane leads to **reduction** in sucrose content.
- Weeds growing within and outside the fields provide shelter to insect pest and disease pathogens of crops and act as host to these both during crop season and off season.
- Weevils survive on ***Solanum*** weed sps.
- **Ergot of Bajra** pathogen survives on ***Cenchrus ciliaris***.
- Stem borer on rice will survive on ***Echinocloa*** as well as ***Panicum.***
- Caterpillar which is a pest on **Redgram**, **Cotton** survives on ***Chenopodium album, Amaranthus* sps, Datura** and so on.
- **Parthenium** causes skin rashes.
- **Ambrosia** *sps*. causes **heyfever**.
- If seeds of ***Argemone mexicana*** mixed with mustard seeds cause **blindness**.
- Examples of thorny and spiny weeds are ***Acanthospermum hispidum*, *Argemone mexicana, Mimosa pudica (Touch me not), Achyranthes aspera*.**
- Certain weeds cause sickness to farm animals and some may prove fatal due to high level of some **alkaloids**.

  Ex: ***Sorghum halepense*** (Johnson grass)

  Tribulus terrestris (produces thorny fruit)
- ***Tribulus terrestris*** causes sours in the hooves (foot) of grazing animals.
- Weeds are good source of organic matter to soil and improve soil fertility.
- Weeds comprise of **2.5 times** more N, **1.5 times** more P, **3.5 times** more K than crop plants.
- **Parthenium, *Eichhornea crassipes*, Eupatorium** are used as compost and also as green manure plants. They should be used before flowering.
- Many of the weeds which are **legumes** enrich the soil fertility by fixing atmospheric nitrogen.
- Weeds which are fodder value to livestock are *Panicum maximum (guinea grass), Panicum repens, Brachiaria mutica (Para grass), Brachiaria reptans, Digitaria sps, Chloris gayana, Cenchrus ciliaris, Eragrostis sps, Dicanthium annulatum, Setaria sps.*

- Weeds which are used as food for human beings are ***Amaranthus viridis, Celosia argentia* (cocks comb weed), *Alternanthera sessilis, Portuluca sps, Digera sps, Chromolina odorata*.**
- ***Centella asiatica*** which is a common weed in **wetland rice** acts as blood purifier and improves memory power.
- All parts of ***Centella asiatica*** have medicinal value.
- ***Phyllanthus niruri*** is used for curing **jaundice**.
- ***Tylophora indica*** is used for curing **asthma** patients.
- ***Solanum nigrum*** and ***Solanum xanthocarpum*** are used to cure **asthma, cough and fever**.
- ***Argemone mexicana*** seeds resemble to that of mustard. Oil is used for **skin treatment**.
- ***Spirulina sps*** (weed in aquatic bodies) is rich in **protein**.
- Weeds serve as soil binders.

  Ex: ***Dicanthium annulatum***, ***Vetiveria zizanoides***
- No soil cover is worse than weedy one.
- ***Hydrilla verticillata*** is used in aquariums.
- ***Lantana camara*** produces beautiful flowers of different colours.
- Very good lawn is developed from ***Cynodon dactylon***.
- Extracts from **parthenium** plant can be used against **pulse beetle**.
- Incorporation of calotrophis, parthenium, Crotalaria into the soil reduces **nematode** population in the soil.
- Weed ***Jatropha gossypifolia*** is used as biofuel.
- Weeds are used as live fences.

  Ex: ***Lantana camara***

  Opuntia dellini
- **2,4-D** is effective for controlling broadleaved weeds.
- ***Lantana camara*** is a **wasteland** weed.
- ***Echinocloa* and *Marsilia*** are wetland weeds.
- **Euphorbiaceae** members produce **milky latex**.
- ***Tribulus terrestris*** possess short spines on fruit.
- ***Solanum xanthocarpum*** has spines on stem and leaves.
- ***Acanthospermun hispidum*** has triangular fruit with spines.

- ***Mimosa pudica*** has short spines on stem.
- ***Oxalis latifolia*** produces **bulbils** in roots.
- ***Cyperus rotundus*** produces **tubers.**
- **Panicum** produces **rhizomes** in root.
- Common name of *Aegeratum conyzoides* is **goat weed**.
- The chief agents of weed seed dispersal are wind, water, animals and man.
- Weed seeds that disseminate through wind possess some structural modifications to help in their dissemination.
- Pappus is a parachute like structure produced by **asteraceae** members.

  Ex: Parthenium, *Sonchus sps*, *Tridax procumbens*, *Aegeratum conyzoides*
- Weed seeds are covered with special hairs (**comose**) in ***Calotrophis gigantea***.
- Weed seeds enclosed in **balloon** like structure which is modification of **calyx.**

  Ex: ***Physalis minima***

  Cordiospermum helicabum
- Seeds of **Orobanche** and **Striga** are so light in weight and easily disperse with windstorm, without any special arrangements.
- Many weedy fruits and seeds are eaten by birds and animals during grazing and above **10-15%** of undigested weed seeds are passed through animal excreta in viable form. This mechanism of weed dispersal is known as **endozoochory**.
- Weed seeds are carried to long distances by clinging to the fur of the animals like **sheep, goat** etc. which are aided by special appendages such as **hooks, sharp spines, sticky glands** etc.

  Ex: ***Achyranthes aspera, Tribulus terrestris,* Spear grass *(heteropogon), Xanthium strumarium***
- **Satellite weeds** are the weeds which resemble to that of crop plant.

  Ex: ***Echinocloa crusgalli***

  Phalaris minor

PERSISTENCE OF WEEDS

- **Persistence** refers to the ability of weeds to invade an environment repeatedly even when it is completely removed from the place.
- **Weed – seed production/plant**

  Amaranthus sps -1,96,000

  Chenopodium album – 72,000

  Striga lutia – 60,000-70,000

  Echinocloa colonum – 40,000

  Parthenium -30,000

  Celosia argentia -11000
- One year seeding is **seven** years **weeding**.
- The viability of seed is the lifespan of a particular seed during which it is able to germinate.
- ***Cynodon dactylon*** seeds retain viability for **2 years**.
- ***Tribulus terrestris*** seeds remain alive for **8 years**.
- ***Cyperus rotundus*** seeds remain alive for **20 years**.
- ***Convolvulus arvensis*** seeds remain alive for **50 years**.
- The % of viability of weed seeds is very high and even the immature seeds are viable that is not so incase of crop plants
- **Seed dormancy** is a protective character that a seed possess for their sustainable survival on the earth.
- Majority of the weed seeds lying below **5cm** soil depth remain dormant and acts as source for future flushes of the weeds.
- **Innate dormancy, enforced dormancy** and **induced dormancy** are the three types of dormancies operating in weed seeds.
- Innate dormancy is a **genetically** controlled character. It is due to presence of **hard seed coat**.

  e.g., Tribulus terrestris

  Ipomea sps

  Xanthium sps.
- **Enforced** dormancy is due to placement of weed seeds deeper than **5cm** in the soils. Weed seeds under this kind of dormancy germinate readily whenever they are brought to the top layers by tillage and provided congenial conditions for their germination.

- **Induced** dormancy results from sudden **physiological** changes takes place in the seed. Even the release of dormancy in weed seeds is erratic.
- ***Alternanthera echinata*** is highly drought resistant.
- Weeds reproduce both sexually and asexually.
- **Weed – mode of reproduction**

  Cyperus rotundus – tubers & seeds

  Cynodon dactylon – Seeds & vegetative propagules

  Convolvulus arvensis – seeds & vegetative means

  Panicum repens – seeds & vegetative means
- Weeds are persistent due to evasiveness. They are not easily destroyable by animals and man because of their bitterness, disagreeable odour, spiny nature

  e.g., Tribulus terrestris

  Chromolina odorata

  Eupatorium sps.
- Weeds possess self regeneration capacity. Weeds are self sown plants. They do not require any preparation of seedbed for their germination, fertilization, plant protection and irrigation.
- Weed seeds readily germinate on undisturbed land or soil under favourable environmental conditions.
- **Ecology** is the study of interactions between the plants and their environment.
- **Weed ecology** is the study of interactions between the weeds and their environment.
- **Aldrich** strongly suggests that weed management must deal with the interactions of all the factors with the weeds.
- Early weed science literature reveals that dominant weed population in many crops specially in small grain crops are **annual broad leaved** weeds.
- After the wide spread use of phenoxy acid group of herbicides (2,4-D) there was a gradual shift from annual broad leaved weeds which are effectively controlled by phenoxy acid herbicides to annual grassy weeds.
- Monocropping and monocultural environment create ecological changes that determine what weeds will succeed.

- **Tillage practices** having influence on **weed flora**, change in the cultivation practices also leads to change in weed flora.
- Understanding **weed crop ecology** will lead to more effective weed prevention, management and control.
- **Yellow nut sedge** does well in **sub humid** and **warm temperate regions**, but it does not thrive well in **temperate areas** with prolonged frost.
- **Purple nutsedge** thrives well in **humid tropics** and **subtropics**.
- **Water hyacinth** an important aquatic weed in **tropics** and **subtropics** is not yet invaded the temperate waters.
- **Soil pH** is an important determinant of which weed plants grow in an area.

CROP WEED COMPETITION/INTERFERENCE

- **Competition** is the struggle for survival and continued existence.
- In plant communities each plant is in a continuous state of war to gain in its competition for various growth factors both above ground and underground.
- **Competition** occurs when plants present in a given area demand a particular growth factor and supply of that factor falls below their combined demand.
- According to **Muller** competition means that one plant utilizes the necessary growth resources resulting in shortage which is harmful to other plant sharing the same habitat.
- According to **Aldrich** competition is the relationship between two or more plants in which the supply of growth factors falls below their combined demand.
- **Competition** does not start as long as growth factor is abundant in supply.
- Weed competition for nutrients, water, light, space, CO_2 etc. is taken as **indirect effect** on crop growth and yield.
- Weeds also release allelochemicals and affect crop growth and yield by a phenomenon called as **allelopathy** is a **direct effect**.
- Crop-weed competition however does not include **allelopathy** which is also a possible mechanism for reduction in growth and yield of crop in the field.

- In ecology, detrimental effect of one plant species on another resulting from interaction with each other is called as **interference**.
- The total detrimental effect of weeds on crop plants resulting from interaction with each other was termed as **interference** by **Harper** which includes both competition and allelopathy.

  Interference = competition + Allelopathy
- Crop weed interference may be more scientific and appropriate than crop weed competition.
- Weed competition is most serious when the crop plants are **young**.
- Competition is relatively greater between the plants of **similar morphology and growth behaviour**.
- Weeds having **similar characteristics** as that of crop plants are often more serious competitors than weeds of dissimilar habit.
- **Grassy** weeds prove more competitive with cereal crops because both of them have fibrous root system of similar spread and depth in soil and similar height and plant architecture.
- **Broad leaved** weeds may put more competition with broad leaved weed crops (pulses, oilseeds).
- A **moderate** infestation of weeds is sometimes serious than heavy infestation.
- In moderate infestation the number of weeds is smaller and thinner, so there is a chance that they may grow vigorously and putout bulky and profuse growth which covers the whole area more rapidly than heavy infestation.
- In **moderate** infestation there is possibility of only **interspecific competition** but in **heavy** infestation both **interspecific** and **intraspecific competition** may occur together.
- Onion is a poor competitor with weeds on account of its inherent characteristic features like **short stature, shallow root system, sparse foliage** and **early slow growth**.
- **Garlic, carrot, beetroot** are also poor competitors with weeds.
- Crops having deep root system, early rapid growth, more branching are the **good competitors** with the weeds having high competitive ability with the weeds.

  Ex: **Potato, field bean, cowpea, maize etc.**

- **Critical period of crop-weed competition** is defined as the shortest time span during the crop growth when weeding is done results in maximum returns. Time of weeding is as important as weeding itself.

  Crop – critical period of CWC

  Onion (transplanted) – 20-40 DAT

  Onion (Direct seeded) – 20-55DAS

  Sugarcane – 30-110 DAS

  Potato-15-30DAS

  Soybean & Sunflower – 30-40DAS

- Weed competition is always **indirect** but weed interference could be **indirect or direct**.
- Plant competition is both under and above the ground for growth factors.
- Competition can be **intraspecific**, **interspecific** between weeds and crops and **intergeneric** under field conditions.

WEED CONTROL EFFCIENCY (%)

- It denotes the magnitude of reduction in **weed dry weight** due to weed control treatments.

$$\text{WCE (\%)} = \frac{\text{DMC} - \text{DMT}}{\text{DMC}} \times 100$$

DMC = Dry matter of weeds in controlled plot (weedy check)

DMT = Dry matter of weeds in treatment plots

WEED INDEX

- Weed index is the **reduction in crop yield** due to presence of weeds in comparison with weed free check plots

$$\text{Weed index (\%)} = \frac{X - Y}{X} \times 100$$

X = Bulb yield or yield from weed free check plot

Y = Yield from treatment plots

NATURE OF CROP WEED COMPETITION

- Weeds usually absorb nutrients faster than many of the crop plants and derive greater benefit.
- Among the plant nutrients **nitrogen, phosphorus** and **potassium** are the limiting ones and among them **nitrogen** is the first nutrient to become limiting due to crop weed competition.
- If soil nutrients are abundant, weed competition for nutrients is less important, but in many tropical and subtropical areas soils are poor in nutrients and competition is critical.
- ***Amaranthus viridis*** accumulates **3.16% N** apart from high levels of **potassium (4.51%)** in their dry matter.
- ***Achyranthes aspera*** and ***Digitaria sanguinalis*** are 'P' accumulators which contain **1.63%** and **3.36% P** respectively
- ***Chenopodium album*** and ***Portuluca quadrifolia*** have preference for **K**. ***Chenopodium album*** contains **4.34%** K, whereas ***Portuluca*** contains **4.57%** K.
- ***Xanthium strumarium* (cocklebur)** and ***Tribulus terrestris*** species utilized 1.5 - 2.2 times more N and 1.7 – 4.0 times more K per kg drymatter higher than grain sorghum.
- **Water** is the primary environmental factor limiting crop production and is the most critical of all the plant growth requirements.
- Weeds compete for water, reduce water availability in the soil and contribute to moisture stress.
- For producing equal dry matter weeds transpire **more** water than most of the crop plants.
- **Sorghum associated weed – transpiration coefficient**

  Amaranthus viridis – 338

  Cynodon dactylon - 813

  Digitaria sps – 693

  Echinocloa colonum – 673

  Tridax procumbens -1402

  Sorghum -394
- **Transpiration coefficient** is the quantity of water (g) necessary for a plant to produce one kg of dry matter.

- Stomata in some of the weeds are less sensitive to the decline in leaf water potential than those of the crops.
- Competition for light may begin at the very early stage of crop if there is shading and smothering effect by dense growth of weeds.
- Similar morphology and growth pattern and more or less similar duration of certain weeds as that of crop results in severe competition with the crop.
- **Annuals** have huge germination, periodicity of germination and more adapted to overcrowding may be **more** damaging to annual field crops than perennials, although **perennials** pose more difficulty in controlling them.
- Weed density and crop yield have a **sigmoidal** and fairly **inverse relationship** with each other.
- Yield **decreases** as weed density increases.
- It has been frequently observed that crop yield becomes **zero** even before attaining **maximum weed density**.
- **Cowpea** due to its initial faster growth and canopy cover smothers the weeds very effectively than greengram and blackgram.
- **Cowpea** has high weed smothering ability.
- **Cereals** because of their tall stature are more competitive.
- **Cowpea, field bean, calapogonium, horsegram, potato, redgram, castor** have **good weed smothering ability**.
- **Greengram, blackgram, soybean, onion, garlic, carrot, groundnut and sunflower** are **poor competitors** with weeds.
- A sufficiently long duration crop like sugarcane, cotton etc. can recover to some extent, the initial damage on growth by weeds if it is made weed free at the later stages. But this sort of compensation on crop growth and yield is hardly achievable in short duration crops.
- **Soil pH, moisture, fertility, texture, structure and topography** to a greater extent determine the weed species composition and magnitude of weed infestation.
- A **good crop** is the best weed killer.

ALLELOPATHY

- The word allelopathy is derived from **greek** words
  Allelo = mutual or each other
  Patho = suffering or to suffer
- The term allelopathy was coined by **Molish** in **1937**.
- **Allelopathy** refers to the inhibitive or detrimental effect of one plant species on the germination, growth and metabolism of another plant species due to release of allelochemicals.
- According to **Rice** allelopathy refers to any direct or indirect inhibitory effect by one plant including microorganisms on another plant through the production of chemical compounds that escape into the environment.
- Allelochemicals includes aliphatic compounds like **oxalic acid, succinic acid, butyric acid**. It also includes **terpenoids, cynogenic glucosides like alkaloids, phenolic compounds, HCN**.
- Source of allelochemicals are **leaf leachates** and **leaf litter, crop residue decomposition** and **root exudation**.
- One crop against other crop allelopathy is likely to operate in multiple cropping systems like intercropping, mixed cropping and agroforestry.
- **Sorghum** is allelopathic against ***Amaranthus hybridus and Setaria viridis***.
- **Sweet potatoes** have allelopathic effect on weeds like ***Cyperus sps***.
- **Cucumber** is allelopathic against ***Echinocloa crusgalli*** and ***Amaranthus sps***.
- **Maize** is allelopathic against ***Chenopodium album***.
- **Parthenium** is having allelopathic interactions on several crops.
- **Euphorbia** is having allelopathic interactions on **flax**.
- ***Chenopodium album*** is having allelopathic interactions on **alfalfa, maize and cucumber**.
- **Parthenium** is allelopathic to many weeds.
- **Parthenium** invades and forms a territory of its own replacing all the existing weed flora because of allelopathic effect.

- ***Amaranthus spinosus, Cassia seracia*** etc. pose a strong allelopathic effect on parthenium.
- **Weed against weeds allelopathy** has enough importance and could be exploited to control some of the poisonous and problematic weeds.
- Parthenium is suppressed moderately (26-50%) by ***Cassia auriculata, Sida spinosa*** **and** ***Hyptis Suaveolens***.
- High suppression (51-75%) of parthenium by ***Croton bonplandianum, Cassia oxidentalis*** **and** ***Cassia tora***.
- Very high suppression (76-100%) of parthenium by ***Cassia sericea and Tephrosia purpurea***.
- Adoption of crops/crop cultivars more allelopathic to weeds may reduce the cost of weed control.
- **Sorghum** residue is incorporated to control weeds in sequence rotational crops.
- Application of residues of allelopathic crop plants as mulch or adoption of allelopathic crop in rotational sequence and allowing the residues to remain in field has enough importance to bring down weed population.
- Selection of companion crop that is selectively allelopathic to weeds has enough bearing towards weed control.

  Ex: Sorghum + cowpea

  Maize + cowpea

  Agroforestry

  Agrisilvipasture system

CHEMICAL WEED CONTROL

- Herbicide is derived from two **latin** words

  Herba = plant

  Caedere = to kill

- Literally the term **weedicide** is correct but technically weedicide is not an appropriate term. It should kill only weeds not others. But at higher doses it loses selectivity and kills all vegetation including crops. Weeds and crops are herbaceous plants. So **herbicide is most appropriate term**.

- First herbicide registered and used for selective control of weeds in crops was **2,4-D**.
- The credit for introduction of 2,4-D goes for **Marth and Mitchell (USDA)** in lawns for control of broad leaved weeds.
- **Common salt** and **inorganic salts of K and Mg** are **non selective** and could hardly be used in crops.
- Kerosene oil also has herbicidal action.
- **Sulphuric acid** is used for weed control in small grain cereal crops.
- **Dilute H_2SO_4** at a conc. of **6-10%** has been used for broad leaved weed control in cereals for a quite long period in Europe.
- In 1900 the herbicidal role of **calcium cyanamide** was discovered and later in 1908 **sodium arsenite** and **chloropicrin (tear gas)** came into use as herbicides.
- In 1919 **sodium chlorate** was first widely used as **soil sterilant** for controlling **perennial weeds**.
- Until recently sodium chlorate used to be recommended as a **total weed killer** on road side, factory premises and non cropped areas.
- The first important discovery in the field of selective weed control was the introduction of **4,6- Dinitro – O - Cresol (DNOC) in France** in 1933 is a **contact herbicide** applied to **cereal crops** to control broad leaved weeds. This was widely used in Netherlands. It is not successable because of phytotoxic effect on crop plants, mammalian toxicity.
- **Pokorny** synthesized 2,4-D in 1940 and described its chemical synthesis in 1941.
- **Zimmerman and Hichcock** too synthesized 2, 4-D in 1942. This event was more highlighted ad taken as first time discovery of 2,4-D.
- **Marth and Mitchell** in 1942 & 1944 from USDA reported its herbicidal activity to selectively control the broad leaved weeds in the lawns.
- **Hammer and Tukey** in 1944 observed that 2,4-D successively control weeds in cereals.
- **2,4-D** is first selective organic herbicide in world because of its widespread use in crops mainly **cereals** all over the world.

- Sister compounds of 2,4-D that is derivates of phenoxy alkanoic acids *i.e.,* MCPA, 2,4,5-T, MCPB, MCPD came into market during late 1940's.
- Between 1945 & 1960's several **photosynthesis inhibitor** herbicides like **urea, triazine, uracil** group of herbicides and **mitotic inhibitors** like **carbamates, dinitroanilines**, **lipid synthesis inhibitors** like **thio carbamates** were developed in the world and the concept of preemergence herbicide originated during this period.
- Now **atrazine** is the principal herbicide used in **maize and sorghum** all over the world.
- In 1970's and 1980's new group of herbicides called **sulfonyl ureas and imidazolinones** were synthesized.
- Sulphonyl ureas and imidazolinones became very popular because of their high **potent nature** and their usage in **very low** quantity. They are ecofriendly because of **low residual** nature.
- In china **butachlor** is the most popular herbicide used in rice. The other most popular herbicide is **pyrazosulfuron ethyl** highly marketed in China, Japan for weed control in rice.
- Herbicide is a chemical mostly organic which selectively kills the weeds when applied to crop area without phytotoxic effect on crops.
- In market any approved herbicide is identified with 3 names
  a) **Common name:** it is technically accepted short name
  b) **Chemical name:** describes chemistry of molecule or reads out complete molecular structure
  c) **Trade name:** given by the manufacturer

Common name	Chemical name	Trade name
2,4-D	2,4-Dichlorophenoxy acetic acid	Agromex, weedor
Glyphosate	N-(phosphomethyl) glycine	Glycel (Excel India crop care ltd) Roundup (Monsanto)

CLASSIFICATION OF HERBICIDES

1) *Based on time of application:*

a) **Preplant incorporation:** Herbicide should be Incorporated 1 or 2 days before sowing or planting of crops

e.g., Fluchloralin, trifluralin

b) **Pre-emergent herbicide:** They are applied directly to the soil prior to the emergence of weeds, applied 1 or 2 days after sowing

e.g., Majority of herbicides

Pendimethalin, alachlor, atrazine, diuron, oxyflourfen, metalachlor, butachlor, isoproturon, pyrazosulfuron ethyl

c) **Post emergent herbicides:** Applied after the emergence of weeds or on grownup weeds. These are sprayed directly on the grownup weeds.

i) **Early post emergent:** These are sprayed when weeds are young *i.e.,* 1 or 2 weeks after emergence of weeds. Weeds are in 2-3 leaf stage. *e.g.,* 2,4-D, Fenoxoprop-p-ethyl, metamfop, cyhalofop-p-butyl.

ii) **Late post emergent**: Applied on foliage of fully grown weeds and they are non selective.

e.g., Glyphosate, paraquat, diquat

2) Based on selectivity

a) **Selective herbicides:** Herbicides which kill selectively target plants (weeds) in a mixed population of crops and weeds. Majority of herbicides are selective.

e.g., Atrazine, butachlor, fenoxoprop-p-ethyl, metolachlor.

Pendimethalin is an excellent herbicide having selectivity to > **60** different crops which includes **cereals, pulses, oilseeds** etc.

- However selectivity of any herbicide is **dose dependent** and **crop dependent**. Therefore herbicide selective to a crop may become non selective if used at higher doses.

b) **Non selective herbicides:** They kill any group or species of plants irrespective of crop and weeds. So they are not used in cropped area and they are used in industrial area, railway track side, bund side, road side.

e.g., Glyphosate, paraquat, diquat

- Even non selective herbicides become selective herbicides when spray is **directed** on to the weeds under controlled conditions.

3) Based on spectrum of weed control

a) **Narrow spectrum herbicides:** They control a particular group of weed flora.

e.g., 2,4-D is basically a broad leaved weed killer

Diclofop-methyl and fenoxoprop-p-ethyl are **grass killers**

b) **Broad spectrum herbicides:** They control wider weed flora consisting of broad leaved weeds, grasses and sedges.

e.g., Glyphosate, paraquat, diquat, atrazine, pendimethalin, isoproturon, oxyfluorfen etc.

4) Based on site of application

a) **Soil applied herbicides:** They are applied to the soil. They kill germinating and sprouting weed seeds, rhizomes, tubers etc.

- All pre-emergent herbicides are **soil** applied herbicides

b) **Foliage applied herbicides:** They are applied on the canopy or the foliage of the weeds. They are applied on the grown up weeds.

e.g., paraquat, glyphosate, 2,4-D

5) Based on residue action in the soil

a) **Residual herbicides:** After application or incorporation in soil, herbicide residues remain in soil for a considerable period of time.

e.g., Atrazine, 2,4-D, pendimethalin

b) **Non residual herbicides:** They leave no or less residue in the soil and gets quickly inactivated or metabolized falling on to the soil. They do not have extended period of activity in soil.

e.g., Glyphosate, Paraquat, Diquat

- **Glyphosate** is systemic in action or nature.
- **Paraquat and diquat** can be used in lakes and ponds because of no residue and adverse effects. They are **contact** herbicides.
- **Glyphosate** takes **12-15 days** for action as it is **systematic**.
- By spraying **contact** herbicides, within a day weeds are burned or killed.

6) Based on chemical structure

a) **Inorganic herbicides:**

e.g., Ammonium sulphate, borate, copper sulphate, sodium chlorate

b) **Organic herbicides:** Most of the herbicides are organic

i) Phenoxy acetic acid group of herbicides:

e.g., 2,4-D (Knock weed – 36% EC)
2,4,5-T (Brush killer -48% EC)
Fluazifop-p-butyl (Fusilade- 12.5% EC)
MCPA (Methyl Chloro Phenoxy Acetic Acid)
MCPB (Methyl Chloro Phenoxy Butyric acid)

- They are called as **old generation herbicides** but till today they have been widely used for weed control.
- They are **hormonal** type of herbicides at lower concentration.
- 2,4-D is **white crystalline** material and it is **auxin** type herbicide. It is used as **preemergent** and **early post emergent** herbicide.
- 2,4-D is effective against **broad** leaved weeds.
- Pulses are highly sensitive to **2,4-D**. Do not use **2,4-D** in pulse crops.
- Dicotyledon crops are highly sensitive to **2,4-D**.

ii) Triazine group

e.g., Atrazine (Atrataf – 50% WP)
Simazine (Gesatop – 50% WP)
Propazine (Gesamil – 50% WP)
Prometryn (Gesagard – 50% WP)

- These are widely used for selective weed control.
- Applied as **pre-emergent spray**.
- They are extensively used for weed control in **Maize**.
- Atrazine is used in **sorghum, maize, bajra, sugarcane**.
- Atrazine is a **broad** spectrum herbicide and controls all weeds.
- They are available as **wettable powder** formulations.
- They are **photosynthesis inhibitors**.
- They are highly **persistent** in soil.

- If we go for pulses after maize it is a problem because of **atrazine**.

iii) Bipyridillium group

e.g., Diquat (Reglone – 20% EC)

Paraquat (Gramoxone – 20% EC)

- They are **non selective herbicides** or total weed killers.
- In **plantation** crops we can use paraquat and diquat for weed control.
- They are used in **aquatic bodies** for weed control.
- They are available in EC formulations.

iv) Pyrimidines (Uracil group)

Bromacil (Hyvar – 80% WP)

Terbacil (Sinbar – 80% WP)

v) Oxadiazone group

Oxadiazon (Ronstar-50% EC)

Oxadiazon is used for weed control in **vegetables.**

vi) Substituted urea group:

e.g., Diuron (Karmex – 80% WP)

Isoproturon (Arelan – 50% WP)

Linuron

Diuron is a very good herbicide for **cotton**.

vii) Sulphonyl urea group:

e.g., Metsulfuron-methyl (10%) + Chlorimuron-ethyl (10%) (**Almix**-Trade Name)

Metsulfuron methyl (**Algrip**)

Bensulfuron methyl (**Londax**)

Pyrazosulfuron ethyl (**sathi**) - used in **aerobic rice**

- These are called as **new generation** herbicides.
- They are **highly potent** herbicides.
- They are applied at a **very low dosage (g/ha)**.
- They are **less persistent** in the soil.
- They are **broad spectrum** in nature.
- They have revolutionized the herbicide usage in the world because of their very low rate of application.

viii) Nitroanilines group (Dinitroanilines):

e.g., Fluchloralin (Basalin – 48% EC)

Pendimethalin (Stomp – 30% EC)

Trifluralin (Treflan – 48% EC)

- This group first introduced in 1960's.
- They are available in **EC formulations**.
- They are **orange yellow** in colour.
- They control wide spectrum of grasses.
- Some of the herbicides which are susceptible to photo decomposition are pre-plant incorporated (**Fluchloralin**).
- **Pendimethalin** is used in cereals, vegetables, pulses, oilseeds and has selectivity for many crops and is available at low cost.

ix) Nitrophenyl ethers:

e.g., Nitrofen (Tok-E-25-25% EC) – used in **groundnut**

Oxyfluorfen (Goal - 23.5% EC) (Oxygold – 23.5% EC)

- Oxyfluorfen is used in **carrot, onion, garlic and potato**.
- For **onion**, oxyfluorfen is the best herbicide.

x) Carbamates:

e.g., Propham (IPC – 50% EC)

Chloropropham (CIPC – 40% EC)

xi) Thiocarbamates

e.g., EPTC (Eptam- 75% EC)

Benthiocarb

xii) Anilides / Amides:

e.g., Alachlor (Lasso- 48% EC)- for **pulse** crops good selectivity

Butachlor (Machete – 50% EC) – for rice no.1 herbicide

Metolachlor (Dual – 50% EC)

Propanil (Stam F 34)

Pretilachlor (Sofit/Refit)- Used in **rice**

- **Sofit is without surfactant** and **refit is with surfactant**

xiii) Organo phosphorus compounds:

e.g., Glyphosate (Roundup – 41% EC) – manufactured by Monsanto

(Glycil – 41% EC) - manufactured by Indofil

Anilofos (Aniloguard – 30% EC) – used in **rice**

- Do not use **glyphosate** in cropped area

7) Based on mode of action

a) Cell division inhibitors: cell division, elongation, tissue differentiation are some of the processes in plants directly affected by some of the herbicides.

i) Microtubule assembly inhibitors:

- During mitosis in metaphase the spindle structures which attach one of the two chromatids of a chromosome and draw them to either of the poles.
- These spindles are composed of filamentous protein called as **microtubulin**.
- Herbicides in sensitive plants binds to the **tubulin** in the cytoplasm and further growth of microtubule ceases and eventually complete loss of microtubules.

  e.g., Dinitroanilines (Pendimethalin, fluchloralin, trifluralin)

ii) Mitosis inhibitors:

- Herbicides block the mitosis in primary meristems. Action relates to mitotic aberrations.

  e.g., Carbamates, thiocarbamates

b) Photosynthesis inhibitors:

- In photosynthesis many herbicides interfere in **hill reaction (light reaction)**. As a result subsequent CO_2 fixation is retarded due to reduced supply of products of light reaction which are essential for dark reaction.
- A large number of herbicides block electron transport in **photo system II**.

  e.g., Triazines, uracils, urea group, Bipyridillium group (Diquat and paraquat)

c) Aminoacid/ protein synthesis inhibitors:

1) Blocking or inhibiting EPSP synthase enzyme :

- **5-Enol Pyruvyl Shikimate 3-Phosphate Synthase enzyme** is involved in biosynthesis of 3 aromatic aminoacids such as **phenyl alanine, tryptophane and tyrosine**.
- **Glyphosate** blocks or inhibits the action of EPSP synthase enzyme.

2) ALS synthase enzyme inhibitors:

- **Aceto lactate synthase** enzyme is involved in biosynthesis of **branched chain aminoacids** such as **leucine, isoleucine and valine**.
- Sulfonyl urea group of herbicides like **chlorosulfuron, Bensulfuron methyl, chlorimuron ethyl, metsulfuron methyl** and **imidazolinones (imazethapyr)** inhibit the action of ALS synthase enzyme.

3) Glutamine synthesis inhibitors:

- **Glutamine synthetase enzyme** is involved in glutamine synthesis. It plays important role in nitrogen metabolism in plant system. By this enzyme ammonia in plant system is converted into aminoacids and glutamic acid.
- **Glufosinate** inhibits glutamine synthesis

d) Lipid biosynthesis inhibitors

- Lipids constitute major components of **cell membranes, tonoplast, cuticular waxes** and **reserved food** in the seeds.
- **Acetyl Coenzyme A carboxylase** is involved in the biosynthesis of fatty acids.

e.g., Clodinafop-propargyl, Diclofop-methyl, fenoxoprop-p-ethyl, fluazifop-p-butyl. These herbicides are grass killers and have good selectivity for dicotyledonous plants.

HERBICIDE SELECTIVITY

- **Selectivity** refers to the phenomenon wherein the herbicide kills the target plant species in a mixed plant population without harming or slightly affecting the other plants.
- **Selectivity** is considered as the greatest single factor that helped the chemical weed control to succeed since the advent of 2,4-D.

Factors achieving selectivity

1) **Differential absorption of herbicide** by crop plants and weeds. Also called as physical selectivity or depth protection selectivity
2) **Differential translocation of herbicides:** After the absorption of herbicide by weed and plant, translocation is **more** in sensitive one (weeds) and less in tolerant one.
   - For 2,4-D the rate of translocation is **very slow in sugarcane** that's why 2,4-D got selectivity in sugarcane. The rate of translocation is **rapid in beans**.
3) **Differential rate of deactivation of herbicide by the plants:**
   - Rate of deactivation differs from plant to plant. In tolerant species rate of deactivation is fast, viceversa

     e.g., atrazine, simazine – deactivation is very fast in maize as well as sorghum
   - Similarly isoproturon is selective to wheat mainly due to its increased detoxification inside the wheat plant , whereas *Phalaris minor* is killed because detoxification is slow
4) **Difference in specific physiology of crop:**
   - The **physiological tolerance** of plants to herbicides may result from its failure to translocate the absorbed herbicide from the site of absorption to site of action. They also differ in rate of metabolism of herbicides.
   - **Conjugation** is the mechanism by which herbicide molecules are transformed to non-toxic form. 2,4-D is transformed to **β-D Glucose ester**.
5) **Chronological selectivity :** Achieved by difference in the time of application of herbicides
   - Chronological selectivity is achieved through time of application of herbicide and dosage
   - Selectivity is also dose dependent

HERBICIDE MOVEMENT IN PLANTS

1) Symplastic movement

- It is source to sink translocation.
- The herbicides move through **phloem** with sugars or photosynthates produced during photosynthesis.
- **Sinks** are the sites where sugars translocated from the source are used for growth process or stored.
- **Source** is nothing but fully expanded and growing leaves
- **Sink** is nothing but buds, growing shoots, roots, flowers, fruits and seeds.
- Sugars while moving from source to sink through symplast carry along some **post emergent** herbicides.
- In all foliage applied and post-emergent herbicides the herbicide movement is called **symplastic movement**.
- It requires metabolic energy and the movement is **basipetal (apex to base).**
- Symplastic movement is always through **phloem.**

  e.g., Glyphosate, 2, 4-D

2) Apoplastic movement

- The herbicides are primarily absorbed by the roots and move predominantly through **xylem and intercellular spaces** in plants.
- They move along with water (**passive movement**) or mineral nutrient ions (**active movement**).
- Therefore the herbicide molecules movement may or may not require metabolic energy.
- In **soil applied or pre-emergent herbicides** the usual basis of herbicide movement is apoplastic movement.

FACTORS AFFECTING THE EFFICIENCY OF HERBICIDES

1) SOIL APPLIED HERBICIDES

a) **Soil moisture:** It is of prime importance to soil applied herbicides. Optimum soil moisture is important. Too dry or too low or very high moisture conditions are undesirable.

b) **Soil texture:** Smaller the soil particles greater the surface area and more absorption of herbicide is likely to occur. Clay will absorb more herbicide than sand.

c) **Organic matter:** Higher the organic matter content greater is the adsorption of herbicide and less herbicide is available for plants uptake and it will reduce herbicide activity. So dose of herbicide should be increased to accomplish desired level of weed control.

d) **Runoff:** Herbicide is subjected to lateral movement with runoff water if it rains immediately or within few days after application of herbicide.

e) **Temperature:** At higher temperature conditions greater uptake and translocation of herbicide is expected to occur because of higher translocation. Metabolism of herbicide may also take place at higher rates.

   Ex: Atrazine

   - Atrazine loses selectivity to **maize** when temperatures are very **low**.

f) Use of recommended herbicide

g) Dosage of herbicide

h) Time of application

2) FOLIAGE APPLIED HERBICIDES

a) **Plant morphology:** Canopy surface, leaf orientation or angle, location of growing points, hairyness, and presence of waxy layer on stem.

b) **Relative humidity:** If the relative humidity is high the spray solution may evaporate more slowly and there will be more opportunity time for the droplets to penetrate the leaves.

c) Spray drift

d) Wash off

HERBICIDE MIXTURES

- Mechanical and chemical mixing of two or more herbicides having different mode of action and varying level of activity and selectivity forms **herbicide mixtures**.
- Herbicides of the **same class** or different classes having **similar mode of action** are not ideal for herbicidal mixture.

- Herbicides having **similar spectrum of weed control** should not be opted for mixing.

Types of herbicide mixtures

1) Factory mix/premix/readymix

It is the mixture of desired herbicides prepared in the **factory** itself with definite proportions.

e.g., Isoguard plus (Isoproturon + 2,4-D)

Aniloguard plus (Anilophos + 2,4-D)

Primaguard (Atrazine + Metolachlor)

Atlantis (Mesosulfuron-methyl + Iodosulfuron methyl sodium)

Almix (Metsulfuron methyl + Chlorimuron ethyl) – used in **rice**

Pursuit plus (Pendimethalin + Imazethapyr)

2) Tank mix/ field mix herbicide mixtures

It is mechanical mixing of two or more herbicides before their application in the **field**.

e.g., Atrazine + Alachlor

Atrazine + Pendimethalin

Isoproturon + Tralkoxydim

Sethoxydim + Chlorosulfuron

EFFECTS OF HERBICIDE MIXTURE INTERACTIONS

1) **Synergistic effect:** It is derived from the **cooperative** action of two or more herbicides in a mixture.

   (AB) > (A) + (B)

   Mixture effect of herbicide is more than the effect of herbicide A and B independently.

2) **Antagonistic effect:** The **decrease in normal biological activity** of one or all component herbicides in a mixture is referred as antagonistic effect.

   If (A) > (B) then (AB) < (A)

3) **Additive effect:** It refers to the **combined action** of component herbicides in the mixture when the total effect of mixture = sum total effect of the component herbicides when applied independently.

   (AB) = (A) + (B)

4) **Enhancement effect:** It generally occurs when adjuvant is mixed with active ingredient in the formulation and it increases the efficacy of herbicide than obtained with active ingredient alone.

e.g., Fenoxaprop-p-ethyl

- Fenoxaprop-p-ethyl is a **grass killer** used in **soybean** under the tradename "**whip super**", while same herbicide is used in **wheat** under different trade name "**pumasuper**".
- The differential action of same herbicide is attributed to different **adjuvants** used in the formulations.

Advantages of herbicide mixtures

- Controls broad spectrum weeds.
- Prevents shift in weed flora.
- Delays development of resistance in weeds.
- Increases the weed control efficiency.
- Reduced dosage of herbicides per unit area.
- Because of reduced rate of application reduced residue in crop and environment.

HERBICIDE MIXTURES FOR CROPS

1) Rice:

Anilophos (0.4 kg) + 2,4-DEE (0.5 kg)/ha

Butachlor (1 kg) + Propanil (2.0 kg)

Anilophos (0.3 kg) + chlorimuron ethyl (0.004 kg)

Anilophos (0.3 kg) + metsulfuron – methyl (0.004 kg)

Pretilachlor + 2,4-DEE for upland rice

2) Wheat and Barley

Diclofop-methyl (750 g) + Isoproturon (500g)

Isoproturon (750 g) + 2,4-D (250 g)

Clodinafop (60 g) + Isoproturon (500 g)

Fenoxaprop – p- ethyl (120 g) + 2,4-D (500g)

3) Maize and sorghum

Atrazine (0.5 kg) + Alachlor (1.0 kg)

Atrazine (0.75 kg) + Pendimethalin (0.75 kg)

Atrazine + 2,4-D

4) Soybean

Pendimethalin + Imazethapyr

Metribuzin + Chlorimuron ethyl

Oxadiazon + Metolachlor

5) Sunflower

Fluchloralin + Metolachlor

6) Cotton

Pendimethalin + Diuron

7) Sugarcane

Atrazine + 2,4-D

FATE OF HERBICIDE IN SOIL

- **Fate** and **persistence** of herbicide although seems to be similar are not synonymous rather they are related with each other.
- If fate processes are considered as **cause** persistent is the effect.
- Of the total herbicide applied to the soil only a small amount is actually utilized for controlling the weeds. The rest of herbicide is subjected to various processes like physical removal or transfer and decomposition.

1) **Physical processes:** These processes take the herbicide away from the root zone of the plant.
   - a) **Adsorption:** Adherence of herbicide molecule on clay colloids and humus and it is unavailable for plant uptake.
   - b) **Leaching:** It is physical movement of herbicide molecule in soil through percolating water.
   - c) **Runoff:** The herbicide molecule gets lost through the surface runoff water.
   - d) **Volatilization:** Some herbicides are lost in gaseous form through volatilization.

     e.g., Fluchloralin

2) Decomposition processes

a) Microbial decomposition: Also called as **biodegradation** process. It is the **major mode** of herbicide decomposition in soil. It is through hydrolysis, alkalization, hydroxylation, oxidation, reduction and conjugation.

- OH^-, $COOH^-$, NO_2^- provide point of attack by microorganisms

b) Chemical decomposition:

- It is **less common mode** of decomposition of herbicide from soil than biodegradation.
- The chemical reaction between **herbicides and soil constituents** tend to inactivate the herbicides.

c) Photodecomposition:

- Some herbicides undergo molecular alteration when exposed to sunlight due to photochemical reaction which results in deactivation.
- An ideal fate of herbicide in the soil on crop plants is the one that brings about selective control of weeds for sufficiently longer period, at the same time allows the herbicide to dissipate from the soil before the close of the crop season so that succeeding crop in the rotation should be planted safely.
- The very rapid loss of herbicide will cause inefficient weed control.

PERSISTENCE OF HERBICIDES

- The length of time that a herbicide remains active in the soil after its initial application is called as **persistence**.
- For effective weed control herbicides must remain in active and available form until the purpose is served. At the same time longer period of persistence pose residual problem in the soil.
- Herbicides injure **sensitive crops** in the cropping sequence.
- Herbicides inhibit the activity of microorganisms in soil.
- Factors influencing the persistence of herbicide are **soil moisture, soil temperature, soil type, organic matter content in the soil and microorganisms activity in the soil**.
- Herbicides cause soil and water pollution

Herbicides	Time of persistence
Phenoxyacid group: 2,4-D Fluazifop-p-butyl Fenoxaprop-p-ethyl Diclofop-methyl	Upto 1 month
Metsulfuron methyl Metolachlor Linuron Prometryne Bromoxynil	1-3 months
Atrazine Simazine Metribuzine Chlorimuron ethyl Alachlor Pendimethalin Oxyfluorfen Oxadiazon Acetachlor	3-12 months
Chlorosulfuron Picloram Bromacil Terbacil	More than 12 months

MANAGEMENT OF HERBICIDE RESIDUE IN THE SOIL

- Use of optimum dose of herbicide.
- Application of organic manures like FYM, compost, green manuring increases surface area so that herbicides gets adsorbed.
- Ploughing the soil increases porosity and soil volume, so that there will be more infiltration and leaching of herbicide.
- Use of herbicide safeners to reduce the phytotoxic effects on crop plants.

- Frequent irrigation leads to leaching of herbicide beyond root zone.
- Use of **activated carbon** which has high adsorptive capacity because of its tremendous surface area. Incorporation of **activated charcoal @ 50 kg/ha** completely inactivate **chlorosulfuron** in the soil.

HERBICIDE FORMULATIONS

- **Active ingredient** is a pure and concentrated form of toxicant present in the formulated product which is responsible for herbicidal activity.
- Active ingredient is expressed in **percentage** and always written on the container of the herbicide.

  e.g., 50% EC, 25% WP, 30% EC

  Atrataf 50% WP
- Many herbicides used are originally **acids** and they are converted into salts, amines and ester products before formulations to reduce the ill effect of acids. Therefore **acid equivalent (ae)** is used to designate the toxic material in formulations in earlier days.
- Most of the herbicides cannot be applied in their original form. These have to be made or formulated in forms suitable and safe for their field use, such forms are called **herbicide formulations**.
- The herbicide formulations are prepared by the manufacturers by blending the toxicant (ai) with substances like **solvents, carriers, surfactants, stickers, stabilizing agents** etc.
- There are two groups of herbicide formulations

  1) Formulations applied after their dilution with water

  a) **Emulsifiable concentrates (EC):** the EC formulations form an emulsion when added to water before spraying. It appears like **milky white**.

  e.g., Pendimethalin, fluchloralin, alachlor, paraquat, diquat, oxyfluorfen, anilophos, metolachlor

  b) Wettable powders (WP):

  It is a finely milled powder which forms a suspension on mixing with water. *e.g.,* Triazine group, atrazine, simazine, phenyl ureas

  - EC and wettable powders are the two most popular formulations present in market

c) Soluble liquids (SL)
d) Soluble powders (SP)
e) Dry flowables (DF)
f) Concentrate emulsion (CE)

2) Formulations applied as such

Granules (G):

- Usually size varies from **0.04 – 1.0 mm.**
- Concentration is usually < **10%.**
- If size of granules is < **0.04 mm** drift problem will be there.
  e.g., Butachlor (machete – 5% G)-used in **wetland paddy**
  Trifluralin
- Butachlor is available in both **EC** and **granular form**.
- Advantages of using granular formulations are ease of application, no drift problem, requires less labour and time.
- Disadvantage of using granular formulations is sufficient moisture should be needed. So granular formulations are best suited for **lowland rice** cultivation.

  Degree of toxicity – indicating colour
  Extremely hazardous – **Red**
  Highly hazardous – **yellow**
  Moderately hazardous – **blue**
  Slightly hazardous – **green**
- Quantity of commercial formulation required

$$\frac{\text{Recommended dosage of a.i of that particular herbicide}}{\text{Active ingredient (a.i)}}$$

HERBICIDE RESIDUE ESTIMATION IN SOIL

- Herbicide residue in soil can be determined by
  1) Biological method/ Bio – assay
  2) Chemical method / Analytical method

1) Biological method (Bio-assay)

Bio-living

Assay – procedure or method to estimate residue in soil

- It simply represents a method of determining the level or amount of herbicide residue present in soil employing highly sensitive crops. It is quantitative as well as qualitative.
- Bioassay may be pot bio-assay or field bio-assay.
- Bioassay remains a major tool for qualitative and quantitative determination of herbicides. It is more economical, less difficult to perform and do not require expensive equipment. The sensitivity of crops to the level of herbicide residue in soil is reflected through variable growth inhibition levels.

Indicator plants for herbicides

Atrazine – cucumber, soybean, mustard

Isoproturon/ Diuron – cucumber, barley, sorghum, millets

Alachlor – cucumber

Metolachlor – rice, sorghum and cucumber

Fluazifop-p-butyl – maize

Metribuzin – maize and sorghum

2,4-D – cucumber, cotton, mustard, tomato, soybean

Sulphonyl ureas – sunflower, maize, sorghum, mung bean

- Germination percentage, root length, shoot length and dry weight of plants are measured.
- Herbicides applied as spray solutions or as granular applications.
- For majority of the herbicides **spraying** is the most common method.
- Sprayers are hand operated and power driven

Sprayer type	Capacity
Low volume sprayer	150-200 litres/ha
Medium volume sprayer	250-300 litres/ha
High volume sprayer	500-750 litres/ha
Ultra low volume sprayer	5 litres/ha

- **Nozzle** breaks spray solution into very fine droplets.
- Nozzle function is to disintegrate or atomize spray liquid into very fine droplets and discharge the liquid in a designed pattern.

- **Cone type nozzle, fan type nozzle, flood jet type** are different types of nozzles.
- Most suitable type of nozzle is **flood jet**, reason is **uniform application** of herbicide application is possible without any gaps.
- In flood jet different types of nozzles are available with nozzle no.24, 40, 60, 78.
- With increase in nozzle number droplet size **increases**.
- Nozzle no.24 droplets are very very small or fine.

HERBICIDE RESISTANT WEEDS

Percentage use of different pesticides

Pesticide	**World**	**USA**	**India**
Herbicides	43%	55%	12%
Insecticides	33%	32%	77%
Fungicides	17%	7%	8%
Others	7%	6%	3%

- Herbicide resistance now has become a worldwide phenomenon continuously expanding its number and frequency.
- Long term continuous use of a single herbicide with similar mode of action may result in weed resistance to herbicides apart from shift in weed flora.
- The first report of weed resistant to herbicide was noticed during 1968 in ***Senecio vulgaris*** a biotype resistant to **triazine** herbicide.
- Among different countries **USA** first in weedicide resistance by weeds then Australia, Canada, France, Spain, UK.
- In India ***Phalaris minor*** **(canary grass)** developed resistance to isoproturon during **1992-93**. This herbicide has been widely used continuously for 10-15 days.
- Due to resistance the control of ***Phalaris minor*** dropped from 78% to 27% within a span of 3 years causing yield loss to the tune of 40-60% in the affected areas.

  1) Atrazine resistant weeds

  Senecio vulgaris

  Chenopodium album

Amaranthus retroflexa

Solanum nigrum

2) **Paraquat resistant weeds**

Solanum nigrum

Bidens pilosa

Eleusine indica

3) **Isoproturon resistant weeds**

Phalaris minor

Convolvulus arvensis

4) **2,4-D**

Daucus carota (wild carrot)

Commelina diffusa

5) **Glyphosate**

Lolium rigidum

Eleusine indica

Ambrosia artemisiifolia (rag weed)

TYPES OF RESISTANCE

1) **Simple resistance:** It is simply the resistance of a weed species due to **continuous exposure** to a particular herbicide. Resistance may be **partial or complete**.

2) **Cross resistance:** It evolves when a weed species already resistant to a herbicide shows resistance to another herbicide of the same herbicide class or same mode of action.

   e.g., Phalaris minor develop resistance to isoproturon in course of time gained cross resistance to diclofop-methyl, fenoxaprop-p-ethyl, clodinafop-propargyl.

3) **Multiple resistance:**

   It is the resistance through which a weed species shows resistance to herbicides of different classes or families having different modes of action.

   e.g., Lolium rigidum resistant to various groups of herbicides first reported in **Australia**.

- Development of resistance in weeds is a complex phenomenon influenced by **weed persistence, herbicide use pattern, cropping practices (monocropping)** adopted for many years.

- Weeds do not change to become resistant instead **weed population** changes. Weed population is extremely diverse in nature even though they are highly similar in morphology or appearance, minor differences exist at **genetic level**. These minor differences confer the variant plants the inherent ability to resist to herbicides.
- The resistant population so called the **biotypes** thus evolve have hardly any eventual differences morphologically with susceptible ones.
- It is difficult to distinguish between the resistant and the susceptible ones. They however may differ **physiologically and biochemically**.
- The possible mechanisms in resistant weeds are
  1) Change in rate of absorption and translocation
  2) Rate of degradation or metabolism of herbicide
  3) Target site alteration

MANAGEMENT OF HERBICIDE RESISTANCE

- Change in the cropping season *i.e* avoid monocropping and adopt crop rotation.
- Abandonment of the herbicide to which the weeds are showing resistance.
- Evaluate alternate herbicides
- Herbicide mixtures may be used
- Herbicide rotation
- Adoption of integrated weed management practices

HERBICIDE RESISTANT CROPS (HRC's)

- Selective herbicide technology in many situations fails to provide a complete control of weeds throughout the season since weeds have periodicity.
- Limitations of selective herbicide technology are
  1) Development of weed resistance for herbicides
  2) Residue problem
  3) Pollution

4) Phytotoxicity
5) Narrow spectrum activity

- Above limitations urged for the development of an ideal herbicide which could render selective control of all the weeds, least phytotoxicity, least propensity for the development of resistance, less residue in the soil, safety to the environment.
- Any herbicide possessing all the above features to satisfy is very difficult to develop. This has called for the research activity towards developing the crops or varieties which are resistant to non selective herbicides.
- **Non selective herbicides** provide complete control of weeds when herbicide resistant crops are used. They are safe to the environment and have least herbicide ill effects.
- HRC's offer tremendous potential towards weed management in crops.
- HRC's should be put to use as an ideal component of integrated weed management system.
- HRC's are **genetically modified crops** to which resistance to certain non selective herbicides such as glyphosate, glufosinate, bromoxynil *etc.* has been conferred through biotechnological tools.
- HRC's were commercially introduced first in **Canada** through **Atrazine resistant canola** variety long back in 1984.

HRC	Herbicide	Trade name	Company
Canola	Glufosinate Glyphosate	Liberty Link Canola Roundup Ready Rape	Agr EVO Monsanto
Maize	Glufosinate Glyphosate	Liberty Link Corn Roundup Ready Corn	Agr EVO Monsanto
Soybean	Glufosinate Glyphosate Sulphonyl urea	Liberty Link Soybean Roundup Ready Soybean STS Soybean	Agr EVO Monsanto Dupont company
Cotton	Glufosinate Glyphosate	Liberty Link Cotton Roundup Ready Cotton	Agr EVO Monsanto

- HRC's are available in rice, tobacco, tomato, potato etc.
- HRC's are very popular in USA, Europe, Canada and Australia.

- Breeding new HRC's is **more economical** than developing a new selective herbicide.
- **Genetic engineering** has made the process in developing HRC's less time consuming process.
- Marketing of HRC's is more market driven since the consult MNC's will sell seed as well as herbicides.

ADVANTAGES OF ADOPTING HRC'S:

- HRC's offer broad spectrum and higher weed control efficiency
- Safe use of non selective herbicides
- Facilitate wider window application
- Higher crop yield is expected through greater reduction in weed competition
- No or less problem of herbicide resistance
- Best suited for reduced or no tillage farming.

LIMITATIONS OF HRC'S:

- Fear of monopoly of MNC's
- Increased dependence on a single herbicide
- HRC's influence on genetic purity of neighboring crops or wild relatives through generation of **super weeds**.
- There is apprehension of possible gene flow from HRC's to its wild relatives and weeds which may develop super weeds through **hybridization**.
- Multidirectional uncontrolled gene flow may result in **gene pollution**.
- Safety of genetically modified crops food is also a concern among the people.
- HRC's may limit the biodiversity
- Abandonment of IWM in course of time

BIOLOGICAL WEED CONTROL

- Antagonism is the balance in the world of nature, where there is life there is antagonism.

- There exists a **pyramid of number** in every ecosystem balancing the population of one individual by other individual.

  e.g., cow-grass

  Insects – plants

  Frog –insects

  Snake – frog
- Existence of each and every individual, host or pest is highly essential on this earth and this preserves biodiversity.
- **Biological control** is defined as the control of an organism employing another living organism or a biological entity to a population lower than what normally occurs in the absence of that organism.
- Biological control of weeds simply means controlling the weeds below their **economic threshold level** using another organism like insects, herbivorous fishes, pathogens, competitive plants.
- Insects are more frequently used than any other bioagents for biological control of weeds mostly under non cropped situations.
- The first effort at biological control of weeds is to control **Cacti in India** in **1863** by cochineal insect known as ***Dactylopius tomentosus***. This insect is able to suppress ***Opuntia dillenii***.
- Worst situation in Australia was 30 m ha land was infested with ***Opuntia inermis***.
- Many ranches were abandoned due to infestation of **prickly pear** in Australia.
- ***Cactoblastis cactorum* (moth)** is effective against ***Opuntia inermis***.
- ***Dactylopius opuntiae*** imported from USA found effective against **prickly pear**.
- ***Lantana camara*** is a shrub native of **Central America** and **Mexico**.
- ***Lantana camara*** was introduced to **Hawaii islands** in **1860**. It invaded large areas of range lands.
- ***Crosidosema lantana* (moth) larvae** bore through flowers, fruits, seeds and foliage of lantana.
- ***Agromyza lantanae*** feeds on seeds of ***Lantana camara***.

- ***Telonemia scrupulosa*** was identified in **India** for control of ***Lantana camara.***
- ***Zygogramma bicolorata*** **(Mexican beetle)** feeds on foliage of parthenium.
- Activity of Mexican beetle is restricted to rainy season and it hibernates in **winter season.**
- ***Epiblema sternuana*** **(gall insect)** is used for control of **parthenium.**
- ***Neochetina eichhornae*** tunnels petioles and stem of **water hyacinth (*Eichhornea crassipes*).**
- ***Neochetina bruchi*** also controls **water hyacinth.**

Features of good bioagent

1) It should be host specific
2) It should have good adaptability
3) It should have high multiplication rate
4) It should be fast feeding on the target plant
5) It should be free from natural enemies

- The regulation of population of an individual pest below the **economic threshold level** is the principal philosophy behind biological control.
- Biological control exercises to limit the infestation to a level at which they will not highly damaging to the crops.

Advantages of biological weed control:

1) Ecofriendly
2) Economical in the long run though initial cost is high.
3) It is self perpetuating and long lasting.
4) It is effective in areas which are not easily accessible for man to control weeds.

Disadvantages of biological weed control:

1) High initial cost
2) Chances of bioagent feeding on economic crops

   Ex: ***Zygogramma bicolorata*** which is a bioagent on Parthenium also feeds on sunflower and niger.

   Teleonemia scrupulosa which is a bioagent on ***Lantana camara*** also feeds on **teak.**

3) Limited use in crop yield which witnesses composite culture of weeds.
4) Slow in action
5) Adaptability of bioagent to the new area.
6) Narrow span of activity. They will not be active throughout the year.

BIOHERBICIDES/MYCOHERBICIDES

- **Bioherbicides** are the native pathogenic (fungal spores) inoculums sprayed on the target weeds to control.

Devine:

- Developed in **USA**
- Contains fungal extracts of ***Phytopthora palmivora***.
- It is effective against **strangle vine weed**.

Collego:

- Contains fungal spores of ***Colletotrichum gloeosporioides***.
- Effective against **joint vetch weed**.
- It is predominant weed in **rice** and **soybean** fields.
- It causes **stem blight**.

Biomal:

- Developed in **Canada**
- Contains fungal extracts of ***Colletotrichum gloeosporioides***.
- Effective against ***Malva pusilla***, which is a major weed in **wheat growing regions in Canada.**
- It causes **anthracnosis.**

ABG-5003

- Contains spores of ***Cercospora rodmanii***
- Effective against ***Eichhornia crassipes***
- It causes **leaf spot**

Characteristics of Bioherbicides

- Bioherbicides are living inoculums of plant pathogens mainly the fungus.

- They are capable of invitro culturing in artificial media.
- They are applied directly on the target weed.
- They are commercially formulated and sprayed like herbicides over the weeds.

PARASITIC WEEDS

- **Parasitic weeds** are defined as weeds, which depend partly or fully for their growth on their host
- **> 2500** plant species known as parasitic weeds.
- Reasons for arising of parasitic weeds are **monocropping, shortened fallow period due to intensive cultivation**.
- Nutrient and water transported *via* **haustorium (physiological bridge)**.
- Parasite connects its vascular system to the host plant.
- **Cuscuta** is a complete stem parasite.
- **Loranthus** is a partial stem parasite.
- **Orobanche** is a complete root parasite.
- **Striga** is a partial root parasite.
- **30-70%** yield loss in **tobacco** due to **Orobanche** infestation in India.
- **94%** yield loss in rice fallow pulse crop in AP due to infestation of **cuscuta**.
- **37-42**% yield reduction in **teak** in Kerala due to **Loranthus** infestation.
- Trapcrops for striga are **sunflower, castor, linseed, cotton, cowpea, pea, soybean, groundnut, sunhemp**.
- Striga infestation in sorghum reduced with increase in **soil nitrogen**.
- Striga can be controlled by preplant incorporation of **fluchloralin** @ **0.5-0.75 kg/ha** or by post emergence application of **2,4-D** @ **0.5-1.0 kg/ha**.
- Orobanche has very well developed **xylem and phloem** continuity with tobacco.
- In **striga** phloem is lacking.

- Trap crops for Orobanche are **garlic, castor, linseed, green gram, cowpea, french bean, soybean, pea**.

Chemical control of Orobanche:

a) **Pre-plant incorporation**

Imazethapyr @ 50-100 g a.i/ha

Imazaquin @ 100 g a.i/ha

Imazabyr @ 20 g a.i/ha

b) **Postemergence**

Imazethapyr @ 60 g a.i/ha

- Orobanche is controlled by the phytophagous insect ***Phytomyza orobanche***.
- By spraying some of the natural as well as synthetic stimulants to the soil striga seeds germinate. After germination due to non availability of host plants striga seeds will die. This is called **suicidal germination of Striga**.
- **Cuscuta** infests **zizyphus, citrus**.
- Loranthus infests **teak, mango, citrus, custard apple, eucalyptus, guava, apple, peach**.

AQUATIC WEED MANAGEMENT

- Aquatic weeds are those plants which grow in and around water bodies.
- ***Monochoria vaginalis*** – carpet weed
- ***Salvinia molesta*** **(water fern)** – floating weed
- Examples of emergent weeds are ***Typha angustata*** **(cat tail), *Ipomea carnea, Marsilea quadrifolia.***
- ***Pistia stratiotes*** – water lettuce
- Examples of submerged weeds are ***Hydrilla verticillata, Potamogeton*** **(pond weed), *Vallisnaria spiralis*** **(Eel grass).**

Chapter 18

Cropping and Farming Systems

- A **system** consists of several components which are closely related and interacting among themselves.
- **System** is an arrangement of components which process inputs into outputs. Consists of boundaries, components, interactions between components, inputs and outputs.
- **Crop system** is an arrangement of crop populations that transform solar radiation, nutrients, water and other inputs into useful biomass.
- **Crop system** is a subsystem of cropping system.
- In Maize crop system, Maize is the dominant crop which is grown in association with other crops.
- **Cropping system** is a land use unit comprising of soils, crops, weeds, pathogen and insect subsystems that transform solar energy, water, nutrients, labour and other inputs into food, feed, fuel and fibre.
- **Cropping system** is a sub system of farming system.
- Cropping system is also defined as cropping patterns used on a farm and their interaction with farm resources, other than farm enterprises, available technology and environment (physical, biological and socio economic) which determine their makeup constitute cropping system.
- Livestock system is a land use unit comprising of livestock and auxiliary feed sources transforming plant biomass into animal products.
- **Farming system** is a decision making and land use unit comprising of farm house hold, cropping and livestock systems that produce crop and livestock products for consumption and sale.

- **Farming system** is the scientific integration of different interdependent and interacting enterprises for efficient use of land, labour and other resources of a farm family which provides year round income to the farmers specially in the handicapped zone.
- Enterprises that could be included in farming system are crops, vegetables, livestock, fruits, flowers, dairy, poultry, pig, goat, sericulture, bee keeping, mushroom cultivation, agroforestry, silviculture, agrobased industries and food processing.
- Farming system is a resource management strategy to achieve economic and sustained production to meet diverse requirements of farm house hold while a system is preserving resource base and maintaining a high level of environmental quality.
- **Agro-ecosystem:** Agro-ecosystems are ecological systems modified by human beings to produce food, fibre or other agricultural products.
- Agro-ecosystems are structurally and dynamically complex and the complexity arises from interaction between socioeconomic and ecological processes.
- **Agro – Ecological zone** is an area of similar soil, vegetation and population density characteristics resulting in a similar type of cropping system.
- Efficient cropping zone is the zone where both **yield and spread indices** are maximum.

$$\text{Yield index of a crop} = \frac{\text{Avg. yield of crop in zone / state}}{\text{Avg. yield of crop in country}} \times 100$$

$$\text{Spread index of a crop} = \frac{\text{Area of crop in state/zone}}{\text{Area of crop in country}} \times 100$$

- Most efficient zone of a crop is where both the indices are **above 100** and least efficient zone of a crop is where the indices are below 100.
- **Cropping pattern** means the proportion of area under various crops at a point of time in a unit area. It indicates the yearly sequence and spatial arrangement of crops or of crops and fallow in a given area.
- **Cropping pattern** is crop rotation practiced by majority of farmers in a given area.

- **Crop rotation** refers to recurrent succession of crops on the same piece of land either in a year or over a longer period of time.
- **Crop rotation** is the key of modern scientific agriculture which aims at producing maximum yield by maintaining soil productivity.
- **Leys** are temporary, short term two to five years specially sown pastures consisting of grasses and legumes.
- **Ahlgren** defined **ley farming** as a system of farming in which grasses and legumes are included in proper rotation for hay, silage and pasture to care for maximum livestock needs and to improve and conserve soil fertility.
- In traditional agriculture the objective to increase production is by two means
  1) Increasing the area of cultivation
  2) Increasing productivity per unit area of crop
- But in modern agriculture two more dimensions are added
  1) Increasing the production per unit time
  2) Increasing production per unit space
- **Mixed farming** is a system of farming on a particular farm which includes crop production, raising livestock, poultry, fisheries, bee keeping etc. to sustain and satisfy as many needs of the farmer as possible.
- Objective of mixed farming is **subsistence**.
- **Sole cropping/solid planting** is the cultivation of one crop variety alone in pure stand at normal density in a certain time and place.
- **Cropping scheme** is the plan according to which crops are raised on individual plots of a farm with an objective of getting maximum returns from each crop without impairing soil fertility.
- Soil fertility and crop yields are important factors in determining which cropping programme to follow.
- **Amount of labour** and **capital required, prices in relation to resources** influence adoption of a particular cropping scheme.
- Repetitive growing of same crop on same land year after year is called **monoculture or monocropping**.
- **Cropping Intensity/Index** = No. of crops grown in a year in a piece of land × 100

- **Intercropping** is growing two or more crops simultaneously on same piece of land, base crop necessarily in distinct row arrangement.
- In intercropping cropping is intensified in time and space dimensions.
- **Annidation** is complementary interaction between intercrops in space and time dimensions. In multistorey cropping annidation in space occurs (different crops occupy different layers in space). In green gram and maize intercropping annidation in time occurs (nutrient requirement at different times).
- **Parallel cropping** is the cultivation of crops which have different natural habit and zero competition.

  e.g., Maize + Blackgram/Greengram

  Black gram/Greengram has peak nutrient demand at 30-35DAS whereas peak nutrient demand of Maize is 50DAS.
- In **companion cropping**, production of both intercrops is equal to that of its solid planting. Production of none is hardly affected.

  e.g., Sugarcane + Onion/Potato/Mustard
- In **synergistic cropping** yield of both crops is more than that of their pure crops on unit area basis.

  e.g., Sugarcane + Potato
- In **additive series intercropping** population of base crop or main crop is same as that of intercrop. Intercrop is introduced by adjusting planting geometry of main crop. Additive series intercropping is **prevalent in India**.

  e.g., Sowing of potato in Sugarcane sown at spacing of 90 cm.
- In **replacement series** intercropping both crops are component crops. Population of both crops are less than their pure stands. This is followed in **western countries**.

  e.g., 10th row of wheat is replaced by mustard, row distance of wheat is reduced to adjust the mustard crop.
- **Strip intercropping** is growing two or more crops simultaneously in strips wide enough to permit independent cultivation and narrow enough to interact agronomically.
- **Relay intercropping** is growing two or more crops simultaneously during the part of life cycle of each.

- In intercropping
  1) Time of peak nutrient demand of component crops should not overlap

     e.g., Maize + urd/Mung

     Peak nutrient demand of Urd/Mung is 30-35 DAS and Maize is 50DAS
  2) Competition for light should be minimum among component crops
  3) Competition for CO_2 and water should be minimum among the component crops.
  4) Difference in maturity of component crops should be atleast 30 days
  5) Complementarity should exist between component crops
- Scientific study of mixed farming was first done by **La-Flitze.**
- **Sequence cropping** is growing two or more crops in quick succession on the same piece of land in a farming year. Harvesting of first crop and sowing of second crop may be done simultaneously in quick succession.

  e.g., Maize – Potato – Chilli
- Ratoon cropping also classified under **sequence cropping.**
- **Relay cropping** is growing two or more crops simultaneously during the part of life cycle of each.
- In relay cropping succeeding crops are planted before the harvest of first crop.

  e.g., Maize – Potato – Raddish

  Potato is planted before harvesting of Maize and Raddish is planted before harvesting of potato.
- Paira cropping (WB & Bihar) and utera cropping (MP) are good examples of relay cropping.
- **Paira cropping or utera cropping** means sowing of Lathyrus or Lentil (generally pulses) before the harvest of paddy in lowland area.
- **SS Bains** suggested following **relay cropping** for North West India

  Mung – Maize – Potato –Wheat.
- **Double cropping** is growing two crops a year in sequence.
- **Triple cropping** is growing three crops a year in sequence.

- **Quadraple cropping** is growing four crops a year in sequence.
- Practice of growing different crops of varying height, rooting pattern, duration is called **multistorey cropping**.
- In multistorey cropping taller component tolerates strong light and high evaporative demand. Shorter component requires shade or relative humidity.

  e.g., Coconut + Black pepper + Cocoa + Pineapple
- **Competition and yield advantage** are assessed by LER, Relative Yield Total, Relative Crowding Coefficient, Aggressivity, Competition Index, Competition Ratio and Competition Coefficient.

Land Equivalent Ratio (LER)

- Land Equivalent Ratio (LER) denotes relative land area under sole crop required to give the same yield as obtained under a mixed or an intercropping system at the same level of management.

$$LER = La + Lb = \frac{Ya}{Sa} + \frac{Yb}{Sb}$$

  La = LER of crop a, Lb = LER of crop b

  Ya and Yb = Yield of individual crops a & b respectively in mixture

  Sa & Sb = yield of individual crops a & b respectively in pure stand
- LER gives an accurate assessment of the biological efficiency of intercropping.
- When **LER>1,** intercropping is beneficial
- The most important index of biological advantage is the **relative yield total (RYT) introduced by de Wit and Van den Bergh** (1965) or **land equivalent ratio (LER) reviewed by Willey** (1979).
- The mixture yield of a component crop expressed as a portion of its yield as a sole crop from the same replacement series is the relative yield of the crop and the sum of relative yields of component crops is called relative yield total (RYT).
- The total land area required under sole cropping to give the same yields obtained in the intercropping mixture is called **land equivalent ratio (LER).**
- RYT and LER are similar.

Relative Crowding Coefficient (RCC)

- Relative Crowding Coefficient (RCC) was proposed by **de Wit (1960).**

- RCC is used in replacement series of intercropping. It indicates whether a species or crop, when grown in mixed population, has produced more or less yield than expected in pure stand.

In 50:50 mixture

$$\text{Kab}(\text{RCC}) = \frac{\text{Mixture yield of A}}{\text{Purestand yield of a} - \text{Mixture yield of B}} = \frac{\text{Yab}}{\text{Yaa} - \text{Yab}}$$

Yab = mixture yield of a crop grown with b
Yba = mixture yield of b crop grown with a
Yaa = yield in pure stand of crop a
Ybb = yield in pure stand of crop b
Zab = proportion of sown spp.a in mixture with b
Zba = proportion of sown spp.b in mixture with a

For all mixture

$$\text{Kab} = \frac{\text{Yab} \times \text{Zba}}{(\text{Yaa} - \text{Yab})\text{Zab}}$$

- **K>1** means **yield advantage** (more yield than expected)
- **K=1** means no difference between intercropping components
- **K<1** means yield **disadvantage** (less yield than expected)
- Crowding coefficient and LER give the yield advantage but only LER gives the magnitude of advantage. Therefore LER is preferred to assess the competition effects and yield advantage in intercropping situations.

Aggressivity:

- Aggressivity was proposed by **Mc Gilchrist (1965).**
- Aggressivity is the measure of how much the relative yield increase in component 'a' is greater than that of component 'b'.

$$\frac{\text{Mixture yield of a}}{\text{Expected yield of a}} - \frac{\text{Mixture yield of b}}{\text{Expected yield of b}} = \frac{\text{Yab}}{\text{Yaa} \times \text{Zab}} - \frac{\text{Yba}}{\text{Ybb} \times \text{Zba}}$$

- Aab = 0 means component crops are equally competitive
- Aab = negative means dominated
- Aggressivity and crowding coefficient can be used only in **replacement series** where as LER used both in **replacement and additive series.**

Competition Index:

- Competition Index (CI) was developed by **Donald (1963).**

- It is a measure to find out the yield of various crops when grown together as well as separately. It indicates the yield per plant of different crops in mixture and their respective pure stand on a unit area basis.

$$CI = \frac{(Yaa - Yab) \times (Ybb - Yba)}{Yaa \times Yab}$$

Competition Ratio (CR):

- Competition ratio of was proposed by **Willey and Rao (1980)**
- It is simply the ratio of individual LERs of the two component crops, but correcting for the proportion in which they were initially sown.

$$CR = \frac{Yab}{yaa \times Zab} \div \frac{Yba}{Ybb \times Zba}$$

$$= \frac{LERa}{LERb} \times \frac{Zba}{Zab}$$

Competition Coefficient (CC):

It is the ratio of relative crowding coefficient (RCC) of any given spp. in the mixture.

$$CC = \frac{\text{RCC of given spp}}{\text{Total RCC of all crops in a mixture}}$$

Crowding coefficient is used to find out the relative crowding from which maximum yield can be obtained without any adverse effect on any of the species.

Land use and productivity in multiple cropping are assessed by Multiple Cropping Index, Cropping Intensity Index, Cropping Intensity, Specific Crop Intensity Index, Cultivation Land Utilization Index, Diversity Index, Rotational Intensity, Harvest Diversity Index, Area Time Equivalent Ratio etc.

Multiple Cropping Index (MCI):

- Proposed by **Dalrymple (1971)**.
- Multiple Cropping Index measures the sum of areas planted to different crops and harvested in a single year divided by total cultivated area times 100.

Cropping Intensity Index (CII):

- Proposed by **Menegay et al.,** (1978)

- CII assesses a farmer's actual land use in area and time relationships for each crop or group of crops compared to the total available land area and time, including land temporarily available for production.
- Efficient cropping zone is judged by CII and LER.

Cropping intensity:

$$CI = \frac{\text{Total cropped area}}{\text{Net cultivated area}} \times 100$$

$$CI = \frac{\text{Area under kharif + rabi + zaid crops}}{\text{Area under actual cultivation}} \times 100$$

- Specific Crop Intensity Index (SCII) was also proposed by **Menegay et al. (1978)**.
- Cultivation Land utilization Index (CLUI) was proposed by **Chuang (1973)**.
- CLUI is calculated by summing the products of land area planted to each crop, multiplied by the actual duration of that crop and divided by the total cultivated land area times 365 days.
- Diversity Index (DI) was proposed by **Strout (1975) and Wang and Yu.**
- Rotational intensity = $\frac{\text{No.of crops grown in a field}}{\text{Years of rotation}} \times 100$

Area Time Equivalent Ratio (ATER):

- It takes into account the duration of crops and permits an evaluation of crops on yield per day basis. It is modification of LER.

$$ATER = \frac{LA \times DA + LB \times DB}{T}$$

Where, LA and LB are relative yields or partial LER of component crops A and B and DA and DB are duration of crops A and B and T is the total duration of the intercropping system.

Chapter 19

Maturity and Harvesting

- Post-harvest losses are estimated to be about **25** per cent.
- Harvesting cost constitute **20 to 50%** of total production cost in different crops.
- Closer row spacing of **less than 40 cm** helps in increasing the cotton yield, but increases the levels of **non-lint** material in the harvested produce.
- Removal of entire plants or economic parts after maturity from field is called **harvesting**.
- Portion of the stem that is left on the field is known as **stubble**.
- If the crop is harvested early, the produce contains high moisture and more immature grains.
- Late harvesting results in shattering of grains, germination even before harvesting during rainy season and breakage during processing.
- Crops can be harvested at **physiological maturity** or **harvest maturity**.
- Crop is considered to be at **physiological** maturity when the translocation of photosynthates is stopped to economic part.
- **Physiological maturity** refers to a developmental stage after which no further increase in dry matter occurs in the economic part
- In cereals, moisture content of grains is very high during **milking stage** and it gradually decreases due to accumulation of photosynthates.
- The moisture content falls steeply from **40 per cent to 20 per cent** which is an indication of attaining **physiological** maturity.
- At physiological maturity, translocation of carbohydrates is stopped due to formation of **abscission** layer between **rachis and grain**.

- The attainment of physiological maturity can be seen from external symptoms like
    1) **Black-layer** formation in **sorghum** and **maize**
    2) Loss of green colour from glumes in **wheat**
    3) **Bleaching of peduncle** beneath the ear in some varieties of **pearl millet**
    4) Turning of **green pods to brown** colour in **pulses**
    5) **Loss of green colour** from leaves in **soybean**
- **Black layer** formation near sorghum grain attachment coincides with cut-off of assimilate translocation.
- **Desiccation** is an important harvest management practice to hasten harvest especially for hybrids which stay green even at harvest maturity.
- Increased levels of the **stay-green** trait in sunflower may result in desiccation becoming a more common harvest management practice.
- **Paraquat** is applied as a desiccant.
- Harvest maturity generally occurs **7** days after physiological maturity.
- Crop is harvested at **physiological maturity** when there is need to vacate the field for sowing another crop.
- Under all other situations, it is advisable to follow harvest-maturity.
- Harvest-maturity symptoms of important crops

Crop	Symptoms
Wheat	Yellowing of spikelets
Finger millet	Brown coloured ears with hard grains
Groundnut	1) Pods turn dark from light colour 2) Dark coloured patches inside the shell 3) Kernels red to pink 4) On pressing the kernels, oil is observed on fingers
Sugarcane	1) Leaves turn yellow 2) Sucrose content more than 10 per cent 3) Brix reading more than 18 per cent
Tobacco	1) Leaves slightly yellow in colour 2) Specks appear on the leaves

- As maturity depends on **climate**, maturity symptoms are good indicators for deciding the time for harvesting.

- Harvesting date can also predicted by calculating **degree-days**.
- Criteria for harvesting of important crops

Crop	Criteria for harvesting
Rice	1) Green grains <4-9% 2) Milky grains < 1% 3) Moisture content of grains <20%
Sorghum	1) 40 days after flowering 2) Moisture content of grains <28%
Maize	1) Moisture content of grains <22-25% 2) Husk colour turns pale brown 3) 25-30 days after tasseling
Wheat	1) 15% moisture in grain 2) Grains in hard dough stage
Sugarcane	1) The ratio of brix between top and bottom part of cane is nearly one 2) Brix 18-20% 3) Sucrose 15%
Redgram	1) 35-40 days after flowering 2) 80-85% pods turn brown
Cotton	Bolls fully opened
Blackgram and greengram	Pods turn brown or black

- Determination of harvesting date is **easier** for determinate crops and **difficult** for indeterminate crops.
- At a given time, the **indeterminate** plants contain flowers, immature and mature pods or fruits.
- In **indeterminate** crops uniform maturity is induced by spraying **paraquat or sodium salt**.
- In fodder crops when toxins are present, they are generally high in **early** stage.
- In sorghum **dhurrin** is high **up to 30 days** after sowing.
- In fodder crops, **protein** content decreases and **fibre** content increases with the advancement age of the crop.
- **75%** of the **nitrogen** requirement is used by grasses during vegetative stage.
- Nitrogen content of fodder grasses varies from **2-3%** in the initial stages and **0.5-0.75%** at flowering.
- **Protein** content is **high** in fodder grasses during **early stages**.

- For **stall feeding**, fodder crop is harvested when protein content is **high** and also when the fodder is **succulent and leafy**.
- Harvesting is delayed by a few more days to get more dry matter if the purpose is **hay making**.
- Good quality silage with long preservative characters is obtained when fodder contains **more carbohydrates** and **less protein** at the time of harvest.
- Fodder grasses regenerate well when the stubble is left with atleast **two nodes** above ground level.
- In fodder trees, the stubble height has to be around **one metre** for convenience in harvesting at subsequent cuts.
- **Types of grazing**

Continuous grazing	Rotational grazing	Rational grazing/strip grazing
Livestock allowed on the pasture throughout the growing season	• Field is divided into several sub-units • Animals are allowed to graze in sub-units one after the other	• Represents the most intensive grazing system • The idea is to provide a day's ration for the herd and then to a fresh supply of forage the next day
Requires less labour	Cost on labour and fencing are more	More labour required
Animal performance is good	Carrying capacity is **10 to 25% more** over continuous grazing	**15-40% yield increase** over the rotational system
Results in **uneven grazing**	-	-
Livestock likes only new growth that is succulent and palatable and do not feed on more mature material	-	-

- **Soilage** which is cutting grass and stall feeding is not a grazing system, but is an alternative to grazing.
- Combine harvester reaps two to nine rows at a time depending on its size and is equipped with **8 to 10 HP engine**.
- Losses due to shattering in paddy crop were **2.93%** higher during manual harvesting in comparison to combine harvesting.
- Harvesting greengram, blackgram, cotton etc. is known as picking and is done at 15 days interval.
- Problems in harvesting occur especially when it coincides with heavy rain or cyclones.
- Sometimes due to heavy rains or cyclones seeds may start germinate on the plant itself. It can be overcome by growing dormant varieties.
- Most of the rice varieties have few days of dormancy.
- Crops can be saved from heavy rains or cyclones by **spraying 25 % salt solution @ 500 l/ha** which hastens maturity by 8 days.
- Groundnut is harvested by running blade harrows (pedda guntaka) with two pairs of animals.
- Tractor drawn sweep cultivators (with inverted 'V' shaped blades) are also used to harvest groundnut.
- Separating fruits or seeds from the plants or ears is called **threshing**.
- Separating grain or seed from chaff is known as **winnowing**.
- Moisture content of grains at the time of harvesting of crops is **18-20%**.
- In general **4-5** days of sun-drying is required for different produce to bring the moisture to a safe level.
- In tropical regions, one-day drying under full sunshine throughout the day brings down grain moisture content of rice from 24% to 14%.
- Sprouting and moulding of wet grains of rice is overcome by mixing powdered **common salt @ 5kg/100kg** grain.
- Wet paddy can be stored by mixing with **paddy husk** for a period of **7 days**.
- Artificial drying uses steam to dry the produce, but it is expensive.

- Losses due to different pests during storage are estimated to be around **6.5%.**

  Insects - 2.55%

  Rodents - 2.50%

  Birds - 0.85%

  Fungi and microorganisms - 0.68%
- Under storage conditions protein and free amino nitrogen contents **decrease** in rice and sorghum.
- Aflatoxin levels are higher in **sorghum** than rice.
- Quality losses are more in the produce stored in **coastal areas** compared to inland areas due to **higher humidity** in coastal areas.
- Moisture content for safe storage of grains of most crops is **14%.**
- Moisture content of grains for safe storage

Crop	Moisture content (%)
Paddy, raw rice	14
Parboiled rice	15
Wheat, barley, maize, sorghum, pearl millet, finger millet and pulses	12
Coriander, chillies, fenugreek	10
Groundnut pods, rapeseed and mustard	6

- Respiration of grains **increases** with increase in temperature.
- In case of bag storage, stacking is done up to **13 bags** high.
- The stack should be brought to **pyramidal** shape.
- During storage of grains, insecticides for spraying should have low mammalian toxicity (**malathion and dichlorovas (DDVP)**).
- When pest population cannot be controlled by spraying and major pests are more than 2/kg of sample, fumigation is resorted to.
- Generally fumigation is done with **aluminium phosphide** (2 tablets/tonne of produce) or **methyl bromide** (3-5 ml/100kg produce).
- Aluminum phosphide tablets absorb moisture from the atmosphere and release **phosphine** gas.

- Panicles of rice, when drenched in rain water, are dipped in **five per cent sodium chloride (common salt)** solution before threshing.
- The grains thus obtained can be stored in ordinary gunny bags for **10 days** without drying.
- **Wet paddy** can be stored for about **two months** by mixing **powdered salt @ 5%** to the heap.
- Most of the seeds should not be dried at a temperature **above 38°C**.
- Storage life of seeds **decreases** as storage temperature **increases**.
- **Harrington's thumb-rule** states that for every 5°C increase in storage temperature, the lifespan of seeds decreases by **half** within a temperature range of **0 to 50°C**.
- High moisture seeds are **more** susceptible to damage from **high temperature**.
- As moisture content increases, rate of seed deterioration **increases**.
- Harrington's thumb rule states that for seeds of **5 to 14%** moisture content, each 1% reduction in moisture content approximately **doubles** seed storage life.
- Shortage of fodder occurs during summer in South India and during winter in North India due to very high and low temperatures respectively.
- Shortage of irrigation water makes fodder production difficult in summer in South India.
- To overcome this problem, green fodder is stored mainly as **silage** and **hay**.
- **Hay** is any forage crop cut before dead ripe stage and dried for storage.
- **Straw** is less nutritious and palatable than hay.
- Good quality hay should be **leafy**, **pliable**, **green** in colour with characteristic pleasant smell and aroma.
- Hay made from mixed herbage of grass and legume is highly nutritious and palatable.
- Hay can be made from any grass or leguminous fodder crop.

- **Bermuda grass (*Cynodon dactylon*)** is one of the best grasses that are suitable for hay and it is equivalent to **timothy grass (*Setaria sphacelata*)** of western countries.
- Grasses suitable for hay making are **Anjan grass (*Cenchrus ciliaris*), *Dicanthium annulatum, Echinochloa colonum* and *Eleusine flagellifera*.**
- Oats, maize and sorghum can also be made into good hay but **maize** and **sorghum** are **most suitable** for **silage** making.
- **Legumes** are less suitable for hay making though these hays are more more nutritious due to **leaf shedding** during drying and curing.
- **Cowpea** is **less susceptible** to leaf shedding, **lablab and Pillipesara** are **moderately susceptible** and **berseem and shaftal** are **highly susceptible**.
- For most of the grasses, **50% flowering** is the most suitable time for harvesting for hay making.
- Leguminous fodder has to be cut at **full bloom stage** for hay making.
- Optimum time of harvesting for hay making in different crops

Crop	Time of harvesting
Grasses, clover, lucerne	Early bloom to full bloom
Cereals	Soft dough to medium dough stage
Soybean	Pod half grown
Cowpea	First pod maturity

- Loss of fodder and feeding value is unavoidable in hay making.
- When hay is dried in the open field, a minimum loss of 10% in feeding value occurs.
- Under normal conditions, dry matter loss in the field drying of hay may be **10-25%.**
- In wet weather conditions, leaching, bleaching and leaf shedding may account for losses up to **40 to 60%**.
- **Silage** is the product formed by the fermentation of green fodder stored under **anaerobic** conditions.
- Silage can be preserved for **12-18 months**.
- The process of making silage is known as **ensiling**.

- In humid regions, subjected to frequent rains, **ensiling** is easier than hay making.
- Nutrient losses are less in **silage making** than in hay making.
- **Maize** is the most suitable crop for silage making.
- Fodder yield from **maize** is higher than most of the other crops.
- **Sorghum** and **Sudan grass** are also well suited for silage.
- A mixture of **grass and legume** makes good silage.
- Forage legumes such as **Lucerne, cowpea, sunhemp and pillipesara** can also be used for making silage.
- Two types of fermentation processes known as **lactic acid** and **butyric acid** fermentation occurs depending on the conditions during silage making

Lactic acid fermentation	Butyric acid fermentation
Desirable	Silage has disagreeable odour and is not relished by cattle
Occurs when moisture content of fodder is **55-75%** with sufficient sugars in plant juice	Occurs when the fodder is wet with **high protein** and under **cold conditions**
Glucose and fructose(major carbohydrate sources for fermentation) are required at a minimum level of **6-7%** on dry weight basis	-
pH<4.5	-
Organisms responsible are ***Lactobacilli and streptococci***	Bacteria responsible is ***Clostridium sp.***
If the acid rises to about 1% at the initial stage itself, the silage will be of good quality as lactic acid checks undesirable organisms	-

- Preservatives are added to the silage to inhibit **butyric acid** type of fermentation by reducing pH or by the addition of carbohydrates or both.
- Substances such as **molasses**, **cereal grains**, **citrus pulp** etc. act as preservatives by adding **carbohydrates** to the fodder.

- **Sodium metabisulphite** @ 400g/100kg of fodder modifies fermentation process and reduces objectionable odour.
- *Characteristics of good silage are*
  1) Green, fruity with pleasing taste and without moulds, slimyness and objectionable odour
  2) Uniform in colour and moisture content
  3) **pH< 4.5**
  4) **Low ammonia** content
  5) Little or no butyric acid
  6) **Lactic acid content ranges from 3-13%**
- Dark brown colour of silage indicates **excessive heating**.
- To obtain good quality silage, the crop has to be harvested at proper stage, moisture content to be **55-75%** at the time of ensiling, carbohydrate content high and entry of air avoided.
- Silage can be a substitute for green fodder but not equal to it.
- Carbohydrates are lost as carbon dioxide and organic acids due to respiration and fermentation.
- Loss of **carotene** and **vitamin C** occurs when the temperature during fermentation is very high.

Chapter 20

Quality of Agricultural Produce

- **Roughage**s are consumed in large quantities by the animals.
- Important source of roughages is **fodder** and **crop residues**.
- Fodders are **high** in nutritive value compared to **crop residues**.
- Digestible crude protein content is **higher** in leguminous fodder than non-leguminous roughages.
- Haulms of groundnut are important leguminous roughage with high protein.
- Crude protein digestibility is **higher** in **legume straws** than in non-leguminous forages.
- Leguminous forages can be used as nitrogen supplement to improve utilization of low grade roughages.
- Lignin present in **grasses** is more inhibitory to digestion than legume lignin.
- Groundnut haulms contains **less** protein than Lucerne but more fat and nitrogen free extract.
- Crude protein digestibility is highest in **mustard cake (86.9%)**.
- **Fibre** content in food grains helps in reducing **blood glucose** levels and improves digestibility.
- **Anti-oxidants** have the capability to trap **free radicals**.
- The radical trapping antioxidant values are in the order of **sunflower > corn > groundnut > olive**.
- The **highest radical trapping antioxidant value** in **sunflower** is due to very high amount of **alphatocopherol**.
- Olive oil, because of the low content of alphatocopherol, has a low radical-trapping capacity approximately one-third that of sunflower.
- **Polyphenol and phytic acid** are the antinutrients present in wheat, maize and sorghum.

- **Oxalate** is one of the important anti-nutritional factor and it is found as **calcium oxalate** in soybeans.
- **Phytic acid**, the major storage form of P in seeds is believed to have **negative impact** on nutritional quality.
- The maximum permissible limit of aflatoxin B is **4 μg/kg** in European countries and **30 μg/kg** in most of the countries.
- The safe limit for cadmium content is **0.3 μg/kg.**
- **Rice** is a high energy or high calorie food.
- Rice contains **less** protein than wheat.
- Protein content of milled rice is around **6 to 7 per cent.**
- The fat content of rice is **low (2.0 to 2.5 %)** and much of the fat is lost during milling.
- Rice has a low percentage of **calcium.**
- In **milling** of rice **embryo** and **aleurone layer** are removed.
- In rice loss of nutrients can be avoided by **parboiling** process.
- **Wheat** contains more protein than other cereals.
- Wheat has relatively high content of **niacin** and **thiamine.**
- Wheat protein has characteristic substance **gluten** essential for bakers.
- Maize grain contains **10 % protein, 4 % oil**, **70 % carbohydrate**, **2.3 % fibre**, **1.4% albuminoides**, **1.4 % ash.**
- Maize protein zein is deficient in **tryptophan** and **lysine.**
- **Quality protein maize (QPM)** is a high-lysine, high tryptophan variety.
- Lysine content of Quality protein maize is **3.7 to 4.2 g**/100 g protein compared to **2.6 to 3.1 g**/100 g protein in normal maize, but lower than the FAO recommendation of **5.0 g**/100g protein.
- Maize is deficient in **lysine**, **isoleucine** and **tryptophane.**
- Maize is **low** in **calcium** and fairly **high** in **phosphorus.**
- Maize ranks below wheat and sorghum but considerably above rice in nutrition.
- Groundnut is a good source of all vitamins **except B_{12}.**
- **Soybean** protein is **not an ideal protein** because it is deficient in the essential aminoacid **methionine.**
- **Raw soybean** meal contains **digestion inhibitor** and **lectins.**

- Sunflower oil is a rich source **(64%) of linoleic acid** which helps in washing out cholesterol deposition in the coronary arteries of the heart and thus it is good for **heart** patients.
- Sunflower oil cake contains **40-44 %** high quality protein.
- Legumes are good source of **phosphorus** and **calcium**.
- Most potent natural source of **tocopherol** is **vegetable oils**.
- Crude oil contains **more** tocopherol than refined oil.
- Aflatoxins are produced by ***Aspergillus flavus*** and other species.

Chapter 21

Sustainable Agriculture

- **Sustainable agriculture** is a form of agriculture aimed at meeting the needs of the present generation without endangering the resource base of the future generations.
- Sustainable agriculture is minimal dependence on **synthetic fertilizers**, **pesticides** and **antibiotics.**
- It is also considered as a system of cultivation with the use of manures, crop rotation and minimal tillage.
- Sustainable agriculture system has to be economically viable both in the short and long term perspectives.
- Sustainable agriculture is also known as **ecofarming or organic farming or natural farming or permaculture.**
- Sustainable agriculture is known as ecofarming as ecological balance is given importance.
- It is called organic farming as organic matter is the main source for nutrient management.
- Organic farming is a agricultural production system which avoids or largely excludes the use of synthetically compounded fertilizers, pesticides, growth regulators and livestock feed additives.
- To the maximum extent feasible organic farming systems rely upon crop rotations, crop residues, animal manures, legumes, green manures, mineral bearing rocks and aspects of biological pest control to maintain soil productivity and tilth to supply plant nutrients and to control insects, weeds and other pests.

Pest management practices in organic agriculture:

- ✓ Crop rotation
- ✓ Strip cropping to moderate spreading of pests over large areas
- ✓ Manipulation of planting dates, planting crop at optimal time
- ✓ Adjustment of seed rate, high seed rate reduces weeds or insects.
- ✓ Use of appropriate plant varieties

- ✓ Biological control methods
- ✓ Pheromone traps
- ✓ Biological pesticides (*Pyrethrum*)

- Characteristics of sustainable agriculture
  1) FYM, compost, green manures, biofertilizers and crop rotations are used for nutrient supply
  2) Cultural methods, crop rotation and biological methods are used for pest control
  3) High diversity, renewable and biodegradable inputs are used
  4) Stable ecology
  5) Rate of extraction of resources do not exceed rate of regeneration
  6) Food materials are safe
- Ozone concentration of the atmosphere is declining at nearly **0.5%** per year due to release of chlorofluorocarbons, nitrogen oxide and methane.
- For every **one molecule of chlorine** released from chlorofluorocarbon, about **1 lakh molecules** of ozone are removed from ozone layer.
- Carbon dioxide and water vapour are transparent to visible solar radiation and so allow light to pass through, but they prevent infrared radiation from escaping and thus effectively trap solar heat.
- Atmospheric carbon dioxide by trapping solar heat produces greenhouse effect and heats up the atmosphere.
- It is estimated that earth's mean temperature would have been as low as -23°C without CO_2 rather than +15°C as it is today.
- Now CO_2 concentration in atmosphere is around **410 ppm**.
- Out of the total geographical area of 329 mha in India, **265 mha** is suitable for crop production and about **175 mha** is affected by soil related constraints and are classified as **wastelands**.
- Soil erosion by water in the form of rill and sheet erosion is a serious problem in the red and lateritic soils of south and eastern India where about **40 t/ha** of top soil is lost annually.
- Out of **70 m ha** of black soils of central India, **6.7 m ha** are already unproductive due to the development of gullies, ravines and torrents.

- Shifting cultivation practiced largely in the **north-eastern India** has caused serious land degradation over **4.4 m ha** of land.
- Deforestation is estimated to be proceeding at the rate of about **1.5 m ha** per year.
- Earlier forest cover of Himalayas was **60%** and it is now estimated to be only **25%**.
- Due to improper management of irrigation water, **salinization** and **alkalization** of soil takes place.
- An area of **6 m ha** of land is affected by **waterlogging**.
- **7 mha land** is salinised due to faulty irrigation practices.
- Disadvantages of sustainable agriculture are
  1) Low yields
  2) Lack of timely and effective control of weeds, insects and diseases
- Conversion from modern agriculture to sustainable agriculture usually takes **3-6 years**.
- Sustainable agriculture movement started in **1981**.
- The use of limited quantities of fertilizers and discrete application of small quantities of target specific pesticides at critical stages of crop damage will be in agreement with the principle of sustainable agriculture.
- Indices of sustainability may be simple involving one parameter or complex involving several parameters.
- Indices of sustainability were given by **Lal (1994)**.
- Indices of sustainability include
  1) **Productivity (P):** production per unit of resource used

     P = P/R

     P = productivity

     p = total production

     R = resource used
  2) **Total factor productivity (TFP) (Herdt, 1993)**

     It is defined as productivity per unit cost of all factors involved

$$TEP = \frac{P}{\sum_{i=1}^{n}(R_i \times C_i)}$$

P = Total production

R = Resource used

C = Cost of resource

N = Number of resources used in achieving total production

3) **Coefficient of sustainability (Cs) (Lal, 1991)**

It is a measure of change in soil properties in relation to production under specific management system

Cs = F (Oi, ad, Om)

C_s = Coefficient of sustainability

O_i = Output per unit that maximizes per capita productivity or profit

ad = Output per unit decline in the most limiting or non-renewable resource

O_m = Minimum assured output

T = Time

4) **Index of sustainability (Is)(Lal, 1993 & Lal and miller,1993)**

It is a measure of sustainability relating productivity to change in soil and environmental characteristics

$I_s = f(P_i{*}\ S_i{*}W_i{*}C_i)t$

I_s = index of sustainability

S_i = alteration in soil properties

W_i = change in water resources and quality

C_i = modification in climatic factor

t = time

5) **Agriculture sustainability (As) (Lal, 1993)**

$A_s = d\ (P_t{*}S_p{*}W_t{*}\ C_t{*})dt$

A_s = Agricultural sustainability

P_t = Productivity per unit input of the limited or non-renewable resource

S_p = Critical soil property of rooting depth, soil organic matter

W_t = Available water capacity including water quality

C_t = Climatic factor such as gaseous flux from agricultural activity

t = Time

6) Sustainability coefficient (SC)

It is a complex and a multipurpose index based on a range of parameters, and is similar to A_s

$S_c = (P_t*P_d*P_m)t$

$S_c = d\ (P_i*W_t*C_t)dt$

P_t = Productivity per unit input of the limited resource

P_d = Productivity per unit decline in soil property

S_c = Critical level of soil property

W_t = Soil water regime and quality

C_t = Climatic factor

t = Time

Chapter 22

Agroforestry

- National forest policy -**1988**
- Geographical area should be under forest and tree cover – **33%**
- Forest area of hilly districts is **38.85%** compared to desired **66%.**
- National agricultural policy – **2000**
- International centre for research in agroforestry or world agroforestry centre located in **Nairobi, Kenya**.
- ICRAF, Nairobi, Kenya established in the year **1978**.
- National research centre for agroforestry – **Jhansi (1988)**.

- **Agroforestry** is a sustainable land management system that increases overall production, combines agricultural crops, tree crops and forest plants and/or animals simultaneously or sequentially and applies management practices that are compatible with cultural patterns of local population.
- In agroforestry there are **ecological** and **socio-economic** interactions between different components.
- Agroforestry involves two or more species of plants, atleast one of which is a **woody perennial**.
- An agroforestry system has always **two or more** outputs.
- Cycle of an agroforestry system is always more than **one year**.
- **Agroforestry** system is structurally, functionally, socioeconomically more complex than **monocropping**.
- Agroforestry is a form of **multiple cropping** which satisfies three basic conditions.
  1) There exists atleast two plant species that interact **biologically**.
  2) Atleast one of the plant species is a **woody perennial**.
  3) Atleast one of the plant species is managed for **forage**, **annual or perennial crop production**.

- **Social forestry** is planting trees to help the poor people to improve their living and meeting their routine requirements of fuel wood and fodder.
- **Farm forestry** includes bund planting and field boundaries by farmers themselves.
- **Farm forestry** includes integration of farming with forestry practices on the farm to benefit agriculture. This concept originated for making agriculture economically viable.
- **Farm forestry** includes practice of rising small woods on the farm in addition to normal cultivation to derive indirect benefits like protection of crops against high winds, control of erosion, meeting demands of fuel, small timber, grazing, fodder and leaf manure.
- Programmes to promote commercial tree growing by farmers on their own land is **farm forestry**.
- **Community forestry**, a form of social forestry, refers to tree planting activities undertaken by a community on community land or panchayat land.
- Community forest is a **tree dominated** ecosystem managed for multiple uses.
- **Khejri or sami – *Prosophis cineraria***

  Aswattha – *Ficus religiosa*

  Palasa – *Butea monosperma*

  Varana – *Crataeva roxburghii*
- Kangeyam tract of Tamil Nadu – *Acacia leucophloea* + *Cenchrus setigerus*
- Ravines of Yamuna, Chambal for rearing of milk producing jamunapuri breed of sheep and goat – trees/shrubs/bamboos + grasses
- Semiarid area of Tamil Nadu – scattered khejri or mehndi trees + jowar, bajra, chillies
- Common practice in Rajasthan – plantation of khejri trees for various uses.
- Coastal areas – *Casuarina equisetifolia* + crops (for cash and to generate small timber).
- Live hedges – **Mehndi, *Agave sisalina, Euphorbia sps.***

- Leaves of ***Pongamia glabra*** and ***Sesbania grandiflora*** are cut annually and applied as green leaf manure to **paddy fields**.
- In MP and UP application of green manure to paddy field was common.
- In western ghats **Terminalia** leaves harvested, spread on land, burnt and then **paddy, ragi and millets** were sown.
- Multistory homesteads or home gardens were in existence in **Kerala, Karnataka, Tamil Nadu, Tripura, Assam** and other **North Eastern states** as an important agroforestry practice.
- **Water erosion > salinisation > terrain deformation**
- Annual soil loss is **16.35 tonnes/ha**.
- **50 mha** area is degraded due to mining activity.
- Extent of degraded forests in the country is **> 40 mha**.
- Maximum area under wastelands is in **Rajasthan (arid and semi arid regions)** followed by Madhya Pradesh and Maharashtra.
- By the end of this century crop land per head decrease by **19%** due to population explosion.
- There is slight scope to increase food production by increasing the area under cultivation.

Advantages due to agroforestry

- **Microclimate** improvement due to trees particularly shelterbelts and windbreaks.
- Feed for livestock from trees.
- Food for man from trees as fruits, nuts.
- Enhanced food production from crops associated with trees due to nitrogen fixation, better access to plant nutrients (trees with deep roots bring nutrients to surface), improved availability of nutrients due to high CEC of soil and its organic matter and mycorrhizal associations.
- Enhanced sustainability of cropping systems through soil and water conservation by controlling soil erosion and runoff.
- Improvement of soil moisture retention in rainfed croplands due to improved soil structure and microclimate effect of trees.
- Reducing flood hazards by controlling runoff, improvement of infiltration.

- Improvement in water drainage from waterlogged or saline soils by growing trees with high water requirements.
- **Ethanol** is produced from fermentation of high **carbohydrate** fruits.
- Oils, latex, resins available from trees.
- Building materials for shelter construction.
- Provides shade for people, livestock and shade loving crops.
- As fencing
- Windbreaks and shelterbelts
- Raw material for paper and pulp industry
- Wood for agricultural implements
- Fibre for weaving
- **Planning commission (1989)** divided country into **15 agroclimatic zones** on the basis of **climate, soil type, topography, water resources, irrigation facilities.**
- **ICAR** classified India into **20 agroecological regions** and **60 sub regions** based on ***crop growing period, soil groups, geographical boundaries*** etc.
- On the basis of structure agroforestry systems can be grouped in nature of components and arrangement of components.
- Based on nature of components
  - ✓ Agri-silviculture = trees + crops
  - ✓ Boundary plantation = trees on boundary + crops
  - ✓ Block plantation = block of trees + block of crops
  - ✓ Energy plantation = trees + crops during initial years
  - ✓ Alley cropping = perennial hedges + crops
  - ✓ Agri-horticulture = fruit trees + crops
  - ✓ Agri-silvi-horticulture = Trees + Fruit trees + crops
  - ✓ Agri-silvipasture = Trees + crops + pasture or animals
  - ✓ Silvi-olericulture = Trees + vegetables
  - ✓ Horti-pasture = fruit trees + pasture or animals
  - ✓ Horti-olericulture = fruit trees + vegetables
  - ✓ Silvipasture = trees + pasture/animals
  - ✓ Forage forestry = forage trees + pasture
  - ✓ Shelterbelts = Trees + crops

- ✓ Wind-breaks = trees + crops
- ✓ Live fence = shrubs and under trees on boundary
- ✓ Silvi or Horti sericulture = Trees or fruit trees + sericulture
- ✓ Horti-apiculture = Fruit trees + honeybee
- ✓ Aquaforestry = Trees + fishes
- ✓ Homestead = multiple combination of trees, fruit trees and vegetables *etc.*

- In **alley cropping** fast growing legumes that coppice vigorously are intercropped with crops.

Agroforestry for eroded lands:

Woody species: *Acacia nilotica, Azadirachta indica, Butea monosperma, Dalbergia sissoo, Pongamia pinnata, Prosophis juliflora, Zizyphus mauritiana*

Grasses: *Cenchrus ciliaris, Cynodon dactylon, Dicanthium annulatum, Saccharum munja*

Legumes: Stylosanthes, Melilotus etc.

Medicinal Species: Aloe vera, *Jatropha curcas*

Chapter 23

Climate Change

- **Climate change** is a long-term change in the statistical distribution of weather patterns over periods of time that range from decades to million of years.
- Climate change refers to both **global warming** and **global dimming**.
- **Global warming** is the increase of earth's average surface temperature due to effect of green house gases, such as carbon dioxide emissions from burning fossil fuels or from deforestation, which trap heat that would otherwise escape from the earth.
- Global warming is a type of **green house effect**.
- The fourth assessment report of intergovernmental panel on climate change (IPCC) makes it clear that the global average temperature has increased by 0.74°C over the last 100 years and projected increase is about 1.8 to 4°C by 2100.
- **Global dimming/ Global cooling** defined as the decrease in the amounts of solar radiation reaching the surface of the earth.
- The by-product of fossil fuels is tiny particles or pollutants which absorb solar energy and reflect back sunlight into the space.
- **Aerosols** have been found to be the major cause of global dimming.
- **Agriculture sector in India contributes to 28% of the total green house gas emissions.**
- According to Intergovernment panel on climate change (IPCC) the global average emission from agriculture is only 13.5%.
- Emissions from agriculture are primarily due to methane from rice fields (23%).
- **El-Nino** is a narrow current of warm water that appears off the coast of Peru in December.
- The difference of pressure between Tahiti (in French Polynesia representing the Pacific) and Port Darwin (in northern Australia

representing the Indian Ocean) is called the **Southern Oscillation Index (SOI)**. **Negative value (-ve)** of the index (Tahiti-Port Darwin) is the precursor of poor or deficient monsoon in India.

- A negative value of SOI and El-Nino favours a year of deficient rainfall.
- **Climate resilient agriculture (CRA)** is the incorporation of adaptation, mitigation and other practices in agriculture which increases the capacity of the system to respond to various climate related disturbances by resting damage and recovering quickly.
- **Climate-smart agriculture** promotes production systems that sustainably increase productivity, resilience (adaptation), reduces/removes GHGs (mitigation), and enhances achievement of national food security and development goals.
- **Carbon sequestration** refers to the provision of long-term storage of carbon in the terrestrial biosphere, underground, or the oceans so that buildup of carbon dioxide (the principal green house gas) concentration in the atmosphere will reduce or slow.
- Abiotic carbon sequestration is based on **physical and chemical reactions and engineering techniques** without intervention of living organisms (*e.g.*, plants, microbes).
- Biotic carbon sequestration is based on managed intervention of **higher plants** and **micro-organisms** in removing CO_2 from the atmosphere.
- Ocean carbon sequestration is a biological process leading to C sequestration in the ocean through photosynthesis.
- Phytoplankton photosynthesis fixes approximately **45 Pg C yr^{-1}** (Picograms carbon per year).
- **Carbon dioxide equivalent (CO_2e)** is the international standard metric for measuring and reporting GHGs, is used to normalize the global warming potentials of different GHGs so that they can be readily compared.
- CH_4, N_2O and CFC have **25, 298** and **10,900** times Global Warming Potential (GWP) than CO_2, respectively, when considered over a 100 year time horizon.
- **Carbon accounting** refers to processes undertaken to measure amounts of carbon dioxide equivalents emitted by an entity.
- A **carbon credit** represents one tonne of carbon dioxide equivalent either removed, avoided or sequestered.

- Credits are awarded to countries or groups that have reduced their green house gases below their emission quota.
- For example, if an environmentalist group plants enough trees to reduce emissions by one tonne, the group will be awarded a credit.
- If a steel producer has an emission quota of 10 tonnes, but is expecting to produce 11 tonnes, it could purchase this carbon credit from the environmentalist group.
- **Biochar** is a solid material obtained from the carbonization of biomass
- **Biochar** is produced through a process known as pyrolysis, means thermal decomposition of organic material (*i.e.*, wood chips, crop waste and manure etc.) under limited supply of oxygen (O_2) and at relatively low temperatures.
- Biochar formation results in net sequestration of carbon from the atmosphere to the soil
- **Global-warming potential (GWP)** is a measure of the atmospheric heat-trapping ability of a given GHG expressed in terms of an equivalent amount of CO_2.
- GWP of methane is **21**. This means methane is approximately 21 times more heat-absorptive than carbon dioxide per unit of weight.
- GWP of N_2O is **310**.
- **Kyoto Protocol** is an international agreement on climate change that sets a target for signatory countries collective emissions reductions and a mechanism for doing so. The agreement was reached in **1997 in Kyoto, Japan** and came into effect in **February 2005**.
- **National Initiative on Climate Resilient Agriculture (NICRA)** is a network project of the Indian Council of Agricultural Research (ICAR) launched in **February, 2011**.
- **NICRA project** aims to enhance resilience of Indian agriculture to climate change and climate variability through strategic approach and technology demonstration.
- The **Intergovernmental Panel on Climate Change (IPCC)** is a scientific intergovernmental body under the auspices of the United Nations, set up at the request of member governments.

- IPCC was established in **1988** by two United Nations Organizations, the World Meteorological Organization (WMO) and the United Nations Environment Programme (UNEP).
- IPCC is an internationally accepted authority on climate change.
- IPCC producing reports have agreement of leading climate scientists and the consensus of participating governments.
- **Carbon dioxide (CO_2) fertilization** is the enhancement of the growth of plants as result of increased carbon dioxide concentration.
- Depending on their mechanism of photosynthesis, certain types of plants are more sensitive to changes in atmospheric carbon dioxide concentration.
- Plants that produce a **3-carbon compound (C_3)** during photosynthesis including most trees and agricultural crops such as **rice, wheat, soybean, potato and vegetables** generally show a **larger response** than plants that produce a 4-carbon compound during photosynthesis mainly of tropical origin, including grasses and other agriculturally important crops maize, sugarcane, millets and sorghum.
- Sources of CO_2 emission are decay of organic matter, forest fires, volcanoes, burning of fossil fuels, deforestation and land use change.
- Sinks of carbon dioxide are **plants, oceans, atmospheric reactions.**
- Rate of CO_2 evolution is greater from **clay-loam soil** which has a higher organic 'C' content than **sandy soil**.
- More CO_2 emission occurs from a **tilled soil** than undisturbed soil.
- Temperature has marked effect on CO_2 evolution from soil by influencing root and soil respiration and on CH_4 by effecting anaerobic carbon mineralization and methanogenic activity.
- Sources of **methane** are wetlands, organic decay, termites, natural gas and oil extraction, biomass burning, rice cultivation, cattle, refuse land fills.
- Sources of methane in agriculture are animal digestive processes, rice cultivation, manure storage and handling.
- In ruminant animals methane produced as a byproduct of the digestion of feed in the rumen under anaerobic conditions.

- Methane emission is related to the proportion of the diet (grass, legume, grain and concentrates) and the characteristic of different feeds (*e.g.*, soluble residue, hemicelluloses and cellulose contents).
- Mitigation of methane emitted from livestock is most effectively approached by strategies that reduce feed input per unit of product output.
- Upland, aerobic soil does not produce methane.
- Altering water management practices, particularly mid-season aeration by short term drainage as well as alternate wetting and drying can greatly reduce methane emission in rice cultivation.
- Anaerobic decomposition of dung also contributes to methane emission.
- Sinks of methane are soil and stratosphere.
- Sources of nitrous oxide are forests, grasslands, oceans, soil cultivation, nitrogenous fertilizers, burning of biomass, fossil fuels.
- Nitrous oxide is oxidized in stratosphere (sink).
- Soil contributes about **65%** of total nitrous oxide emissions.
- Mitigation measures for reducing nitrous oxide emissions are site specific nutrient management, fertilizer placement, proper type of fertilizer supply of nutrients in accordance with plant demand.
- High temperature changes starch composition which in turn increased stickiness in cooked rice.
- In wheat **4-5 mt** loss of yield for 1°C temperature raise in India.
- Reduction in grain size, protein and micronutrient concentration in wheat due to elevated temperatures.
- Altering water management, use of sulphate containing fertilizers, nitrification inhibitors, use of different rice cultivars are the promising techniques for mitigating CH_4 emissions.
- Wheat variety tolerant to high temperature is **DWR 162.**

Chapter 24

Other Important Concepts

A horizon: Surface layer of a soil profile. This horizon has more organic matter and dense microbial population hence greatest biological activity than other layers or horizons, such as B horizon and C horizon. It is also referred to as the surface mineral horizon with decomposed organic matter. Most important horizon from crop nutrition and microbial activity point of view.

Absolute weed: These are the plants, which are undesirable regardless of time and place.

Absolute Zero: Considered to be the point at which theoretically no molecular activity exists or the temperature at which the volume of a perfect gas vanishes. The value is 0° Kelvin, -273.15^{o} Celsius and -459.67^{o} Fahrenheit.

Acetobacter: N-fixing bacteria found in the roots, stems and leaves of sugarcane with a potential N-fixing capacity of 200 kg N ha^{-1}. It also solubilises insoluble phosphorus. It is recommended for sugarcane.

Acetylene reduction assay (ARA): The quantitative method for estimating biological nitrogen fixation through gas chromatography. The enzyme nitrogenase (N-ase), which is responsible for biological N fixation, can reduce the gas acetylene (C_2H_2) to ethylene (C_2H_4) as well as dinitrogen (N_2) to ammonia (NH_3).

Acid rains: Acid rain contains excessive concentration of acidic compounds, primarily NO^{3-}, SO_4^{2-} and H^+, having pH 5-7, received where atmospheric pollution through industrial activity or vehicular exhaust is high.

Acid sulphate soil:

- Very acid soil (pH<4) in which sulphuric acid is formed by the oxidation of S-bearing pyrite minerals.
- Found primarily in coastal, deltaic and estuarine areas of the humid tropics. Sometimes also called **cat clays**.

Actinomycetes: A group of microorganisms, intermediate between bacteria and true fungi that usually produce a characteristic branched mycelium. These organisms are responsible for earthy smell of the compost.

Activated charcoal: Charcoal, which has been treated to remove impurities. Activation carried out by heating charcoal under partial aeration. Used in chemical analysis.

Additive series: In intercropping, introduction of another plant species without reducing the population of the first species from the optimum.

Adjuvant: Substance added to a formulated pesticide product to act as a wetting or spreading agent, sticker, penetrant, or emulsifier in order to enhance the physical characteristics of the product.

Adsali sugarcane: Sugarcane, which takes **18 months** for harvesting, usually planted in June-July.

Advance time (irrigation): The time it takes the first water applied to a dry irrigation furrow to travel the length of the furrow.

Advection: Advection involves the transfer of heat energy by means of hiorizontal mass motions through a medium.

Aerial root: A root usually arising adventitiously from a stem. **Epiphytes** produce aerial roots which have specialized tissue called velamen for absorbing moisture from the air. Aerial roots may contain chlorophyll and photosynthesize.

Aeroponics: A technique in growing plants wherein the plants derive their nutrients and water from a mist of air and aqueous solution that comes in contact with the roots.

Aerosol: Particulate matter, solid or liquid, larger than a molecule but small enough to remain suspended in the atmosphere. Aerosols can also originate as a result of human activities and are often considered pollutants.

Agricultural lime: Material containing oxides, hydroxides and / or carbonates of Ca and / or Mg, used for neutralizing soil acidity.

Agrobiology: A phase of the study of agronomy dealing with the relationship of yield to the quantity of an added or available fertilizer element.

Agroecology: The study of the interrelationships of living organisms with each other and with their environment in an agricultural system.

(or)

The use of ecological concepts and principles to study, design, and manage agricultural systems.

Agrology: The study of applied phases of soil science and soil management.

Ahu rice: Early rice similar to "Aus"; grown in Assam, India.

Akiochi disease: Japanese word used to describe a disease-like condition of rice plants caused by H_2S toxicity, deficiency of Si, Mg, bases in general and N and K at later stages of plant growth.

Albuminous seed: A seed that contains endosperm at the time of germination, which nourishes the growing seedling.

Aleurone layer: The peripheral layer of endosperm of the grain beneath the seed coat, which envelops the endosperm and contains oil and protein. (or) It is a layer of high-protein cells surrounding the storage cells of the endosperm. Its function is to secrete hydrolytic enzymes for digesting food reserves in the endosperm.

Alfisols:

- Soils with grey to brown surface horizons.
- Medium to high supply of bases and B horizons of illuvial clay accumulation.
- Formed mostly under forest or savanna vegetation in climates with slight to pronounced seasonal moisture deficit.

Alien weeds: When a weed is allowed to move from the place of its origin to a new area, and it establishes itself there, it becomes an introduced weed in its new environment. Such weeds are known as alien weeds or **anthrophytes**.

Alkaloids: Any of a group of organic bases occurring in plants and containing carbon, hydrogen, oxygen and nitrogen for example, Dhurrin/HCN, coumarins, oxalate etc.

Allelo-inhibition: Allelochemicals inhibit more the growth of plants of species other than producer species.

Alley cropping: A farming system in which arable crops are grown in alleys formed by trees or shrubs, established mainly to hasten soil-fertility restoration and enhance soil productivity.

Alley crops: when arable crops are grown in alleys formed by trees or shrubs, established mainly to hasten soil fertility restoration, enhance soil productivity and reduce soil erosion they are known as alley crops.

Such crops should have slight shade tolerance and should be non-trailing. *e.g.,* sweet potato, blackgram, turmeric and ginger in between the rows of *Eucalyptus, Subabool* and *Cassia.*

Alluvial soil: A soil developed from recently deposited alluvium and exhibiting essentially no horizon development or modification of the recently deposited materials.

Alluviation: The process of accumulation of gravel deposits, sand, silt or clay, at places in rivers, lakes or estuaries where the flow is checked.

Alluvium: Sediments deposited by running water of streams and rivers.

Alternative agriculture/farming: A concept of farming based on the exclusion of mineral fertilizers and synthetic pesticides but including mainly organic manures, waste recycling and biological agents, as in organic farming, in contrast to modern agriculture in which optimum use of mineral fertilizers and pesticides is sought to be made.

Alternative crops: Non-traditional crops that can be grown in an area to diversify rotations and increase income.

Alternative energy: Energy produced from sources other than fossil fuels (solar, wind, hydroelectric, geothermal, and biomass).

Altimeter: An instrument used to measure the altitude of an object above a fixed level.

Aman rice: A term used in Bangladesh and East India for lowland rice grown in the wet season during June to November. Water depth does not exceed 0.5 m.

Amino acid: Class of organic compounds containing the amino ($-NH_2$) group and the carboxyl (-COOH) group. Aminoacids are building blocks of proteins. Alanine, proline, threonine, histidine, lysine, glutamine, phenylalanine, tryptophan, valine, arginine, tyrosine, and leucine are the common amino acids.

Amphoteric: A substance that can act as either an acid or a base in a reaction. *e.g.,* Aluminium hydroxide can neutralize mineral acids or strong bases.

Angiosperm: A plant in which the female gamete is protected within an enclosed ovary. A flowering plant.

Anthocyanins: A class of water-soluble pigments that account for many of the red to blue floral and fruit colurs. Anthocyanins are found in the vacuole.

Apical dominance: The phenomenon in the plant where the apical shoot/buds have inhibitory influence on the growth of lateral shoot and buds.

Apomixis: Asexual development of embryo (seed) in the ovary without fertilization.

Arable farming: Farming system that involves the production of crops requiring tillage.

Arable land: Land which is ploughed, and on which crops are cultivated.

Arboricide: Chemical used to kill trees

Arboriculture: Cultivation of woody plants, particularly those used for decoration and shade.

Arboriculture: Cutivation of trees.

Aridisols: Mineral soils that have an aridic moisture regime, an ochric epipedon and other pedogenic horizons but no oxic horizon. These are desert soils.

Aridity index: A measure of the dryness of a region and is expressed as

$$\frac{\text{Number of rainy days} \times \text{Mean precipitation per day}}{\text{Mean temperature} + 10}$$

Arviculture: Crop science

Asexual reproduction: The multiplication of plants by vegetative means through budding, grafting, rooting of cuttings, or division.

Associative Symbiosis: Loose association between the roots of non-leguminous plants (grasses, wheat, maize, rice, sorghum etc.) and nitrogen-fixing soil bacteria, primarily *Azospirillum.*

Augmentation cropping: when subcrops are sown to supplement the yield of the main crops, the subcrops are known as augmenting crops. *e.g.,* Japanese mustard with berseem, Chinese cabbage with mustard. Here the mustard or cabbage helps in getting a higher yield of fodder in spite of the fact that berseem gives a poor yield in the first cutting.

Aus rice: A photoperiod-insensitive, rainfed, drought prone, lowland, or upland rice, broadcast and transplanted during the early part of the wet season from March to September in Bangladesh and from April to August in east India.

Autecology: The study of details of how an individual or a species interacts with its environment.

Autotroph: An organism that can live on very simple carbon and nitrogen sources, such as carbon dioxide and ammonia.

A-value technique:

- Radio-chemical analysis of plants grown on soils which have been treated with fertilizers containing elements such as radioactive phosphorus.
- A – value technique may be used to calculate the phosphorus supply of original soil.
- A-value is defined as available soil nutrient determined in terms of a standard fertilizer used. It is used for the assessment of available P and S in soils expressed as

  $$A = \frac{B(1-Y)}{Y}$$

  B = amount of nutrient in the applied fertilizer

  Y = Proportion of the nutrient in the plant derived from fertilizer
- A-value can only be determined by tracer technique using a labeled fertilizer.
- A-value technique is used in research, not for farm advisory purposes.

Avenue crops: These crop plants are grown along the farm roads and fences such as *Pigeonpea, Sisal, Glyricidia* and *Tephrosia.*

Azolla: Azolla is a fresh water fern found in ponds, ditches, canals and paddy fields. It fixes N in symbiotic association with cyanobacterium (BGA) Anabaena azollae. It fixes 25-40 kg N ha^{-1} $crop^{-1}$. Azolla is an excellent food for fish, ducks, pigs, poultry and line stock. (Sheep, good, cow, etc.

Azomonas: It is a non-symbiotic aerobic nitrogen-fixing bacteria under the family Azotobacteriaceae. Its optimum temperature for growth is 20° – $30^{o}C$ and pH range is 4.5 to 9.0 (optimum 7.0-7.5). *Azomonas* has three species: *Azomonas agilis, Azomonas insignis* and *Azomonas macrocytogenes.*

Azorhizobium: A stem-nodulating bacterium, which is capable of forming root nodules as well as stem nodules on tropical legume *Sesbania rostrata.* Grouped under *Azorhizobium* in **Rhizobium** classification. *e.g., Azorhizobium caulinodans.*

Baby corn: A young finger like unfertilized cob with 1-3 cm emerged silk preferably harvested within 1-3 days of silk emergence depending upon the growing season. It is a good source of fibrous protein and easy to digest.

Bagasse: The mill residues from the cane sugar industry consisting of crushed stalks from which the juice has been extracted, often used as a fuel in sugar factories.

Bahar treatment: Regulation of flowering and fruiting in fruit crops *viz;* guava and pomegranate, which flower more than once a year, by cultural, mechanical and chemical means.

Base exchange capacity: The extent to which the soil can adsorb exchangeable cations other than hydrogen and aluminium. It is an indicator of soil fertility.

Bast fibre: The fibre obtained from vegetative parts or phloem of a plant. e.g., Jute and Mesta.

Baule unit:

- Baule unit is a unit of fertilizer or any other growth factor to be taken as that amount necessary to produce a yield of 50% of the maximum possible.
- Baule unit for N is 223 lb/acre

  P_2O_5 is 45 lb/acre

  K_2O is 76 lb/acre

Beijerinckia: Anaerobic nitrogen-fixing bacteria.

Beushening in paddy: It involves cross ploughing the young crop 4-6 weeks after sowing with a light country plough in 5-10 cm standing water once or twice depending on the weed density and crop stand. If there are too many weeds then it is followed by planking. Locally known as beushening in Odisha and biasi in Madhya Pradesh, Bihar, West Bengal, Assam and Uttar Pradesh.

Biochemical oxygen demand (BOD): A measure of the amount of oxygen consumed by natural, biological processes that break down organic matter, such as those that take place when manure or saw dust is put in water. High levels of oxygen-demanding wastes in waters deplete dissolved oxygen thereby endangering aquatic life. Sometimes referred to as biological oxygen demand.

Biodiversity: It is the variety and variation among plants, animals, and microorganisms and their ecosystems.

Biogas: A mixture of gases containing methane, carbon dioxide, hydrogen and traces of few others produced by the anaerobic fermentation of easily decomposable cellulosic materials in the presence of methane – forming bacteria. Most commonly made from animal dung and other excreta. Major component is methane.

Bio-climatic law: Hopkins (1928) attempted to express the **importance of latitude, longitude and altitude** in the distribution and rate of development of plants by means of a bioclimatic law. The law may be stated as a biotic event in temperate north America will in general show a lag of **4 days** for each degree of latitude, 5° of longitude and 400 feet of altitude, northward, eastward and upward in spring and early summers.

Biological yield: Refers to total dry matter produced by a plant or a crop in a unit land area.

Biological amplication/Biomagnification: Increase in concentration of toxic fat-soluble chemicals in organisms at successively higher trophic levels of a grazing food chain or food web because of the consumption of organisms at lower trophic levels.

Bio-farming: A farming system in which only the living organisms are involved.

Bio-fortification

- **Bio-fortification** is the process by which the nutritional quality of food crops is improved through agronomic approaches, traditional breeding practices and modern biotechnology.
- Biofortified seeds help in reducing anemia, cognitive impairment, and other malnutrition related health problems that affect billions of people.
- **Genetic bio-fortification** is the process of developing food crops that are capable of absorbing more micronutrients, such as zinc and iron and synthesizing more vitamins.
- **Agronomic bio-fortification** involves the application of fertilizers to seeds, soil and/or foliage, at rates greater than those required for maximum yield, to increase the uptake of micronutrients into the plants and its translocation into seeds.
- **Golden rice** is a variety of *Oryza sativa* rice produced through genetic engineering to biosynthesize **beta – carotene**, a precursor of **vitamin – A**, in the edible parts of rice.

- Golden rice was created by transforming rice with only two beta-carotene biosynthesis genes.
  1) **Psy (*Phytoene synthase*)** from **daffodil (*Narcissus pseudonarcissus*)**, **crt I (Carotene desaturase)** from the soil bacterium ***Erwinia uredovora.***
- Prof. **Ingo Potrykus and Prof. Peter Beyer** responsible for this wonder product called **golden rice**.
- Crown gall bacterium ***Agrobacterium tumefaciens*** provided the plasmids that served as gene couriers into rice tissue.

Biosalinity: It is the study and practice of using saline water for irrigating agricultural crops.

Biosphere: The portion of earth and its atmosphere that can support life.

Biosuper: A fertilizer containing elemental S and rock phosphate. It is inoculated with S-oxidising bacteria which convert elemental S to sulphuric acid and the acid inturn solubilizes rock – phosphate.

Bitter pit : A disorder of apple caused by calcium deficiency which is characterized by small, brown, necrotic zones in the flesh 3-5 mm in cross section, more frequent towards the calyx portion of the fruit and sometimes visible through the skin as dark green or brown in flesh.

Biuret (NH_2–CO–NH–CO–NH_2): Undesirable compound synthesized during urea manufacture. Commercial urea usually contains less than 1.5% but for foliar spray should not contain more than 1.0 – 1.5% of it. Biuret is a good source of non-protein N for ruminants.

Black tip: A disorder of mango caused due to brick – kiln fumes and is characterized by blackening and hardening of the distal end of fruits which ripe prematurely.

Blind cultivation: Cultivation before the crop is emerged especially practiced in potato and sugarcane.

Blossom – end – rot: A disorder of tomato due to calcium deficiency characterized by a black sunken spot develops at the blossom end of the berry which later on spreads with water soaked region around it.

Bolting or shooting: Refers to significant stem elongation that precedes flowering in many plants.

Boot: The sheath of the last (flag) leaf through which the inflorescence emerges.

Boro rice: An irrigated, high yielding, cold-tolerant, relatively pest-free and photoperiod insensitive rice cultivated during the winter months in India and Bangladesh. Generally transplanted in December-January and harvested in April-May.

Brace root: A type of adventitious root that grows from above ground parts of the stem and serves to support the plant. Brace roots are frequently seen in corn. Also called prop roots.

Bradyrhizobium: It is name of a new genus of erstwhile Rhizobium, which is slow growing. Important in tropical legumes. Example: *Bradyrhizobium japonicum.*

Brake crop: These crops are grown to break the continuity of the agro-ecological situation of the field under multiple cropping systems. The inclusion of such crops in the cropping system helps to reduce the inoculum of soil-borne harmful biotic agents such as weeds, pests, pathogens and parasites and improves soil conditions for crop growth.

Bray's nutrient mobility concept: As the mobility of a nutrient in the soil decreases, the amount of that nutrient needed in the soil to produce a maximum yield (the soil nutrient requirement) increases.

Brix: It refers to the **total solid** in any solution but in case of sugarcane it is used for assessing the maturity of canes. The brix is measured with the help of **hand refractometer** and the values over **16** indicate that the canes are approaching maturity and they may be harvested for milling.

Bronzing: Development of bronze/copper colouration on the plant tissue. A common nutrient deficiency symptom.

Brown rice: Rice grain with its hulls removed but not polished.

Brown manuring:

- It is the practice of co-culture of rice and green manure crop of Sesbania together for 25-35 days before Sesbania is knocked down with 2,4-D.
- It acts as a mulch and manure.

C_3 plants: Plants in which the first product of CO_2 fixation is the 3-carbon compound phosphoglyceric acid. These are usually temperate plants. Generally characterized by lower dry matter per unit water used, occurrence of photo-respiration and need for greater CO_2 concentration (**25-100 ppm**) as compared to C_4 plants. Photosynthetically these are less efficient than C_4 and CAM plants. *e.g.* wheat, rice, barley, sugarbeet, legumes, oilseeds etc.

C_4 plants: Plants in which the first product of CO_2 fixation is the 4-carbon compound **oxalo acetic acid**. These are usually tropical plants. Characterized by higher dry matter production per unit water used, absence of photo-respiration and ability to utilize lower CO_2 concentrations (0-10 ppm) resulting in higher net assimilation rates and photosynthetic efficiency as compared to C_3 plants. e.g. sugarcane, maize, sorghum, pearlmillet, finger millet, tropical grasses etc.

Caffeine: It is the purine base alkaloid found in tea and coffee which works as a stimulant.

Calcifuge: Plants suited to grow on acid soils.

Canola: Seed, oil and meal from *Brassica napus* and *B. campestris* that contain **<2%** of the total fatty acid as erucic acid **< 22 µmol** of aliphatic glucosinolates per gram of oil free meal.

Capillary fringe: The vertical distance above a water table along which moisture content varies from full saturation to field capacity.

Carbon dioxide (CO_2) fertilization:

- The enhancement of the growth of plants as a result of increased atmospheric carbon dioxide concentration.
- Depending on their mechanism of photosynthesis, certain types of plants are more sensitive to changes in atmospheric carbon dioxide concentration.
- In particular, plants that produce a three-carbon compound (C_3) during photosynthesis including most trees and agricultural crops such as rice, wheat, soybean, potato and vegetables generally show a larger response than plants that produce a four-carbon compound (C_4) during photosynthesis mainly of tropical origin, including grasses and the agriculturally important crops such as maize, sorghum, millets and sorghum.

Cash crops: These crop plants are grown for sale to earn hard cash. The processing of such crops after harvest is beyond the means of individual farmers, for instance jute, tobacco, cotton and sugar cane.

Catch crop/emergency crop/contingent crop: These are the crops, which are cultivated to catch the forthcoming season. They replace a main crop that has failed due to biotic or climatic or management hazards and utilize the remaining period of the season. *e.g.*, mungbean, urdbean, cowpea, pearlmillet, spinach, radish, coriander, onion.

Cation exchange capacity: The sum total exchangeable cations adsorbed by a soil expressed in milliequivalents per 100g (Cmol (P^+)/kg) of soil.

Check dam: Small dam built across a gully or other small watercourse at suitable points to control water levels and regulate downstream discharges.

Check row planting: The process of planting in which row to row and plant to plant distances are uniform and plants across the rows are also in line.

Chemical oxygen demand (COD): It is a measure of the oxygen consumed when organic or inorganic matter is oxidized in water chemically, rather than biologically.

Chlorophyll meter: Also known as Soil – Plant Analysis Development (SPAD) meter. Used to measure **chlorophyll content** of leaves and is a non-destructive method to determine the right time of N top dressing for rice.

Chlorophyll: Green pigment functioning as receptors of light energy in photosynthesis; consist of magnesium-porphyrin complex.

Chloroplast: Chlorophyll-containing photosynthetic organelle in eukaryotic cells.

Cleaning crops: These are crop plants whose agronomic practices make the field clean from weeds and stubble, for instance potato, groundnut, ginger, turmeric and colocasia which require considerable earth work such as earthing up, preparation of irrigation and drainage channels, placement of top-dressed fertilizers and harvesting by digging which helps to disturb the soil surface, the site of weed growth.

Climacteric fruit : Fruits in which the respiration rate is **minimum** at maturity and remains rather constant even after harvest which gradually increases at the beginning of ripening followed by a sharp rise to a peak (climacteric peak) and then slowly decline (post climacteric stage). *e.g.,* sapota, mango, banana, custard apple etc.

Clinometer: A simple instrument for measuring vertical angles or slopes.

Clostridium: An anaerobic bacteria commonly found in soil. Some species of Clostridium can fix atmospheric N_2. ***Clostridium pasteurianum*** was the first non-symbiotic N-fixing bacteria to be reported.

Clothesline effect: Horizontal heat transfer from a zone of warm upwind over a relatively cool irrigated crop field.

Cloud burst: Highly concentrated rainfall over a small area lasting a few hours.

C:N ratio:

- The ratio between organic C and N in organic materials or soils.
- When C:N ratio of crop residues is **below 20**, there is a net gain (release) of mineral N.
- If C:N ratio **>30**, there is a **net immobilization** of mineral N and the crop may even face a temporary N-deficiency.
- C:N ratio between **20 and 30**, there is **no mineralization or immobilization**.
- C:N ratio in sawdust > 100:1

  Rice straw 66:1

  FYM 16:1
- FYM is better manure than saw dust and rice straw.
- Application of N_2 fixing biofertilizer improves C:N ratio. That is why N-rich legume residues decompose faster than N-depleted cereal residues.
- C:N ratio of upper 15 cm of arable land ranges from 8:1 to 15:1

Coarse grains: Generally refers to cereal grains other than wheat and rice.

Coenzyme: An organic factor required for the action of certain enzymes; often contains a vitamin as a component, a substance necessary for the activity of an enzyme.

Cole crops: These crop plants are essentially cold weather crops belonging to the Cruciferae family capable of withstanding considerable frost such as cabbage, cauliflower and Brussels sprouts. Colewarts is the ancestor of wild cabbage from which the name cole has been derived.

Colluvium: Unconsolidated, unsorted earth material being transported or deposited on side slopes and/or at the base of slopes by mass movement.

Colza oil: Oil from rapeseed

Commensalism: An inter-organism interaction in which one organism is aided by the interaction and the other is neither benefitted nor harmed.

Commercial farming: Specialized farming enterprise that is capital-intensive and aimed at profit maximization.

Companion crop: In intercropping situations when subsidiary crops are usually of a shorter duration in a long duration main crop *i.e.,* the main crop gets the company of a short duration crop for a certain period at the early stages of its growth, for instance potato, onion and spinach in autumn planted sugarcane, lady's finger and *Amaranthus* in spring planted sugarcane; radish in potato; cowpea, ricebean, mungbean in napier.

Conjugated protein: A protein containing a metal or an organic prosthetic group, or both.

Conjunctive water use: The joining together of two sources of irrigation water, such as ground water and surface water, to serve a particular piece of land.

Conservation agriculture:

- A concept of resource saving agricultural crop production that strives to achieve acceptable profits together with high and sustained production levels while concurrently conserving the environment.
- It emphasizes minimum soil disturbance, permanent soil cover through crop residues or other cover crops and diversified crop rotation using a legume.

Contiguous drought: Drought resulting from irregular precipitation patterns which cause a moisture deficit during the rainy season.

Contract farming: Contract farming can be defined as an agreement between farmers and processing and/or marketing firms for the production and supply of agricultural products under forward agreements, frequently at predetermined prices.

Convection: A process by which heat, solutes, or particles are transferred from one part of a fluid to another by movement of the fluid itself; also called advection.

Co-operative farming: Co-operative farming means a system under which all agricultural operations or part of them are carried out jointly by the farmers on a voluntary basis; each farmer retaining right in his own land. The farmers pool their land, labour and capital. The land is treated as one unit and cultivated jointly under the direction of an elected management. A part of profit is distributed in proportion to the land contributed by each farmer and the rest of the profit is distributed in proportion to the wages earned by each farmer.

Cotton fibre: An elongation or outgrowth of an epidermal cell of the seed coat. Fibres are made from cellulose. The long outgrowth forms the **staple or lint** while the shorter outgrowth forms the **fuzz**.

C:P ratio:

- The ratio between organic carbon and phosphorus in organic materials, soil etc.
- **Net mineralization** (release) of organic P results if the C:P ratio < **200**.
- **Net immobilization** of P above C:P ratio of **300**.
- Application of biofertilizer improves (narrows down) C:P ratio.

Crassulacean Acid Metabolism (CAM) plants: Plants in which the first product of CO_2 fixation is the *4-carbon compound oxalo acetic acid* or malic acid. These are mostly succulents. Generally characterized by very high dry matter production per unit water used, absence of photo respiration and ability to utilize very low CO_2 concentration (0-5 ppm) resulting in very high NAR and photosynthetic efficiency as compared to C_3 and C_4 plants. PEP carboxylase in the cytosol of CAM plants is the enzyme responsible for CO_2 fixation into malate at night but rubisco becomes active during daylight as in C_3 and C_4 plants. *e.g.,* pineapple, century plant (*Agave sisalina*), *Aloe vera* etc.

Crop associated weed : Non-parasitic weed associated with a specific crop *e.g.,* chicory (*Chicorium intybus*) and swine cress (*Coronopus didymus*) in berseem and Lucerne, wild rice (*Oryza sativa fatua*) in paddy and wild oats (*Avena fatua*) and canary grass (*Phalaris minor*) in small grain crops.

Crop bound weed: A parasitic weed that partially or fully depends for its growth on some nutrients drawn from its host plant *e.g.,* Dodder (*Cuscuta spp.*), loranthus (*Dendroptheae falcata*), broomrape (*Orobanche spp.*) and witch weed (*Striga spp.*).

Crop ecology: The study of the relationships between crop plants and their environment.

Crop lodging : The falling down of a crop due to strong winds, common in long stature crops such as sugarcane, pearl millet, sorghum, maize, tall wheat etc. in sugarcane, it can be prevented by trench planting, earthing up, wrapping and propping.

Crop logging: A record of the progress of crop growth from its start until harvest. Approach developed by **HF Clements** in Hawaii in sugarcane.

Widely used to monitor the progress of crops like sugarcane and to suggest mid term corrective measures such as nutrient application.

Crop residue management: use of the non-commercial portion of the crop for protection or soil improvement activities.

Cropping index: The number of crops grown per annum on a given area of land multiplied by 100.

Crop water use efficiency: The ratio of crop yield to the amount of water depleted by the crop plants through evapo-transpiration.

$$\text{Crop water use efficiency} = \frac{\text{Yield (kg / ha)}}{\text{Evapotranspiration (mm)}}$$

C:S ratio:

- The ratio of organic carbon to sulphur in organic materials, soils etc.
- At C:S ratio of **less than 200, net mineralization** (release) of organic S is expected in the soil
- C:S ratio > **400** favours **net immobilization** (tying up) of mineral S.

Cupping: The upward turning of leaf edge to form a cup – like structure as seen in case of Mo deficiency.

Darcy's law:

- Darcy's law states that the velocity of a fluid in permeable media is directly proportional to the hydraulic gradient.
- In this law, hydraulic conductivity (K) is taken as proportionality constant.
- Darcy stated that the rate of flow increases with an increased depth of water above the bottom of the soil and decreases with an increased depth of soil, through which water flows.

Dead furrow: An open trench left in between adjacent strips of land after completion of ploughing

Deciduous: Used in reference to trees that loses their leaves every year, as distinguished from evergreens.

Deep soil: A soil having a solum depth of more than 100 cm.

Denitrification:

- The biochemical reduction of nitrate or nitrite to gaseous nitrogen in the soil either as molecular nitrogen or as an oxide of nitrogen usually carried out by denitrifying bacteria, which result in escape of nitrogen to the atmosphere.
- Denitrifying bacteria break down nitrates anaerobically to produce nitrogen.

Diara land/Recession farming: It is a system in which crops are planted in flooded areas as the rainy season ends and water recedes. This system takes advantage of silt and nutrients left behind by flood water.

Diffusion: The tendency of molecules to move from higher concentration to lower concentration.

Diversified cropping: A cropping plan in which no single crop contributes 50% or more towards the total crop production or monetary income (comparable equivalents).

Double cropping: Taking two crops a year in sequence on the same piece of land.

Drosometer: Instrument for measuring dew.

Drought year: If the annual rainfall is less than or equal to 75 per cent of the normal, that year is said to be a drought year.

Ecosystem: A major interacting system that involves both living organisms and their physical environment.

Ecotype: A group of biotypes especially adapted to a specific environmental niche.

El Nino: It is a band of warm ocean water temperatures that periodically develops off the **pacific coast of South America**.

- Typically this anomaly happens at irregular intervals of **two to seven years**, and lasts **nine months to two years**.
- The average period length is **five years**.
- When this warming occurs for only **7 to 9 months** it is classified as **El Nino "conditions"**. When it occurs for more than that period, it is classified as **El Nino "episodes"**.
- El Nino is **Spanish** for **"the boy"** and the capitalized term El Nino refers to the **Christ child, Jesus**, because periodic warming in the pacific near South America is usually noticed around Christmas.
- When the trade winds weaken, **EL Nino** develops.

- Meteorologists refer to the two phenomena of El Nino and Southern Oscillation that are atmospheric and oceanic parts of global system of climatic fluctuations as **ENSO**.
- El Nino is a disruption of the ocean-atmosphere system in the **tropical pacific** having important consequences for weather around the globe.
- Among these consequences are **increased rainfalls** across the **southern tier of the USA and in Peru**, which cause destructive flooding, and **drought** in the regions of **west pacific**, sometimes associated with devastating bush fires in Australia.
- Though the effects of the ENSO are global, the most pronounced anomalies occur in the **Indian ocean-tropical pacific sector**.
- West Pacific – Indian ocean monsoon regions such as **Australia, Indonesia, Philippines and India** experience **drought** during El Nino years resulting in crop losses.
- El Nino causes a massive flooding in the arid zone of Peru.
- Maize production has been found to be much higher in Argentina during El Nino years.
- El Nino and La Nina classified based on Southern Oscillation Index and Sea surface temperature.

Eluvial horizon: A soil horizon that has been formed by the process of eluviation.

Eluviation: The removal of soil material in suspension (or in solution) from a layer or layers of a soil. Usually, the loss of material in solution is described by the term leaching.

Energy crops: Crops grown specifically for the fuel value. These include food crops such as corn and sugarcane, and non food crops such as poplar trees and switch grass.

Energy farming: The process of using land to grow crops, woody or otherwise, that provide fuel, for example, close-planted, fast growing tree species such as poplar (temperate) or Leucaena (tropical).

Enriched Compost:

- **Compost** fortified with the addition of fertilizers (urea, SSP, rock phosphate) during its production to raise its nutrient content and narrow down the C:N ratio.

Entisol: Mineral soils that have no distinct subsurface diagnostic horizons within 1 m of the soil surface. These soils have little or slight development and properties that reflect their parent material. They include soils on steep slopes, flood plains, and sand dunes. Example: Alluvial soils. Such soils can be deficient in sulphur, boron, zinc, iron and manganese.

Epinasty: Increased growth on the upper surface of a plant organ or part (especially leaves) causing it to bend downwards.

Epiphyte: A plant which grows on another plant but does not secure nourishment from it.

Eutrophication:

- A process of water enrichment with some nutrients particularly **nitrogen and phosphorus**, resulting in abundant aquatic plant growth.
- Such water is deficient in oxygen.
- It is the promotion of growth of plants, animals and micro organisms in lakes and rivers.
- If the growth is uninterrupted, a deficiency of O_2 results and favours anaerobic organisms, and life of aerobes including fish is endangered.

Evergreen revolution: A term coined by **Dr M.S. Swaminathan** to denote the green revolution based on sustainable methods of intensification and diversification.

Exhaustive crops: These are crop plants, which on growing leave the field exhausted because of a more aggressive nature, for instance sorghum, maize, sesame, brinjal and linseed.

Feni/Fenny/Fenim: A fermented product of the juice from cashew nut or cashew apple.

Fertilizer salt-index: The ratio of the decrease in osmotic potential of a solution containing a fertilizer compound or mixture to that produced by the same weight of sodium nitrate ($NaNO_3$) x 100.

Field water use efficiency:

- It is the ratio of crop yield to the total amount of water used in the field.
- Field water use efficiency = **yield/water used in field**

Flood recession farming:

- It is the practice of growing crops on land that is flooded annually and crops are grown during the recession period.
- By way of sediment deposits, soil fertility is improved.

Fodder: Coarse grasses such as maize and sorghum harvested with the seed and leaves green or live, cured and fed in their entirety as forage.

Forage: All browse and herbaceous food that is available to livestock. Material such as pasture, hay, silage and green feed in contrast to the less digestible plant material known as roughage.

(or)

Edible parts of plants, other than separated grain, that can provide feed for grazing animals, or that can be harvested for feeding.

Fortified fertilizer: A fertilizer to which another compound has been deliberately added which enhances its nutrient value. Several common fertilizers can be fortified with compounds of nutrients such as S, B and Mo. Example: Boronated SSP, Zincated urea.

Fouling crops: These are crop plants whose cultural practices allow the infestation of weeds intensively, for instance maize, cotton and direct seeded upland rice as they have low covered over the ground at their earlier stages of growth and wider spacing.

Frankia: The nitrogen-fixing actinomycetes under the family frankiaceae. It is capable of inducing root nodules with non-leguminous woody plants (e.g. *Alnus, Casuarina, Datisca, Myrica* etc. in temperate, tropical and sub tropical regions. Known also as *Actinorhizal endophyte*. Capable of fixing **50-200 kg** N/ha/year.

Fuel crops: These crop plants are grown to obtain fire wood or solid fuel as a by-product along with their economic yield, for instance jute, sugarcane, pigeonpea, cotton, mustard and sesame.

Fuzz: The unmarketable and non-separable lint or fibre attached with cotton seeds. These are non-marketable fibres and their greater proportion shows an inferior quality of the variety.

Gamma-ray attenuation technique: When a narrow beam of gamma-radiation is passed through the soil, the rays are attenuated depending upon the **thickness of soil mass**, the **bulk density** and **water content** of soil following the principle of **Beer's law**. If the **thickness** and **bulk density** of soil are known, water content of the soil can be determined.

Ginning: The process of separating lint from seed cotton in ginning factory.

Ginning percentage: The weight of cotton lint obtained from seed cotton expressed in terms of percentage of seed cotton or percentage of lint obtained from 100 unit of seed cotton by weight. It can be calculated as follows.

$$\text{Ginning percentage} = \frac{\text{Yield of lint in tonnes / ha}}{\text{Yield of seed cotton in tonnes / ha}} \times 100$$

Glucosinolates: These are a class of organic compounds that contain sulphur, nitrogen and a group derived from glucose, which provide pungency, strong smell and bitterness in oils and onion.

Glutelins: Proteins that are insoluble in neutral solutions but soluble in weak acidic or basic solutions. These proteins are mostly formed in cereal grains, for example, glutenin from wheat and oxygenin from rice.

Gluten: Wheat proteins are collectively called as gluten.

Gossipol: A phenolic pigment in cotton seed that is toxic to some animals.

Grassland: A plant community in which grasses are dominant, shrubs are rare and trees absent.

Green power: Electricity that is generated from renewable energy sources is often referred to as green power.

Green revolution: A term used to describe the success in increased crop production throughout Asia, commencing in the 1960s as a result of high-yielding rice varieties developed by IRRI and wheat varieties by CIMMYT.

Gross cropped area: The total area covered with crops during a year. When three crops are grown on same land during one year, the same land area is counted thrice.

Gross irrigation water requirement: The net water requirement plus distribution and application losses in operating the system. Gross irrigation requirement (GIR) is the net irrigation requirement plus water application losses or the total amount of irrigation water to be applied through irrigation.

$$\text{Gross irrigation requirement} = \frac{\text{Net irrigation requirement}}{\text{Efficiency of irrigation system}}$$

Guano: The name given to the collected droppings of seabirds, bats, and seals.

Guar gum: A substance made from the seeds of the guar plant, which acts as a stabilizer in food sytems. Is found as a food additive in cheese, including processed cheese, ice cream and dressings.

Guard crops: These crop plants help to protect another crop from trespassing or restrict the speed of wind and thus crop damage such as safflower in gram, *Saccharum munjo* around the crop fields situated on the banks of torrential rivers.

Haulm: The stems and leaves of a crop left after harvest, *e.g.* in potato.

Hay: It is dried grass or legumes cut, stored, and used for animal feed, particularly for grazing animals like cattle, horses, goats and sheep.

Heading: Emergence of the panicle out of the flag-leaf sheath is called heading. It occurs after booting.

Hedge: Bushes or shrubs or trees planted in a row and trimmed. Used to separate one piece of land from another.

Hedgerow: A barrier of bushes, shrubs or small trees growing close together in a line. A hedge is similar but pruned.

Herbigation: It refers to application of herbicide with irrigation water.

Heterotroph: An organism able to derive carbon and energy for growth and cell synthesis by utilizing organic compounds.

Horizontal revolution in agriculture: Increased land use by expanding cultivated land area through the utilization of fallow and marginal lands and reclaiming cultural wastelands, thereby increasing land-use intensity.

Hull/husk: The outermost covering of the rice grain, which provides protection to the rice caryopsis composed of lemma and palea.

Hulling: The removal of the husks or hulls from the rice grain; converting rough rice or paddy into milled rice. It may be calculated by the following equation.

$$\text{Hulling percentage (\%)} = \frac{\text{Weight of rice}}{\text{Weight of paddy}} \times 100$$

Hydrocyanic acid (HCN): Poison, also called prussic acid, produced as a glucoside by several plant species, especially *Sorghum* and common sudangrass.

Hydrology: The science dealing with the distribution and movement of water.

Hydromorphic rice: Rice that is grown where the water table is very close to the surface.

Hydrophilic: Molecules and surfaces that have a strong affinity for water molecules.

Hydrophilic: Water loving

Hydrophobic: Molecules and surfaces that have little or no affinity for water molecules.

Hydrophobic: Water hating

Hydroponics: The technique of growing plants in aqueous solution of essential nutrients.

Hyetograph: Graphical representation of rainfall intensity against time.

Hypoxia: A state of low oxygen concentration in water/soil and sediments, relative to the needs of most aerobic species.

Ideotype: Ideal type plant of a particular crop which performs in a predictable manner in a particular environment.

Illuviation: The process of deposition of soil material removed from one horizon to another in the soil; usually from an upper to a lower horizon in the soil profile.

Illuvial horizon: A soil layer or horizon in which material carried from an overlying layer has been precipitated from solution or deposited from suspension. The layer of accumulation.

Inceptisol: Mineral soils that have one or more pedogenic horizons in which mineral materials other than carbonates or amorphous silica have been altered or removed but not accumulated to a significant degree. Soil order representing moderately developed soils of the humid region. Soils showing development in between that found in Entisols and Alfisols. Example: Alluvial soils. Such soils can be deficient in sulphur, boron, zinc, iron and manganese.

Income equivalent ratio (IER): The ratio of the area under sole cropping needed to produce the same gross income as one hectare of intercropping at the same management level. IER is the conversion of the land equivalent ratio (LER) into economic terms.

Infiltration rate/flux: The volume of water entering a specified cross-sectional area of soil per unit time; expressed in mm/h or mm/day.

Infiltration: The downward entry of water into the soil, which is a surface phemenon.

Integrated weed management: A weed control program that combines two or more weed control methods. Methods commonly considered prevention, eradication, mechanical, cultural, biological and chemical control.

Intensive cropping: Maximum use of the land by means of frequent succession of harvested crops.

Intensive farming: A system of farming with the aim to produce the maximum number of crops in a year with a high yield from the land available and to maintain a high stocking rate of livestock.

Inverse nitrogen yield concept: According to Willcox, the yield of the crop is inversely proportional to its nitrogen content, *e.g.,* $Y = K^{-n}$; where Y = yield; n = N(%) in crop, K = constant (**318 lb/acre**)

Iron oxidizing bacteria: Bacteria that derive energy by oxidizing ferrous iron (Fe^{2+}) to ferric iron (Fe^{3+}). Example: *Thiobacillus ferroxidans.*

Irrigation frequency: Time interval between irrigations.

Irrigation interval: Number of days between two successive irrigations during the peak period of consumptive use of the crop is known as **irrigation interval**.

Irrigation period: The number of hours or days that it takes to apply one irrigation to a given design area during the peak consumptive-use period of the crop being irrigated. It is the basis for designing the capacity of an irrigation project.

Isobar: Lines on a map joining points of equal atmospheric pressure.

Isobath: Line connecting points of equal water depth on a chart.

Isodrosotherm: The line drawn on a weather map connecting points of equal dew point.

Isohel: A line drawn through geographic points having equal duration of sunshine or another form of solar radiation during a specified time period.

Isohyet: A line on a chart or diagram drawn through places or points having the same rainfall or precipitation over a stated period.

Isomorphous substitution: The replacement of one atom by another of similar size in a crystal structure without disrupting or seriously changing the structure. When a substituting cation is of a smaller valence than the cation it is replacing, there is a net negative charge on the structure.

Isonephs: A line on a weather map or chart connecting points having the same amount of cloudiness.

Isopleth: Any line on a chart or diagram drawn through places or points having the same value of a meteorological element.

Isotach: A line connecting equal wind speeds.

Isotherm: Lines on a map joining points of equal temperature.

Kelvin scale: Scale for measuring temperature. In this scale, absolute zero is 0 Kelvins, water boils at 373.15 Kelvins and freezes at 273.15 Kelvins.

Kharif crops: Crops grown during the main monsoon season (April to September), such as *kharif* sorghum, maize, bajra, rice, cotton *etc.*

Kilopascal (kPa): Unit for measuring force and pressure. Equivalent to 10,000 dynes cm^{-2}.

Kirchoff's law: This law suggests that good emitters of radiation are also good absorbers of radiation at specific electromagnetic radiation wavelength bands.

L – value: A measure of the quantity of available P in the soil, defined by Larsen.

Lambert's law: The intensity of radiation passing through a material decays exponentially with path length b.

La Nina: The reverse phenomenon of the cooling of the eastern pacific is called as La Nina (The Girl).

- It is the climatic opposite of the **El Nino**.
- Less heating leads to colder sea waters off western South America coast, thus making it a high pressure zone which pushes the moist sea winds towards the Indian ocean therefore, increasing chances of normal or excessive rainfall in the Indian subcontinent.

Laser land leveling:

- It is a prerequisite for adopting conservation agriculture practices in any field.
- It alters fields having a constant slope of 0 to 0.2% using laser equipped drag buckets and gives a smooth land surface ($\pm$ 2 cm).
- Large horsepower tractors and soil movers equipped with global positioning system (GPS) or laser-guided instrumentation help to move soil either by cutting or filling to create the desired slope.

- Laser leveling provides a very accurate, smooth and graded field, which helps in saving of irrigation water up to 20% and improves the use-efficiency of applied N.

Latent heat of condensation: The amount of heat energy released to the environment when a gas changes its state to a liquid. For one gram of water, the amount of heat energy released is 540 calories at a temperature of 100° Celsius.

Latent heat of vaporization: The amount of heat energy required from the environment to change the state of a liquid to a gas. For one gram of water, the amount of heat energy required is **540 calories** at a temperature of 100° Celsius.

Lateritic soils:

- Soils formed insitu by the leaching out of the bases from the parent rock under monsoon conditions of alternate dry and wet seasons.
- These are characterized by poor fertility and deficient in N,P, K and Ca.

Laterization:

- Process of leaching out completely of calcium at or near the surface of the soil in heavy rainfall areas under tropical conditions, due to intense weathering taking place to a great depth.
- Iron and aluminium concentrate at or near the surface of the soil.

Lathyrism: Paralytic condition of animals caused by consumption of forage or seed of certain plants of genus ***Lathyrus***.

Leaching: Removal of a nutrient or non-nutrient substance by downward movement with percolating waters out of reach of plant roots.

Legumin: Protein found in the seeds of legumes.

Length of growing period (LGP): It is the duration of rainy season plus the period for which the soil moisture storage at the end of post rainy season and winter rainfall can meet the crop water needs.

LGP	Cropping system
Less than 75 days	Perennial vegetation
75 to 140 days	Sole cropping of short duration varieties
140 to 180 days	Intercropping
More than 180 days	Double cropping

Climate	Length of growing period
Arid	< 75 days during *kharif* 75-140 days during *kharif*
Semi arid	75-140 140-180 >180
Sub humid	75-140 140-180 >180
Humid	140-180 >180
Ecosystem	**LGP**
Arid ecosystem	< 90 days
Semi arid ecosystem	90-150 days
Sub humid ecosystem: Northern plains Central highlands Eastern plateau	150-180 days
Sub humid ecosystem: Western Himalayas	180 – 210 + days
Humid per humid ecosystem	210 + days
East coast plain	90 – 210 + days
Coastal ecosystem	210 + days
Island ecosystem	210 + days

Ley crops: These consist of any crop or combination of crop plants that is grown for grazing or harvesting for immediate or future feeding to livestock, for instance marvel grass + berseem, Dinanath grass + cowpea, berseem + mustard.

Ley farming: Farming system involving a rotation of arable crops requiring annual cultivation and pastures occupying the field for 2 or more years, before the arable crops are raised again. The legume component of the pasture is a major source of nitrogen for sustaining ley farming.

Ley pasture: A sown pasture used for a specific period of time and which is alternated with crops.

Ligand: An organic molecule, which can form a chelated complex with a metal cation. Also called chelating agent. Example: EDTA, DTPA, EDDHA.

Lignin: Important constituent (10-40%) of soil organic matter. It also constitutes 25-30% of the wood of tree. A resistant material which is difficult to decompose.

Limnology: The scientific study of physical, chemical, meteorological, and biological conditions in fresh waters.

Lint index (LI): The weight of lint per seed cotton or 100 seeds.

$$LI = \frac{\text{Weight of 100 seeds}}{\text{Ginning percentage}} \times 100$$

LISA (Low-Input Sustainable Agriculture): It is an alternative method of agriculture that reduces the application of purchased inputs such as fertilizer, pesticides, and herbicides. Methods include crop rotation, mechanical cultivation to control weeds, integrated pest management strategies, application of livestock manures, municipal sludge, and compost for fertilizer and over seeding of legumes into maturing fields of grain crops.

Local Mean Time: The surface of the earth is divided into 24 time zones. The time established in each zone is **'standard time'**. The Indian Standard Time (IST) is the Local Mean Time (LMT) for the longitude of **82°50' E**, which passes through **Allahabad**. The LMT is based on the transit of the mean sun. To calculate LMT from IST, it is essential to know the **longitude** of the season.

The relation between IST and LMT is as follows:

$$LMT = IST - 4(\lambda_s - \lambda)$$

Where, λ_s = standard longitude (82°50' E) passing over Allahabad

λ = longitude of the station for which local time is calculated

Loess: Material transported and deposited by wind and consisting of predominantly silt-sized particles.

Lopping: Cutting one or more branches of a standing tree, Example, for fuel or fodder.

Lowland rice: Rice grown on fields where water is held by bunds. About 30% of the world's rice is grown as rainfed lowland; about 45% as irrigated lowland. Some areas are flooded lowlands.

Luxury consumption/uptake: Absorption of a nutrient by a plant well in excess of the quantities required. Common in case of N, K and Cl but can also occur in Zn. A waste from farmer's view point since the excess nutrient absorbed does not lead to extra yield increase. Reduces the physiological nutrient use efficiency through increased crop recovery of added nutrients.

Lycopene: Lycopene is a carotenoid related to the better known beta-carotene. Lycopene gives tomatoes and some other fruits and vegetables their distinctive red colour. Nutritionally, it functions as an antioxidant.

Major project (irrigation): A project which can irrigate more than 10,000 ha of land.

Mangroves: Open or closed stands of trees and bushes occurring in the tropics in inter-tidal zones, usually around the mouths of rivers, creeks and lagoons where soils are heavy textured and have a fluctuating salt content and soil level.

Marginal land: Land which is not suitable, economical or productive in most circumstances for a generalized type of land use (agriculture, forestry, intensive grazing) due to the presence of climatic, soil associated or geographic constraints.

Medium project: An irrigation project irrigating an area between 2,000 to 10,000 ha.

Methemoglobinemia : A condition associated with nitrate toxicity as a result of consuming nitrate – rich water. Nitrate transforms ordinary oxyhaemoglobin into inactive methemoglobin and infants suffering from this condition have been referred to as blue babies due to development of grayish – blue skin and the problem as **blue baby syndrome**.

Midseason correction:

- It is a contingent management practice to overcome unexpected or unfavourable weather conditions.

  e.g., Thinning or population adjustment according to the availability of moisture in the dry spell.

Milled rice: Rice from which the hull and bran have been removed.

Milling yield/recovery: The estimate of the quantity of head rice (whole rice or nearly whole kernels) and of total milled rice that can be produced from a unit of rough rice. It is generally expressed as percentage. Rice milling yield refers to the amount of polished white rice obtained from unhusked rough rice.

Milling: The process of separating the hull or husk and bran from the paddy or rough rice into milled rice and bran-and-chaff.

Mimosine: An alkaloid toxic to animals, which is contained in some members of the legume family (*Mimosaceae*) including *Leucaena leucocephala.*

Modelling: The construction of physical, conceptual or mathematical simulations of the real world. Models help to show relationships between processes (physical, economic or social) and may be used to predict the effects of changes in land use.

Moisture adequacy index: It is the ratio of actual to potential evapo-transpiration.

Moisture index (I_m): obtained by comparing the water need at a given place with the moisture surplus and deficit. The generalized moisture index is computed as:

$$I_m = \frac{100\ s - 60\ d}{n}$$

where n = water need, s = surplus and d = deficiency

Mollisols:

- Soils with nearly black organic rich surface horizons and high supply of bases.
- They have mollic epipedons and base saturation greater than 50% in any cambic or argillic origin.
- Lack the characteristics of vertisols.
- Must not have oxic or spodic horizons.

Monoecious : A condition when male and female flowers are borne separately on the same plant.

Muck: Organic soil material in which the original plant parts are not recognizable.

Nano Technology: It is the manipulation or self assembly of individual items, molecules or molecular clusters into structures to create materials and devices with new or vastly different properties.

- Nano is greek word meaning dwarf
- Nanotechnology utilizes structures of 0.1 to 100 nm in size.
- Nano-structured catalysts will be available to increase the efficiency of pesticides and herbicides with lower doses.

Natural farming: Natural farming reflects the experiences and philosophy of Japanese farmer Masanobu Fukuoka. His books ***The one-straw Revolution: An Introduction to Natural Farming*** and ***The natural Way of Farming: The Theory and Practice of Green Philosophy*** describe what he calls "do-nothing farming". His farming method involves no tillage, no fertilizer, no pesticides, no weeding, no pruning, and remarkably little labour.

Niche: Adaptive role that a species has in a habitat. This includes its behaviour and interactions with other species.

Nipping or topping: Pruning of top branches of the plant to encourage reproductive growth. Commonly practiced in chickpea at 50-60 days after sowing (DAS) either by a flock of sheep or with spray of 2,3,5 – tri iodo benzoic acid (TIBA) @ 75 ppm.

No-till farming: A method of planting crops that involves no seed bed preparation other than opening the soil to place individual seeds in holes or small slits; usually no cultivation during crop production; chemical weed control is normally used. No-till may be referred to as slot tillage or zero cultivation.

Notorious herbicides: It refers to the herbicides, which affect the crops in rotation even after two seasons of its application at normal rates.

Noxious weed: A plant arbitrarily defined by law as being especially undesirable, troublesome and difficult to control. *e.g., Cynodon dactylon, Cyperus rotundus, Sorghum halepense.*

Nurse crop: A companion crop, which nourishes the main crop by way of nitrogen fixation and/or adding the organic matter into the soil, *e.g.* cowpea intercropped with cereals or new plantations of fruit trees. These crop plants help in the nourishment of other crops by providing shade and acting as climbing sticks such as rai in peas, jowar in cowpea, *Tephrosia, Glyricidia, Crotalaria* in tea.

Non-climacteric fruits : Fruits showing a gradual decline in respiratory rate with ripening. e.g., grapes, ber, citrus *etc.*

Oasis effect: The exchange of heat between a growing crop and hot air whereby air over the crop is cooled.

Objectionable weed: Troublesome weed whose seeds once mixed with crop seeds are extremely difficult to separate.

Obligate aerobe: An organism that grows only in the presence of oxygen. Example: *Rhizobium, Azotobacter, Azospirillum.*

Obligate weed: Weed of cropland incapable of surviving in a wild community.

Olericulture: A branch of horticulture which deals with cultivation of vegetables.

Opportunity cropping: The practice of placing primary emphasis on the use of stored soil moisture while determining whether or not to establish a crop.

Osmosis: Bulk flow of water through a semi-permeable membrane into another aqueous phase containing a solute in a higher concentration.

Outer/guard/border crop: The crops which are grown around the field boundaries in narrow strips with twin objectives of protecting the main crop from stray cattle and producing livestock feed and /or seed are called outer or guard crops ***e.g.,*** *Sesbania* or *Leucaena* on boundaries of field / plantation crops and castor around spring planted sugarcane.

Oxylophytes: Plants tolerant to high acidic soil conditions.

Paddock: A grazing area that is a subdivision of a grazing management unit, and is enclosed a separated from other areas by a fence or barrier.

Paira/utera crop: A crop sown broadcast in the standing crop of low land rice before its harvest where the residual moisture is used for the establishment of paira/utera crop. *e.g., Lathyrus*, gram, lentil etc. in standing crop of rice.

Paired row planting: In this technique two adjacent rows of the base crops are paired, reducing the inter-row space in the pair narrow enough to create some interspace between pairs of base crop rows but wide enough to minimize undue competition among plants.

Papain: The latex exudated from the unripe papaya fruit having proteolytic activity.

Parallel crops: These consist of two or more crops which are grown simultaneously but do not have inter-competitive effects *i.e.*, they are parallel with respect to competition, for instance maize + cowpea, jowar + pigeonpea.

Parboiled rice: Rough rice soaked overnight or longer in water at ambient temperature, followed by boiling or steaming the steeped rice at 100°C to gelatinize the starch. The rice is then cooled and dried before storage or milling. In this way part of the vitamins and minerals of the bran permeate the endosperm and are thus retained in the polished rice.

Partial factor productivity (PFP): The average productivity of a single factor, measured by grain output divided by the quantity of the factor applied.

Pasture: Fenced area of domesticated forages, usually improved, on which animals are grazed.

Pearling index (PI): An index used to determine the hardness of grain. A higher value of pearling index denotes less kernel hardness and vice-versa. The PI is determined as follows:

$$\text{Pearling Index} = \frac{100-(x-y)}{x}$$

Where, x = Initial sample weight which is normally 20 grains

y = Weight of the material left on mesh sieve

Peat soil: An organic soil in which the plant residues are recognizable.

Pedology: The scientific study of soils and their weathering profiles.

Phosphobacteria: Bacteria able to convert organic phosphorus into orthophosphate. *e.g., Bacillus megatherium var.phosphaticum.*

Phyllosphere: The surface of above-ground living plant parts.

Phytin: Main organic phosphorus compound in seeds. Occurs as the Ca and Mg salt of phytic acid. This is the source of P for new seedlings till they can absorb P from the soil.

Plant tissue test

- Refers to rapid chemical testing of plant tissue for colorimetric determination of the levels of nitrate, phosphorus and potassium in the sap of fresh plant tissue.
- Sometimes tests are also carried out for Mg, Ca, Mn and Zn.

Plough layer: The top 15-20 cm of soil normally ploughed or disturbed with tillage operations.

Ploughpan (hard pan): A hard layer of soil at 15-20 cm depth developed through continuous ploughing at the same depth.

Plough-sole depth: Ploughing up to a depth of 15 cm.

Podzolization (Silication): The chemical migration of aluminium and iron/organic matter resulting in the concentration of silica (i.e., silication) in the layer eluviated.

Point source pollution: Pollutants discharged from any identifiable point or pollution that can be traced back to a definite source, including pipes, ditches, channels, sewers, tunnels, and containers of various types.

Popping: A physiological disorder in groundnut due to calcium deficiency in which pods are without kernels or unfilled pods.

Pressmud: A by-product of sugar factories. Residue obtained by filtration of the precipitated impurities, which settle out in the process of clarification of the mixed juice from sugarcane.

Propping: Tops of the adjacent rows are brought close to each other and tied with a long rope running the full length of rows and fastened at either end by strong bamboo support. Commonly practiced in sugarcane to prevent it from lodging in cyclonic belts.

Psammophytes: Plants, which prefer or tolerate sand, particularly fine to medium sand, as a habitat.

Quadratic response: A growth rate in which the output goes on increasing linearly up to a certain level of input and then starts decreasing when input is increased further. In such cases the response is said to be quadratic or curvilinear and is given by: $Y = a + bx + cx^2$.

Quartz: One of the most common minerals in the earth's crust. Made up of silicon dioxide (SiO_2), also called silica.

Quick lime/burned lime/oxide lime: Calcium oxide (CaO) with or without magnesium oxide (MgO). Ground limestone is heated in a kiln to drive off CO_2.

Rabbing: It is a traditional practice of raising seedlings of rice in which undisturbed soil nursery area is heated by low burning of dry cow dung, dry leaves, branches of trees and dry grass spread layer-wise. This practice, though leads to destruction of organic matter, cow dung and favourable microorganisms, provides effective weed control and prevents immobilization of nutrients by the soil microorganisms.

Rabi crops: Crops which are grown during the winter season (October – November to March – April) with irrigation or on conserved soil moisture *e.g.*, wheat, barley, oats, chickpea, safflower etc.

Rainforest: Generally, a forest that grows in a region of heavy annual precipitation. There are both tropical and temperate rainforests.

Rainy day: A 24 hour period in which > **2.5 mm** is recorded.

Ranching: Commercial raising of grazing animals, mainly for meat, under extensive production systems usually with controlled boundaries and paddocks.

Range or rangeland: A kind of land on which the native vegetation, climax or natural potential consists predominately of grasses, grass-like plants or shrubs. Rangeland includes lands re-vegetated naturally or artificially to provide a plant cover that is managed like native vegetation. Rangelands may consist of natural grasslands, savannahs, shrub lands, most deserts, tundra, alpine communities, coastal marshes, and wet meadows.

Ratoon cropping: the cultivation of an additional crop from the regrowth of stubbles of previous main crop after its harvest, thereby avoiding reseeding/replanting such as in sugarcane, sorghum, rice, fodder grasses etc.

Recession farming (diara land farming): It is a system in which crops are planted in flooded areas as the rainy season ends and water recedes. This system take advantage of thoroughly saturated soil profile and also has the advantage of silt and nutrients left behind by flood water.

Red rice: A rice kernel that has a red seed coat frequently found in African rice *Oryza glaberrima* or some *Oryza sativa* cultivars.

Red soils: Comprise vast area of Tamil Nadu, Karnataka, Goa, Daman and Diu, south eastern Maharashtra, Madhya Pradesh, Odisha and Chhotanagpur. In the north it includes the Santhal Paraganas in Bihar, the Birbhum district of West Bengal, the Mirzapur, Jhansi and Hamirpur district of Uttar Pradesh. The ***ancient crystalline and metamorphic rocks on weathering have given rise to the red soils***. The red colour is due to the wide diffusion of iron than to the high proportion of it. They are generally poor in nitrogen, phosphorus and humus. These soils are poorer in lime, potash, iron oxide and phosphorus than the regur soils. ***The clay fraction of red soils is rich in kaolinite***.

Regolith: The unconsolidated material overlying rocks is known as regolith and includes A, B and C horizons.

Regur: An intrazonal group of dark calcareous soils high in clay, which is mainly montmorillonitic, and formed mainly from rocks low in quartz; occurring extensively on the Deccan Plateau of India.

Relative weed: These are crop plants which when grow at the places where these are undesirable.

Respiratory Quotient: The number of molecules of CO_2 liberated for each molecule of O_2 consumed.

Respiratory quotient for carbohydrates is 1.0

Respiratory quotient for Proteins and fats < 1.0

Respiratory quotient for Organic acids >1.0

Restorative crops: These are crops, which provide a good harvest along with enrichment or restoration or amelioration of the soil, such as legumes. They fix atmospheric nitrogen in root nodules, shed their leaves during ripening and thus restore soil conditions.

Retting: Retting is a microbial process in which aerobic and anaerobic bacteria and fungi loosen the fibre by decomposing and dissolving the pectin, hemicelluloses and other cementing agents. It completes in about 8-30 days. The optimum temperature for jute retting is **34°C**. Slow moving clear water is best for good retting. *Sesbania aculeata* and *Crotolaria juncea* are added as an activator for hastening the retting process.

Rhizosphere: Volume or zone of soil immediately surrounding plant roots which is most influenced by root activity and metabolism.

Rice husk: Outer covering of the rice grain. It constitutes about 25% of paddy or rough rice and finds various uses. It can be used in agriculture as a carrier of biofertilizer and as raw material for compost making. It is also burnt and the ash used on the seed bed to protect from pest and disease infestation.

Riparian crops: These crop plants are grown along irrigation and drainage channels or water bodies such as water-bind weed (*Kalmi sak*), pepperwort (*sushni sak*), para grass, Sesbania, bhabhar or babui (*Elaliopsis binate*). They help to protect the soil from erosion.

Roughage: Plant materials containing a low proportion of nutrients per unit of weight and usually bulky and coarse, high in fibre and low in total digestible nutrients. Roughage may be either dry or green.

Runoff farming: When the collected runoff water is directly applied to the cropped area during the rainfall event, the system does not use long-term storage. The soil profile serves as a water reservoir and the method of irrigation is called runoff farming.

Salt index: It is a measure of the relative tendency of a fertilizer to increase the osmotic pressure of the soil solution as compared to the increase cause by an equal weight of sodium nitrate ($NaNO_3$) as a reference material.

Salt tolerance: The degree to which a plant species can tolerate salt concentration in the medium without large adverse effect on yield. Can range from EC of 16 in barley (salt tolerant) to 2.5 in beans (low salt tolerance).

Satellite weed: Weed that has become an integral part of a crop ecosystem.

Sedges: Members of the family Cyperaceae. They bear a close resemblance to the grasses and can be distinguished by a thin **triangular stem**, the absence of ligules, and the fusion of leaf sheaths forming a tube around the stem.

Seed plot technique: It is a technique of disease free seed material of potato particularly virus free in northern plains of the country.

Shifting cultivation:

- Forest land cleared and cultivated.
- Same crop is grown year after year, so soil productivity is lost
- Crop is shifted to another slashed and burnt land
- Crop is fixed but land is rotated
- Causes soil erosion
- Practiced in northeastern states, hilly regions, Chotanagpur area of Jharkhand, MP

Siderophore: A non porphyrin metabolite secreted by certain microorganisms that forms a highly stable coordination compound with iron.

Smother crop: A dense growing crop which can suppress or stop the growth of a less competitive crop; it is grown for the suppression of weeds.

Soilage: Forage produced to be chopped green and fed directly to livestock.

Solubor: A boron fertilizer particularly for foliar spray. Formula $Na_2B_4O_7.5H_2O + Na_2B_{10}O_{16}.10H_2O$ containing 19% B.

Sorghum injury: Poisoning of livestock resulting from feeding of young sorghum plants containing hydrocyanic acid (HCN). HCN concentration is more at seedling stage.

Sorghum sickness: Temporary locking of the next crop after sorghum cultivation.

Specific leaf area: Area of a leaf per unit leaf weight; expressed as square decimeters or centimetres per gram.

Specific leaf weight: Dry weight of leaf per unit area. Expressed by the formula Dry weight of leaf (g)/Area of the leaf (cm^2).

Spectrophotometer: An instrument for measuring the amount of light absorbed by a sample.

Spent wash: A distillery effluent. A type of polluting industrial wastes. It has high BOD and COD values and low pH (4-5). Can be used as an ingredient in composting.

Spillman's equation: According to Spillman plant growth increases with increasing application of limiting element but increase in growth is not in direct proportion to the amount of growth factor added. The increase in growth with each successive addition of the element in question is progressively smaller.

Spodosols: Soils with subsurface illuvial accumulations of organic matter and compounds of Al and usually Fe. These soils are formed in humid and mostly cool or temperate climates.

Spudding: Removal of weeds by cutting off below the soil surface.

Stale seed bed: A seed bed left unsown to let a heavy flush of weeds appear and be destroyed with herbicide before seeding the crop, without any further tillage.

Steppe: Term usually applied to areas with rainfall of <500-600mm per year and a dry season of 8-9 months.

Stoke's law: Velocity of fall of a particle (v) with the same density is directly proportional to the square of the radius (r) and inversely proportional to the viscosity of the medium.

Stover: Mature, cured stalks of such crops as maize, sorghum or millets from which grains have been removed, a type of roughage.

Straight fertilizer: A traditional term referring to fertilizers, which contain one major nutrient as opposed to multi-nutrient carriers.

Strip tillage: Tillage operations performed in alternate strips of tilled and untilled soil.

Sublimation: Process where ice changes into water vapour without first becoming liquid. This process requires approximately 680 calories of heat energy for each gram of water converted.

Subsistence farming: Growing crops and, where appropriate, keeping animals so as to provide food (cereals, pulses, vegetable and fruits), shelter materials, and possibly other products (fibres, medicinal) for family use.

Subtropical: The region between the tropical and temperate regions, an area between 35 and 40 degrees North and South latitude.

Sugar and starch crops: Crops grown for the production of sugar and starch are sugarcane, sugarbeet, potato, sweet potato, tapioca and asparagus.

Surfactant: A substance that lowers the surface tension of a liquid. It imparts spreading, wetting, dispersability or other surface-modifying properties.

Synecology: The ecology of populations and communities. (or) The study of groups of organisms that are associated as a unit.

Synergism: A phenomenon where the combined effect of two inputs is greater than the sum of their individual effects on a crop.

Tal lands: Beyond the natural levees there are bowl-shaped depressions geologically known as back water, which though inundated are not subjected to erosion.

Taungya system: Method of raising forest trees in combination with agricultural crops. Used in the early stages of establishing a forest plantation. It not only provides some food but also can lessen the establishment costs.

Temperate climate: Climate with distinct winter and summer seasons, typical of regions found between the tropic of cancer and capricorn and the arctic and antarctic circles.

Tensiometer: A device for measuring the soil-water matric potential 'in situ' (or) An instrument for measuring the amount of energy needed to extract water from the soil. (or) It is a device used to determine matric water potential (soil moisture tension) in soil.

Test weight: It denotes the weight of 1000-grains of field crops. In some crops, 100-seed weight is also considered.

Time-domain reflectometry: A method that uses the timing of wave reflections to determine the properties of various materials, such as the dielectric constant of soil as an indication of water content.

Toddy: A sugar containing juice which is obtained by tapping the unopened spadix of coconut palm.

Topping (tobacco): The removal of the terminal bud with or without some of the small top leaves just before or after the emergence of a flower bud.

Transgenics: The transfer of an unrelated desired gene from one organism to another or non-crossable species is called transgenics. The transgenic plants or animals so derived are called genetically modified organisms.

Trap crops: These crop plants are grown to trap soil borne harmful biotic agents such as parasitic weeds, Orobanche and Striga that are trapped by Solanaceous and sorghum crops, respectively. These weed seeds germinate when they come in contact with roots of these crop plants. Thereafter the destruction of this crop reduces the inoculums of such parasitic weeds. Similarly, some solanaceous crops trap nematodes. On uprooting crop plants, nematodes are pulled out from the field soil.

Trashing: Stripping of lower leaves of sugarcane crop is known as trashing.

Truck crops: Crops which yield in tonnes and grown for distance market requiring heavy transport. Truck crops include those crops that are not processed before selling and directly used or sold fresh such as lettuce, celery and flowers.

Ultisols: Soils that are low in bases and have subsurface horizons of alluvial clay accumulation.

Urease: Enzyme which catalyses the hydrolysis of urea to produce ammonium carbamate and ammonia. Abundantly present in soils with greatest activity in the rhizosphere. Micronutrient **nickel** is a component of urease.

Ureide: Ureides (allantoin and allantoic acid) are important storage and translocatory forms of N in nodulated legumes. These are synthesized within the nodules. Many tropical legumes including soybean export N from the nodule in the form of ureides.

Vermiculture: The activity of growing and multiplication of earthworms.

Vernalization: Method of inducing early flowering in plants by pre-treatment of the propagating material with very low temperature.

Vertical mulching: Incorporation of vegetative mulch in a band in the soil for the purpose of harvesting rain water and conserving soil and water.

Vertical revolution in agriculture: Maximising production per unit land area per unit of time using intensive cropping systems, high production inputs and improved management practices.

Virgin soil: A soil that has not been significantly disturbed from its natural environment.

V-notch: A type of weir containing a V-shaped notch used for gauging discharge in small streams.

Void ratio: The ratio of the volume of soil pore space to the Solid particle volume.

Ware crops: These crop plants are grown for temporary storing as intact in ware-houses for future use or sale, for instance potato, beet, carrot, onion. They are in general, fleshy fruits or roots of higher values.

Water yield: It is the total annual runoff volume

Wet year: If the rainfall exceeds twice the normal deviation at a particular place, that year is said to be a wet year.

Zaid: A relatively short crop season (April-June) in between the two main seasons *Rabi* and *Kharif.*

Zaid or summer crops: Crop plants grown during February-March to May-June such as blackgram, greengram, sesame and cowpea. They require warm dry weather for their major growth period and longer day-length for flowering.

Chapter 25

Agricultural Statistics

- **Statistics** is a branch of science which deals with collection, classification, analysis and interpretation of data for drawing sound and valid scientific conclusions. It is a mathematical analysis of data when data is collected in theory of probability.
- **Variable** is a quantity which varies from one observation to another observation.
- Any character which is considered to collect the data in an experiment is called as **variable**.
- **Continuous variable** takes successive values, including fractions or which takes any numerical value with in certain range.

  e.g., plant height, rainfall measurement, leaf area etc.
- **Discrete or discontinuous variable** takes only exact value. Here the variable is counted. It does not read the fractions.

  e.g., number of leaves, branches, tillers, flowers etc.
- **Population** is an aggregate of all individual units.
- Sample is a part of population or miniature of population, which represents that population.
- If the data is collected at an entire population and if estimation is made then the value is called as **'True value" or "Parametric value"**.
- Characteristics of frequency distribution
  - ✓ *Central tendency*
  - ✓ *Dispersion/ spread/ variability*
  - ✓ *Skewness*
  - ✓ *Kurtosis*
- The tendency of the data to concentrate at certain values is called as central tendency. Methods to determine **central tendency** are mean, median and mode.

- Among these three, mean is considered as better measure, in most of the estimations mean is commonly used.

$$\text{Mean} = \frac{\Sigma x}{n}$$

- Sum of all the deviations is equal to zero.
- The extent to which individual items in a particular distribution are scattered around the central tendency is called **dispersion**.
- Methods to determine dispersion are
  - ✓ Range
  - ✓ Average deviation or mean deviation
  - ✓ Standard deviation
  - ✓ Variance
  - ✓ Coefficient of variability
- **Average deviation** is the mean sum of deviation by ignoring the sign.
- Standard deviation is the square root of mean sum of squares of individual deviation.
- **Skewness** indicates the direction of scatteredness i.e., whether more items are attracted towards higher values or lower values. The values of observation are spread evenly or not.
- **Kurtosis:** Extent to which the distribution is more peaked or more flat topped than the normal distribution. There are three types of kurtosis
  - ✓ Lepto kurtic
  - ✓ Meso kurtic
  - ✓ Platy kurtic
- ANOVA is a technique of partitioning the total variability present in a set of observations into different components of variability produced by different sources some 'known' and other totally 'unknown'.
- ANOVA was developed by **RA Fisher of England**.
- The technique of ANOVA tries to isolate the amount of variation attributed to the known and unknown causes.
- **One-way ANOVA:** If the total variation is accounted by only one assignable reason then it called one-factor or one-way ANOVA.

- **Two-way ANOVA:** If the total variation is explained by two assignable reasons or factors then it is called as two-factor or two-way ANOVA.
- Degrees of freedom is the total number of independent deviations or it is the number, which are free to vary, or it is the number, which has more number of choices.
- Minimum degrees of freedom required to conduct an experiment is **12**.

Assumptions of ANOVA:

- ✓ All observations are independent
- ✓ The observations should follow normal distribution
- ✓ Homogeneity of error variance or the experimental errors should be homogenous in nature. This can be tested using Bartlett's test.
- ✓ Various components of variation are additive

- **Hypothesis** is a tentative explanation made for an observed phenomenon scientifically the acceptance or rejection of a hypothesis which depends on verification of facts.
- **Null hypothesis** is the hypothesis with no differences, denoted as A=B=C *i.e.,* the treatment mean differences are non significant. The differences observed are only due to error effect and not due to treatments.
- **Alternate hypothesis** is the hypothesis with difference, *i.e.,* atleast one treatment is different from others. The differences observed are due to treatments.
- **Test of significance** is a test criteria which indicates whether or not there is significant differences 'among' or 'between' the treatment means.

Tests of significance

Types of test	Usage
Students t test	Small samples
Z test	Large samples
F test	To test the proportions and variances
Chi square	Test of independence Test of goodness of fit Test of homogeneity

- F-Test is a test criterion indicate whether or not there is a significant difference **among** the treatment means.
- t-Test is a test criterion indicates whether or not there is a significant differences **between** the treatment means. It is also known as 'Student's t-test' and was discovered by **W.S.Gosset**.
- t-test is used
    - ✓ to test the differences of two means
    - ✓ to test the superiority of one mean over other
    - ✓ to test the significance of correlation coefficient
    - ✓ to test the significance of regression coefficient
- **One-sample t-test:** It can be used to know the significant difference between sample mean and population mean or hypothetical value or Standard value.
- **Two sample t-test:** It can be used to know the significant difference between two independent sample means.
- **Paired t-test:** It can be used to know significant difference between two related samples which are pre and post score of an experiment.
- Calculated F = larger variance/smaller variance

$$\text{Calculated F} = \frac{\text{Mean sum of squares due to treatment}}{\text{Mean sum of squares due to error}}$$

- If calculated F value is **far away from one** then there is treatment effect and if it is nearer to the value 'one' then there is **no treatment effect**.
- Level of significance is a demarcation line indicating whether or not there is significant differences among or between the treatment means.
- **Critical difference** is that least difference between any two treatment means which decides whether or not there is significant difference between that two treatment means
- Experimental design is a plan of layout of an experiment according to which the treatments are allocated for the plots based on theory of probability, with a certain set of rules and procedure so as to obtain appropriate observations.
- The main objective of the experimental design is to reduce the experimental error as low as possible and thereby increase the precision of the experiment.

- Basic principles of experimental design are randomization, replication and local control.
- These three basic principles are the devices to eliminate the systematic error completely and control/reduce the random error as low as possible.
- These three basic principles are in a way complementary to each other in trying to increase the precision of an experiment.
- Randomization eliminates the **systematic error** completely.
- Replication reduces the **random error** as low as possible.
- Replication improves the precision by reducing the **standard error mean**.
- Soil heterogeneity can be over come to some extent by replication.
- In the absence of **randomization**, any number of replications may not control the error.
- For almost all types of experiment, it is absolutely essential that all other factors other than treatments be maintained uniformly for all experimental units. It is almost impossible. So the important ones be watched closely to ensure that variability among experimental plots is minimized. This is the primary concern of local control.
- **Local control** is the control of all factors except the one about which we are investigating. This can be achieved by grouping, blocking and balancing.
- Soil fertility variations can be reduced by **local control**.
- Replication and local control, both try to reduce the **random error** as low as possible.
- **Completely Randomized Design** is the basic and most simplest design. In this treatments are allocated randomly to the entire experimental plot without any restrictions.
- CRD is more appropriate for experiments with **homogenous experimental** material. Commonly used in **laboratory** experiments where environmental effects are easily controlled. Not suitable for field experiments where more heterogeneity exists.
- In CRD **unequal number** of replications may be included for various treatments.
- CRD is used when the experimental material is **limited in quantity**.

- CRD is not suitable for large number of treatments as homogeneity of experimental material cannot be obtained.
- In CRD missing plot technique is used to estimate missing data.

Randomized Complete Block Design:

- **Most widely used** design of all the experimental designs in agricultural research due to its simplicity, flexibility and validity.
- Used when there is **one directional variation** in the experimental material.
- In this design technique in local control principle is adopted by using **one way blocking** in field experiments and one way grouping in animal experiments.
- Missing plot technique is possible
- More number of treatments (up to 12), compared to CRD and LSD.

Latin Square Design (LSD):

- Used only when there is **two directional variation** in the experimental material.
- **Two-way blocking or two-way grouping** is adopted
- Number of treatments = number of replications = number of columns = number of rows
- Highly restricted randomization is followed
- Missing plot technique is possible
- Less than five treatments does not provide enough degrees of freedom
- **Not flexible** as number of treatments, replications, rows and columns should all be equal.

Factorial experiments:

- **More than one factor** is considered at a time.
- The main interest is to know the simultaneous effect of many factors at a time.
- Gives additional information on the interaction effect.
- Missing plot technique will have more severe implications.

Split Plot Design:

- This design involves the testing of two factors at a time while the **first factors are assessed at a lower precision** and the **second factors are assessed at a greater precision**.
- The experimental plots in each replication are equally divided into number of main plots which are equal to number of main-plot treatments, which need larger plot sizes for the treatment imposement.
- The mainplots are further subdivided into sub-plots which are equal to number of sub-plot treatments.
- Main-plot treatments are randomly allocated to the main-plots first.
- Each set of sub-plot treatments are randomly allocated to each main plot, and randomization should be done afresh to each main plot.
- Sub plot treatments are assessed with greater precison because of less variation due to soil heterogeneity.

Strip Plot design:

- This is also a two factor experimental design.
- If **factors require larger plots** then we use Strip Plot design.
- It is an arrangement of 2 sets of factors in which one set of factors are superposed over the others as right angles.

Error degrees of freedom

Design	Error degrees of freedom
CRD	N – t
RBD	(t –1) (r – 1)
LSD	(m – 1) (m – 2)
Split	m(r – 1) (s – 1)
Strip	(r – 1) (a – 1) (b – 1)
2^2	3(r – 1)
2^3	7(r – 1)

Chapter 26

Recent statistics and General Agriculture

- Total number of KVKs in India is **680**.
- CACP – Commission for Agricultural Costs and Prices
- NAFED – National Agricultural Cooperative Marketing Federation of India Limited
- SFAC – Small Farmers Agri Business Consortium
- Minimum support prices of *rabi* crops for 2016-17 season

***rabi* crop**	**MSP for 2016-17 season**
Wheat	1625/-
Barley	1325/-
Bengal gram	4000/-
Masur(Lentil)	3950/-
Rapeseed/Mustard	3700/-
Safflower	3700/-

- Minimum support prices of *kharif* crops for 2016-17 season

Crop	**MSP for 2016-17 season**
Paddy (Common)	1470/-
Paddy (Grade A)	1510/-
Jowar (Hybrid)	1625/-
Jowar (Maldandi)	1650/-
Bajra	1330/-
Maize	1365/-
Ragi	1725/-
Tur (Arhar)	5050/-
Moong (green gram)	5225/-

Contd...

Crop	MSP for 2016-17 season
Urad (Black gram)	5000/-
Groundnut in shell	4220/-
Soybean	2775/-
Sunflower seed	3950/-
Niger seed	3825/-
Sesamum	5000/-
Cotton (Medium staple)	3860/-
Cotton (Long staple)	4160/-

- Parampragat Krishi Vikas Yojana (PKVY) to promote organic farming and develop potential market for organic products.
- Pradhan Mantri Krishi Sinchai Yojana was started with objective of creating sources of assured irrigation.
- Kisan channel started by Doordarshan on **May 26, 2015**.
- Per capita availability of rice is **199 g/day**.
- Per capita availability of wheat is **183.1 g/day**
- Per capita availability of total cereals is **444.1 g/day**
- Per capita availability of pulses is **47.2 g/day**
- Per capita availability of food grains is **491.2 g/day**
- Estimated annual precipitation (including snowfall) in India is **4000 BCM**
- Average annual potential in rivers in India is **1869 BCM**
- Percapita water availability (2010) is **1588 m^3**
- Estimated utilizable surface water is **690 BCM**
- Estimated utilizable ground water is **433 BCM**
- Estimated total utilizable water is **1123 BCM**
- Ultimate irrigation potential is **139.9 mha**
- Reported area in India is **305.67 mha**
- Gross irrigated area is **87.26 mha**
- Net irrigated area is **62.3 mha**

- Net irrigated area by source is given below
  - Canals – 16.5 mha
  - Tanks – 2 mha
  - Wells – 37.8 mha
  - Others – 6 mha
  - Total – 62.3 mha
- Total volume of water on earth – **1.4 billion Km^3**
- Percentage of fresh water in total water is **2.5%**
- In fresh water **68.9 %** is ice or permanent snow, **29.9%** is ground water, **0.3%** is in lakes, rivers and **0.9**% is present as soil moisture, swamp water.
- **1000-3000** litres of water is required to produce 1 kilogram of rice
- **2000 to 5000** litres of water is required to produce one person's daily food
- Extent of land under irrigation in the world is **277 mha**.
- Due to climate change, Himalayan snow and ice, which provide vast amounts of water for agriculture in Asia, expected to decline by **20%** by 2030.
- Irrigated agriculture contributes **40%** of world's food production.
- Use of freshwater in world
  - For irrigation -70%
  - For industry – 22%
  - For domestic use – 18%
- River basin having highest catchment area is **ganga** followed by Indus, Godavari, Krishna, Brahmaputra, mahanadi, narmada, barak and others.
- Average water resources potential highest in **Brahmaputra basin** (537.24 BCM) followed by Ganga (525.02 BCM) and Godavari.
- Utilizable surface water resources highest in **Ganga (250 BCM)** followed by Godavari and Krishna.
- Most of the areas under tanks, lakes and ponds lie in states of AP, Karnataka, Arunachal Pradesh, West Bengal account for 56% of total area under ponds and tanks in the country.

- Maximum rainfall recorded in **coastal Karnataka (379.8 cm)**, followed by Kerala (281.6 cm), Konkan and Goa (273.8 cm) and Andaman and Nicobar (261.4 cm).
- Less than 50 cm rainfall in Rajasthan east and west, Punjab and Haryana, Chandigarh and Delhi.
- Higher number of dams in **Maharashtra (1821)**.
- Indian Meteorological Department (IMD) established in **1875**.
- Head quarter of IMD was first located in Kolkata, then shifted to shimla later to Pune and now it is located in New Delhi.
- Types of weather forecasting

Now casting :

- Forecasts up to a few hours ahead (but less than 24 hours). Provides details about current weather

Short range forecasting :

- Valid up to 72 hours ahead

Medium range forecasting :

- Valid for a period of 4 to 10 days
- Average weather conditions and weather on each day will be prescribed with progressively lesser details and accuracy than that of short range forecasts.

Long range forecast:

- Forecast from 30 days up to one season's description of averaged weather parameters
- Monthly and seasonal forecast comes under long range forecast

✓ Seasonal reversal of winds and the associated rainfall is called **monsoon**.

✓ Withdrawal of south west monsoon – **1st September**.

✓ When spatial coverage of drought is more than **40%** it will be called as All India Severe **Drought year**.

✓ Speed of tornado is **20 to 90 km/h**.

✓ Greatest concentration of Ozone occurs at an altitude of about **25 km**.

✓ Clouds located at high altitude are **cirrus, cirrocumulus, cirrostratus**.

- ✓ Clouds located at medium height are **altocumulus, altostratus and nimbostratus.**
- ✓ Clouds located at low height are **stratocumulus, stratus, cumulus and cumulonimbus**.
- ✓ **Geostationary orbit:** satellite moves in a circular orbit around the earth at a height of **36000 km** above the equator and move in time with earth. Satellites in this orbit are called geostationary because they are stationary with respect to the earth and appear to be fixed in sky
- ✓ Satellites to monitor weather of Indian region are **Kalpana-1 and INSAT-3A**.
- ✓ **146.82 mha** of land is degraded in India.
- ✓ Water erosion is the major cause **(63.8%)** of land degradation.

  Soil acidity – 10.9%

  Waterlogging – 9.7%

- Wind erosion is the major cause of land degradation in **Haryana and Rajasthan**.
- Waterlogging is the major cause of land degradation in **Goa and Kerala**.
- Soil acidity is the main cause for land degradation in **Mizoram, Manipur, Tripura and Meghalaya**.
- Minister of food processing industries is **Harsimrat Kaur Badal**.
- Minister of food processing industries for state is **Sadhvi Niranjan Jyothi**
- Minister of water resources, river development and Ganga rejuvenation is **UmaBharathi**
- Minister of chemicals and fertilizers is **Ananth Kumar**
- Minister of chemicals and fertilizers for state is **Ravi Anand**
- Central Agriculture Minister is **Radha Mohan Singh**
- State Agriculture Minister
  1) SS. Ahluwalia
  2) Parshottam Rupala
  3) Sudarshan Bhagat
- Minister of state in the ministry of environment and forest and climate change is **Anil Madhava Dave**

- State minister for water resources – **Sanwar Lal Jat**
- Present DG of ICAR **– Trilochan Mohapatra**
- Chairman of FCI – **Yogendra Tripathi**
- Chairman of National Knowledge commission – **Sam Pitroda**
- Chairman of Tea Board of India – **Santhosh Sarangi**
- Chairman of National Commission for Farmers – **Dr. M.S. Swaminathan**
- Chairman of Neeti Ayog – **Narendra Modi (PM)**
- Vice- Chairman of Neeti Ayog – **Arvind Panagariya**
- CEO of Neeti Ayog – **Amitabh Kant**
- Governing council of Neeti Ayog – **Chief Ministers of all states**
- Full time members of Neeti Ayog
    1) Bibek Debroy
    2) V.K.Saraswat
- Production of urea in 2015-16 is **24.5 mt**
- Import of urea, DAP and MOP was of the order of **8.47 mt**, **6.01 mt** and **3.24 mt** respectively, during 2015-16
- Total consumption of fertilizers in India in 2015-16 is **27 mt**
- NPK use ratio in India in 2015-16 is **7.5 : 3.0 : 1**
- Per hectare consumption of fertilizers in India during 2015-16 is **138.9 kg/ha**
- Fertilizer (NPK) use per ha is highest in Punjab state (228 kg/ha) in India during **2014-15**.
- Percentage share of area under food grains to gross sown area is **70%**.
- Net cultivated area of food grains is **127 mha**.
- Food grain production in 2015-16 is **252.2 mt**.
- Food grain yield (kg/ha) in 2014-15 is **2129 kg/ha**.
- Production of food grains declined by **4.7%** during 2014-15 from 265 mt in 2013-14.
- Urea price per tonne is **Rs. 5360**
- Rice production during 2015-16 was **104.3 mt.**
- Wheat production during 2015-16 was **93.5 mt**.
- Coarse cereals production during 2015-16 was **37.9 mt**.

- Pulses production during 2015-16 was **16.5 mt**.
- Oilseeds production during 2015-16 was **25.3 mt**.
- Cotton production during 2015-16 was **33.8 million bales**.
- **33%** of total foreign exchange is from cotton export.
- Cotton area in India in 2015-16 was **10.68 mha**, reduced to **8.61 mha** in 2016-17.
- Cotton productivity in India is **438.79 kg/ha**.

Revolution	Field
Green revolution	Food grains
White revolution	Milk
Blue revolution	Fisheries
Brown revolution	Food processing/Fertilizers
Yellow revolution	Oilseeds
Golden revolution	Horticulture
Round revolution	Potato
Rainbow revolution	Overall development of agriculture sector
Black revolution	Petroleum products
Silver revolution	Egg production

- First DG of ICAR - **Dr B.P.Pal**
- First President of ICAR - **Habibullah**
- First Director of IARI - **Dr. Vishwanathan**
- Present DG of ICAR - **Trilochan Mohapatra**
- Present President of ICAR - **Radha Mohan Singh**
- Present Director of IARI - **Dr. A.K.Singh**
- Father of Green Revolution- **N.E.Borlaug**
- Father of Green Revolution in India - **M.S.Swaminathan**
- Father of White Revolution in India - **Verghese Kurien**

Science	Father
Agricultural Chemistry	Liebig
Modern Agronomy	Pietro de' Crescenzi
Pedology	Dokuchaev
Agroclimatology	Koppen
Safeners	O.L.Hoffman

Contd...

Science	Father
Bacteriology	Leeuwenhoek
Microbiology	Louis Pasteur
Plant Physiology	Stephen Hales
Indian Ecology	R.Mishra
Organic farming	Albert Howard
Biodynamic Farming	Rudolf Steiner
Natural farming	Masanobu Fukuoka
Agrometeorology in India	L.A Ramdas

Plant Group	Preference
Halophytes	Plants that prefer saline conditions
Sciophytes	Plants that prefer shady condition
Lithophytes	Plants that grow on rock surface
Psammophytes	Plants that prefer sandy soils
Calciphytes	Plants which require large quantity of Ca
Xerophytes	Plants that grow in desert
Acidophiles	Plants that grow well under acidic condition
Chamaephytes	Plants growing under extremely cold climate
Cryophytes	Plants growing on ice or snow
Hemicryptophytes	Plants suitable for grassland condition
Amphiphytes	Plants which grow both on land and water
Calcifuges	Calcium sensitive plants
Chasmophytes	Plant roots capable of penetrating into rock fissures
Epiphytes	Plants that grow on other plants for physical support
Gypsophytes	Gypsum loving plants
Heliophytes	Light loving plants
Basophiles	Plants that prefer alkali soils
Hydrophytes	Water loving plants
Oxylophytes	Plants tolerant to acidic soil condition
Petrophytes	Plants able to grow on rocks

Contd...

Plant Group	Preference
Phanerophytes	Plants grown in warm and moist climate
Pteridophytes	Seedless vascular plants
Spermatophytes	Seeded vascular plants
Therophytes	Plants growing in hot and dry conditions

Vegetation (Grasslands):

Region	Type of grassland	Remarks
USA	Prairies (steppe)	Temperate treeless grasslands
Eurasia	Steppe	Temperate treeless grasslands
Hungary	Pustza	Temperate treeless grasslands
South America (Argentina)	Pampas	Temperate treeless grasslands
South Africa	Veldts	Temperate grasslands
Africa, South America, Australia, India, Madagascar and Myanmar - Thailand	Savanna	Tropical grasslands with scattered trees under hot-dry conditions
Australia	Downs (Rangeland)	Temperate grasslands
Brazil, Paraguay, Uruguay	Campos	Humid-sub tropics rich in plant species
New Zealand	Rangeland	Temperate grasslands

- **Fischer** coined the term remote sensing in 1960 AD.
- **Remote sensing** is the acquistion and recording of information about an object without being in direct contact with that object.
- **Geographic information system** is a computer based system for storing very large amount of data (collected based on spatial location), retrieving, manipulation and displaying them for easy interpretation.
- **GPS** is a computer based versatile navigational aid. Key components in GPS are satellites.
- Kisan day – **December 23rd**

- World water day-**March 22nd**
- World environment day – **June 5th**
- Water year starts from **October 1**
- **2015** is called International year of **soils.**
- **2016** is called international year of **pulses.**
- Percapita forest area in India is **0.07 ha.**
- **Food prizes**

Year	Awarded to	Contribution
1989	Dr. Verghese Khurien	Founder of operation flood, the largest development program in the world made the farmer the owner of his cooperative, cutting out middle men
2000	Dr. Surinder K. Vasal and Dr. Evangelina Villegas	Developed high quality protein maize
2014	Dr. Sanjaya Rajaram	Developed disease resistant varieties of wheat
2015	Sir Fazle Hasan Abed, Bangladesh	Founder of BRAC, world's largest NGO, working on reducing poverty in Bangladesh and 10 other countries
2016	Dr. Maria Andrade Dr. Robert Mwanga Dr. Jan Low Dr. Howarth Bouis	Developed the single most successful example of micronutrient and vitamin biofortification – the orange-fleshed sweet potato (OFSP).

- Irish famine-**1845**
- Black tip of mango – **B deficiency**
- Half life of P^{32} is **14 days**
- Calcium requirement highest in **legumes.**
- Maximum CEC at root surface noticed in **legumes.**
- Maximum infiltration in soil at bulk density **1.1**
- At saturated condition in soil matric potential is **zero.**
- Mn toxicity is found in **Assam.**

- Deposition of material with the action of gravitational force is called **colluvium.**
- As the soil changes from acid to alkali redox potential **decreases.**
- Fools gold – pyrite
- **First world food prize** was awarded to **Dr. M.S.Swaminathan (1987)** for introducing high yielding wheat and rice varieties to India starting Indian green revolution.
- 1 kpa = 10 mb
- 1° latitude = **111 km**
- Thermometer discovered by **Tricolle.**
- **Epigeal germination** – greengram, bean, castor, mustard, tamarind, sunflower, papaya, cotton, gourd, onion, guar, cucumber.
- **Hypogeal germination** – chickpea, groundnut, wheat, pea, mango, monocotyledons, arecanut, coconut, Runner bean (*Phaseolus coccineus*)
- In remote sensing optical wavelength used is **0.3 – 15 µm.**
- Biodiversity act – **2002**
- Insecticide act – **1968**
- Cellulose content in humus – **21%**
- Nitrogen content in humus – **5 to 5.5%**
- Primary electron acceptor in photosystem II is **pheophytin**
- Recommended safe limit of land slope for border irrigation in medium soils is **0.2 – 0.4%**
- Element required for stabilizing various enzyme systems in plants is **phosphorus**
- Plant quarantine order passed in **2003**
- Square root transformation is done when observations follow **poisson distribution.**
- Movement of water molecules from a solution with higher concentration towards lower concentration solution through semi permeable membrane is called **osmosis.**
- Gypsum equivalent of iron pyrite is **0.63.**
- Most suitable system for arid regions is **pasture development.**
- Agroforestry system suited in low rainfall areas is **silvipasture.**

- Earth emits **long wave radiation.**
- Albedo is highest for **fresh snow.**
- CO_2 compensation point in C_4 plants is **0-10 ppm.**
- CO_2 compensation point in C_3 plants is **30-70 ppm.**
- Photosynthetically active radiation (PAR) – **400 to 700 nm**
- Visible radiation – **390 to 760 nm.**
- Climate where low temperature in winter and high temperature in summer prevails is **Subtropical climate.**
- Largest canal for the purpose of irrigation in world is **Indira-Gandhi canal.**
- In India contribution of herbicides in pesticide consumption is **16%**
- Protection of plant varieties and farmer rights authority – **New Delhi**
- Anti gibberellins in action = **Absciscic acid**
- Nitrate is commonly absorbed by **phloem**
- Endocytokinin is derivative of **adenine (purine)**
- Balanced fertilizer ratio for legumes is **1:2:2**
- Blue colour triangle on insecticide container represents **slightly toxic.**
- Mechanical analysis of soil makes use of **stokes law.**
- First KVK at Pondicherry started in **1974.**
- Humic acid which is a fraction of humus is **souble in alkali, insoluble in acid.**
- Average content of **Si** in soil – **27%**
- Fulvic acid → Humic acid → Recalcitrant biopolymers → humin acid
- **Humic acid** is aromatic with high molecular weight
- Humus fraction lightest in colour is **Fulvic acid**
- Humus forming fungi includes the genera ***Alternaria*** and ***Aspergillus.***
- **Fulvic acid** is soluble both in acid and alkali.
- Calibrated device used for measuring flow of water in open conduit is **Parshall flume.**

- National agriculture policy aims the growth rate of > **4%** per annum.
- Term evergreen revolution given by **M.S.Swaminathan**.
- Phytohormone involved in nutrient mobilization is **cytokinin**.
- Floral abnormality is present in **white rust of crucifers**.
- Floral abnormality absent in **downy mildew of mustard**.
- Illite is rich in **potash**.
- Phosphorus is not found free in nature.
- **Phosphorus rocks** are present in Australia, France, Belgium, Spain, Morocco, Tunisia, Algeria and Florida, Tennessee, Wyoming, Utah, Idaho states of US.
- According to US geological survey 50% of global phosphorus reserves are in **Arab nations**.
- Large deposits of **apatite** located in China, Russia, Morocco, Florida, Idaho, Tennessee and Utah.
- Potash is mined in Canada, Russia, Belarus, Germany, Israel, United States, Jordan and Great Britain.
- Antisenecence phytohormone is represented by **gibberellins**
- **Al^{3+}** has higher aggregation capacity in soil.
- **Na^{+}** has low adsorption capacity on clay compared to H^{+}, Ca^{2+}, Fe^{2+}.
- Slow growing species of legume root nodule bacteria included in the bacterial genus ***Bradyrhizobium***.
- Seed work board is required for **seed blending**.
- Soil structure improved by application of **superphosphate**.
- Approximate weight of 15 cm surface soil over 1 ha is **2.24×10^{6} kg**.
- **Paddy** causes maximum reduction in soil alkalinity.
- Flow of water in saturated soil is described by **Darcy's law and Poiseuille's law**.
- True density of most mineral soils is **2.65 g/cm^{3}**.
- Rainfed authority of India – **New Delhi**.
- Average rainfall of India – **1190 mm**.
- Maximum K fixation takes place in **Vermiculite**.

- Fast growing tree species – **Euclayptus.**
- *Albizzia lebbek* – **multipurpose** trees species
- Rainfed area in the country is **65 mha.**
- Preventing fruit drop in grapes by spraying **NAA @ 20 ppm.**
- Casparian strip is present in **endodermis.**
- Most effective instrument for measuring soil moisture content insitu is **TDR.**
- Freezing point depression of a chemical solution is measured by **osmometer.**
- Average human labour power in India is **0.1 KW.**
- Maximum area under fruit cultivation in the state – **Maharashtra**
- Transgenic crop having maximum cultivated area in the world is **Soybean.**
- In cereals grain startch consists of **amylase and amylopectin.**
- Highest Zn containing fertilizer is **ZnO.**
- Apical dominance in sugarcane controlled by **cytokinins.**
- Water soluble vitamins – **B, C**
- Fat soluble vitamins – **A, D, E, K**
- According to area requirement Basin > Catchment > Watershed
- Member countries in WTO – **164 no.**
- **Monosaccharides** – Glucose, Galactose, Ribulose
- **Disaccharides** – Maltose, Lactose, Sucrose, Cellobiose
- **Non reducing** sugar – **sucrose**
- Sugar largely found in **germinating** seeds – **Maltose**
- Glucose + Galactose = **Lactose**
- Glycogen is present only in **animal cells**
- Positively charged aminoacid is **lysine**
- Sugar sweetest among all sugars is **fructose**
- Enzyme for conversion of ammonia to aminoacid is **glutamine synthetase**
- In plants genetic material is present in **nucleus, chloroplast, mitochondria.**
- Main function of endoplasmic reticulum is **protein synthesis.**

- Enzyme associated with decarboxylation reaction in photosynthetic reaction of C_4 plants is **Malic enzyme**.
- RNA synthesis in nucleus participates in protein synthesis in **cytosol**.
- Site of chemical activity in cells, perhaps over half of cells metabolism is **mitochondria**.
- Photorespiration is high in **C_3 plants.**
- Spherosomes are related with **fat.**
- Ribosomes are produced in **Nucleolus.**
- Pigments that produce the colour of many flowers or red of red maple leaves are stored in **vacuoles**.
- Ultimate electron donor in mitochondrial electron transport chain is **ubiquinone**.
- Latent heat of vapourisation (water to vapour) of water is **586 cal**.
- Latent heat of fusion (ice to water) is **80 cal**.
- Important radiant generated in Pentose phosphate pathway of glucose degradation is **NADPH**.
- Glyoxysomes function is breakdown of fattyacids.
- Maximum free radicals production takes place in **senescence**.
- Precursor for ethylene biosynthesis is **methionine**.
- In a rapidly transpiring plant the water column in xylem will be under **negative pressure**.
- Transpiration is measured by **potometer**.
- Proteins that bind to tata box in promoters region are **transcriptional factors**.
- Chemical nature of GA_3 is **terpene**.
- Site of oxidative electron transport in cell is **mitochondria**.
- Guttation is not favoured under **low root pressure**.
- Xylem and phloem elements in plant are surrounded by a layer of living cells called **pericycle**.
- Part of root that absorbs water and minerals is **root hairs**.
- Stage of seeds showing no germination bacause of internal conditions of seed is known as **dormancy**.
- Plant hormone which is primary regulator of abscission process is **ABA**.

- Most of the wheat cultivars are **qualitative long day** plants.
- Rice grain is deficient in **lysine**.
- Critical concentration of micronutrients needed in tissue is equal to or less than **100ppm**.
- Storage of elements in vacuoles occurs under **luxury consumption**.
- Chelates are **organic** in nature.
- Siderophores produced by bacteria and fungi in the soil are source of **iron.**
- Iron stored in chloroplast as iron protein complex called **phytoferritin**.
- Initiation of protein synthesis in eukaryotic mRNA requires a **5' cap**.
- The first sign of switchover from vegetative stage to reproductive stage in wheat is **double ridge stage**.
- Abundant phosphorus in plants is related with **delayed maturity** and accumulation of **anthocyanin pigments**.
- Increase in temperature at anthesis stage in wheat results in **decreased grain size**.
- Ideal type of rice with small, thick and erect leaf was proposed by **Yoshida**.
- Increase in wheat yield potential so far results from increase in **harvest index**.
- Most commonly grown crop plants are included in **glycophytes**.
- Acetylene reduction to ethylene is measured as **nitrogen fixation**.
- **Mn deficiency in crops:**
  1) Grey speck of oats
  2) Marsh spot of peas
  3) Speckled yellows of sugarbeet
  4) Pahala light of sugarcane
- **Boron deficiency in crops:**
  1) Heart rot of sugarbeet
  2) Droughtspot of apple
  3) Stem crack in celery
  4) Watercore in Turnip

- **Zinc deficiency in crops:**
  1) Little leaf of cotton
  2) Rosette of apple
  3) Whitebud of Maize
- Under excessive light level the synthesis of **Zeaxanthin** increases.
- Dieback disease in cotton is the result of **copper** deficiency.
- For the synthesis of auxins micronutrient essential is **Zinc**.
- Direct reduction of O_2 by photosystem I lead to the formation of **H_2O_2**.
- Optimum pH of nutrient solution culture is **6**.
- Acid rains are due to **NO_2 and SO_2**.
- Association of fungi with roots of higher plants – **mycorrhiza**.
- Vesicular Arbuscular Mycorrhizae mostly used in **perennials**.
- If the accumulation ratio in absorption of nutrients is greater than 1 then it is **active absorption**.
- Most harmful pollutant by automobiles is **carbon monoxide**.
- C^{14} has a half life of **2530 years**.
- Mass flow mechanism proposed by **Munch**.
- Isotopes differ in number of **neutrons**.
- The process in which sugars (carbohydrates) are raised to high concentration in phloem cells close to a source is known as **phloem loading**.
- **Catabolism** is the breakdown of large molecules to small molecules and this process often releases energy.
- Climacteric rise in respiration is observed in **mango**.
- Callus is induced to form roots in the medium of **more auxins than cytokinins**.
- Sulphur containing aminoacids are **methionine and cysteine**.
- Group of enzymes which form double bond by elimination of a chemical group is **Lyases**.
- Electrophoresis was developed to separate **proteins**.
- Ripening is delayed by the synthesis of **antisense ACC synthetase RNA** in tomato.

- **Blue light** is always **less efficient** in photosynthesis **than red light**.
- Recognition site of t-RNA is **anticodon**.
- Wavelength of visible light is **390-760 nm**.
- Chlorophyll is green because it **reflects green colour**.
- Plastocyanin protein contains **copper**.
- Z-scheme of electron transport was first proposed by **Hill and Bendall**.
- Number of photons required to produce 1 molecule of oxygen is **8**.
- In C_3 plants **RUBISCO** first reacts with CO_2 to form Phospho Glyceric Acid (PGA).
- Hormone associated with acid growth theory is **auxin**.
- Nitrate reductase is found in **cytoplasm**.
- Natural inhibitor of IAA oxidases is **coumaric acid**.
- In C_4 plants first stable product of photosynthesis is **oxalic acid**.
- Close association of chloroplast, peroxisomes and mitochondria in a leaf cell are associated with **photorespiration**.
- Number of ATP required to produce 1 mole of hexose in photosynthesis is **18**.
- Instrument used for measuring stomatal pressure is **porometer**.
- Scientist related to Biological clock – **Bunning**
- Most dangerous gas for depletion of ozone layer is **CFC**.
- Photorespiration is also known as glycolate pathway.
- In C_4 plants enzyme responsible for synthesis of malic acid is Phospho Enol Pyrivate **(PEP) carboxylase**.
- Element required for dehydrogenases is **Zinc**.
- Most striking feature of CAM plants is formation of **malic acid at night**.
- **Tropical rain forest** has highest net primary productivity per unit area.
- The irradiance at which photosynthesis is equal to respiration rate (Net CO_2 exchange is zero) is **light compensation point**.
- CO_2 concentration at which photosynthetic fixation just balances respiratory loss is **CO_2 compensation point**.

- Transpiration ratio is highest for **C_3 plants**.
- Photosynthesis inhibited by 21% oxygen in **C_4 plants.**
- Optimum temperature for photosynthesis in C_3 plants is **15-25°C**.
- Respiratory coefficient of **carbohydrates** is **1**

  Fatty acids is **0.7**

  Organic acids is **1.33**
- End product of glycolysis is **pyruvic acid**.
- Glycolysis takes place in **cytoplasm.**
- Krebs cycle produces **30 ATP**.
- First time IAA from human urine was isolated by **Kogl**.
- Scientists related to **skototropism** : **Strong and Ray**.
- **Letham** isolated zeatin from corn seed.
- **Phaseoline** is the storage protein in Beans.
- Main organic acid in pineapple is **malic acid**.
- Sulphate reduction in leaves takes place in **chloroplast**.
- Polymer of cellulose is **β-D glucose**.
- In C_4 plants PEP carboxylation takes place in **mesophyll cells**.
- Cyanide resistant respiration follows **pentose phosphate pathway**.
- Aminoacid produced in photorespiration is **serine**.
- In monocots and dicots accumulation of **ethylene** causes collapse and lysis of mature cortical cells in root and formation of tissue with large air spaces.
- Aerenchyma is related with **ethylene**.
- When starch reacts with iodine produces **blue colour**.
- Under anaerobic conditions microbes grow slower but utilize more sugar and produce more CO_2 and ethanol, this phenomenon is known as **Pasteur effect**.
- Enzyme used to cut double stranded RNA is **restriction endonuclease**.
- H^+ cannot pass across membrane by **diffusion**.
- In many species gradual decrease in respiration is reversed by sharp increase known as **climacteric**.
- Conversion of organic nitrogen to NH_4 by soil microbes is called **ammonification**.

- Denitrification occurs in **waterlogged** soils.
- C_3 cycle of carbon fixation takes place in **stroma** of chloroplast.
- The process by which N_2 is reduced to NH_4^+ is called **nitrogen fixation.**
- Electrons required for conversion of NO_2^- to NH_4^+ are **6.**
- Mature root nodule made largely of **tetraploid cells.**
- Nitrogen fixation is carried out by the enzyme **Nitrogenase.**
- Nitrogenase consists of **Fe-Mo protein.**
- Dormin is coined by **Wareing.**
- Kranz type of anatomy found in **sorghum (C_4 plant).**
- **6 calvin cycles** needed to produce **1 molecule of glucose.**
- **Ureides** (Allantoin and allantoic acids) are the major nitrogen compounds transported from root nodules to other parts of plant in **soybean.**
- Number of quanta in 1 micro Einstein is **6.02×10^{17}.**
- **Pascal** is the SI unit of pressure.
- In the process of nitrate reduction oxidation number of nitrogen changes from **+5 to -3.**
- Reduction of nitrite to ammonium catalysed by nitrite reductase in **chloroplast and proplastids of roots.**
- Flowering stimulus is perceived by **leaves.**
- **1-amino cyclopropane 1-carboxylic acid (ACC)** is a close precursor of ethylene.
- First step of sulphate assimilation is catalysed by **ATP sulfurylase.**
- Coconut fat is a rich source of **lauric acid.**
- Antimicrobial compounds synthesized by plants when infected with microbes are called **phytoalexins.**
- **Phytoalexins** – pisatin, phaseolin, isocoumarin

National Board/authority	Place
Tea Board	Kolkata
Coffee Board	Bangalore
Biodiversity Authority	Chennai

Contd...

National Board/authority	Place
Rubber Board	Kottayam, Kerala
Spices Board	Kochi, Kerala
Fish and Fish product Board	Hyderabad, Telangana
Tobacco Board	Guntur, AP
Central Silk Board	Bangalore, Karnataka
Coconut Board	Kochi, Kerala
Agricultural Scientists Recruitment Board	New Delhi

Concept	Person/Father
Golden rice	Ingo potrichus
Super rice	G.S.Khush
Hybrid rice	Yuvan Long Ping
Super wheat	S. Nagarajan
Bt-cotton in India	C.D.Mayee
Proteto (protein rich potato)	Ashish Dutta

Concept/Term	Person
Rainbow revolution	Nitish Kumar
Evergreen revolution	Swaminathan
Green house effect	J.B.Fourler
Drip irrigation	Symcha Blass
Tillage	Jethro Tull

Crop	Bale (kg)
Cotton	170
Jute	180
Mesta	181

- Growth towards gravity – **Gravitropism**
  Growth towards light – **Phototropism**
  Growth towards solid objects – **Thigmotropism**
  Heliotropism – Response to sunlight
- Grow more food campaign started in the year **1942-43**
- High yielding variety programme started in the year **1965-66**
- Drought prone area programme started in **1970-71**
- Agricultural Technology Management Agency (ATMA) started in **May 2005**
- AICRP on Maize – **1957**

Project/Mission	**Started in the year**
AICRP on Maize	1957
National Agricultural Research Project (NARP)	1979
Technology Mission on Oil Seeds	1986
National Agricultural Technology Project (NATP)	1998
National Agricultural Innovation Project (NAIP)	July, 2006
National Horticultural Mission (NHM)	2005-06
National Food Security Mission (NFSM)	2007-08
National Initiative on Climate Resilient Agriculture (NICRA)	Feb 2011

Dam/reservoir	**River**	**State**	**Purpose/Remarks**
Bhakra Nangal	Sutlej	Haryana, Punjab and Rajasthan	India's biggest multi-purpose river valley project
Beas	Beas-Sutlej link	Haryana, Punjab, Rajasthan	Irrigation
Bargi	Bargi	Madhya Pradesh	Irrigation
Bhadra	Bhadra	Karnataka	Irrigation and electricity
Farakka	Ganga, Bhagirathi	West Bengal	Preservation and maintenance of Kolkata port

Contd...

Dam/reservoir	River	State	Purpose/Remarks
Chambal	Chambal	M.P. and Rajasthan	-
Damodar valley	Damodar	West Bengal, Bihar & Jharkhand	Multipurpose
Gandak	Gandak	Bihar, UP & Nepal	Irrigation and power
Hirakud	Mahanadi	Odisha, Chattisgarh	World's longest dam, multipurpose
Karanj	Karanj	Gujarat	Irrigation
Nagarjuna Sagar	Krishna	A.P.	Multipurpose
Tawa	Tawa	MP	Irrigation
Tehri dam	Bhagirathi	Uttarakhand	Multipurpose
Ukai	Tapti	Gujarat	Irrigation and drinking water
Sardar Sarovar	Narmada	Gujarat	Multipurpose
Indira Sagar	Narmada	M.P.	Irrigation & Electricity
Mettur	Kaveri	TN, Karnataka, Pondicherry	Irrigation

Selected References

Agronomy Terminology – Indian Society of Agronomy

An Introduction to Agriculture – A.K. Vyas and Rishi Raj

Cropping and Farming Systems – S.C. Panda

Definitional Glossary of Agricultural Terms – Dinesh Kumar and Y.S. Shivay

Hand Book of Agriculture – ICAR

Internet

Principles of Agronomy – S.R. Reddy

Principles of Agronomy – T.Yellamanda Reddy and G.H. Sankara Reddi

Soil Fertility and Nutrient Management – S.S.Singh

Text Book of Plant Nutrient Management – Rajendra Prasad